ANNUAL REPORTS: DELIVERING YOUR CORPORATE MESSAGE TO STAKEHOLDERS

ANNUAL REPORTS: DELIVERING YOUR CORPORATE MESSAGE TO STAKEHOLDERS

John Stittle

GOWER

Published by
Gower Publishing Limited
Gower House
Croft Road
Aldershot
Hampshire GU11 3HR
England

Gower Publishing Company
Suite 420
101 Cherry Street
Burlington, VT 05401–4405 USA

British Library Cataloguing in Publication Data
Stittle, John
Annual reports : delivering your corporate message to stakeholders
1. Corporation reports 2. Corporations – Investor relations
I. Title
658. 1′512

ISBN 0 566 08494 5

Library of Congress Cataloguing-in-Publication Data
Stittle, John.
Annual reports : delivering your corporate message to stakeholders / John Stittle.
p. cm.
Includes bibliographical references and index.
ISBN 0-566-08494-5 (alk. paper)
1. Corporation reports. I. Title

HG4028.B2S78 2002
657′.32--dc21 2002045228

Typeset in 11 point Palatino by IML Typographers, Birkenhead, Merseyside, and printed in Great Britain by MPG Books Ltd., Bodmin, Cornwall

Contents

List of figures

Preface

Annual reports and accounts have a vital role to play in the life of all companies and also of many other organizations. While annual reports play an especially important role in larger public companies, they are essential not only in furthering accountability but also in communication and image projection for all companies.

It is commonly believed that annual reports are mere booklets of dry and dusty figures, which are only relevant to highly technically-minded accountants and financial analysts. However, this view is utterly and completely wrong. The days of a simply typed annual report, perhaps with a black and white photograph of the chairman, are long gone.

Today's society is all about image, impression and creating a positive and dynamic profile. All organizations are concerned about making statements, creating an image and constructing a presence. Business reporting is far more than producing accounts and a few supporting explanations. Indeed, annual reports still contain the accounting statements and other technical and regulatory information, but this information is only just one small part of a very much larger story.

Annual reports have become a key way of projecting a self-image – a way of portraying the corporate personality and, most importantly, a way of delivering both implicit and explicit messages. Recent legislative changes have permitted companies to additionally make their annual reports available in electronic form, either by placing them on their websites or by sending them electronically to those groups entitled to receive them. Nevertheless, annual reports in hard-copy format will still continue to be (legally) made available and will be a major means of communication and accountability for the foreseeable future.

In many ways, an annual report is 'the company'. It is the corporate voice delivering corporate messages not only to shareholders and debenture-holders but also to the wider world, including potential investors, employees and the general public.

These messages are not always necessarily explicit statements. Messages, opinions, and images can often be portrayed and delivered in a far more effective way than by mere plain written statements. They can be conveyed by various means such as the report's style, use of photographs, page layout and design, use of colour, quality of paper and printing type and so on.

This book examines ways in which companies can use the annual report to portray their corporate 'self' and convey corporate messages and themes to shareholders and other interested parties. While it will be of interest to accountants who may well wish to improve the communicative power of corporate reports, it should also appeal to many other groups of specialists and professionals who are, or should be, involved in drafting the report. These groups include designers, lawyers, company secretaries, directors, managers and many other people in corporate life. This book will assist, suggest, guide and advise this mixed group of experts and professionals.

Shareholders will also find the book useful, as it will not only help explain the procedures and planning that underlie their company's published annual report, but will also help them to analyse the messages and 'signals' that their companies are trying to convey to them.

Annual Reports: Delivering Your Corporate Message to Stakeholders leads the reader through the key stages in the report's planning, preparation and production stages and also identifies the managerial skills needed to design a successful report. A background and discussion to the main financial statements are provided, together with supporting statements and reports from chairpeople and directors. Other increasingly relevant areas that are examined include corporate governance and environmental issues. As many companies are now using the Internet to convey their information, a section is included on delivering your message by the World Wide Web.

In many smaller companies, the directors and shareholder-owners are often the same people. In some ways, the annual report is not always as essential to these groups in terms of image projection and conveying messages. Companies that are legally classified as being 'small' or even 'medium' are not required to publish the same level of detail as large listed companies. Nevertheless, directors and managers of small companies may still find value in reading this book. Many of these smaller businesses may need to produce accounts and reports for other interested parties, such as banks and potential purchasers. There are still occasions when even smaller companies need to project their image and deliver their own vital messages.

This book does not explain every technical and legal detail involved in producing an annual report – there are plenty of accounting and legal reference books available – but it does highlight the key areas that must be considered and reflected upon in its preparation and publication. Understanding the nature of annual reports and accounts, and exactly how they can be used to explain and portray a company's image and corporate 'personality', is important for anyone interested in company reporting.

Annual Reports: Delivering Your Corporate Message to Stakeholders explains the nature and purpose of annual reports and will help all readers to deliver the vital messages that they wish to convey.

John Stittle
University of Essex
Colchester
July 2002

Acknowledgements

The author gratefully acknowledges the following organizations for permission to use extracts of their annual reports and other information.

Abbey National plc
Allied Domecq PLC
AstraZeneca plc
British Airways plc
Kingfisher Group plc
Manchester and District Housing Association
Marks and Spencer plc
Royal National Lifeboat Institution
Tate & Lyle PLC.

I would like to express my grateful appreciation to Guy Loft at Gower for his invaluable advice, guidance and assistance. I am also greatly indebted to Linda Cayford for her editing expertise and for the invaluable changes she has suggested to my draft manuscript. Any errors or omissions are, of course, entirely mine.

Part 1
Framework and context

1 The message

Every year thousands of companies go through the routine of producing their annual report. They have no choice – it is a legal requirement. But the publication of this report is far more than just a legal or accounting formality; it should capture the very spirit and personality of a company, forming the basis of the company's image and projecting the essence of a company's identity and direction. The annual report should be a means of portraying themes and corporate character. Above all, it should deliver a clear and unequivocal message: your message – the corporate message.

Content

A company's annual report and accounts, normally just termed 'the annual report', is essentially a financial and narrative report for the previous 12 months of a company's trading activities and its position at the year-end. It comprises many parts and its content is mainly dictated by legislation, accounting rules and stock exchange regulations. (The stock exchange regulations, under the auspices of the UK's Financial Services Authority, only apply to companies that are listed on the London Stock Exchange.)

Significantly, a vital component of the annual report is the company's accounts – normally termed the financial statements. These key statements include, *inter alia*:

- the profit and loss account
- the balance sheet
- the cash flow statement

- the statement of total recognized gains and losses.

However, in addition, there is extensive supporting information concerning the notes to the accounts, explaining issues such as accounting policies and practices. Information is also given about the company in the form of a directors' report, a chief executive's report and chairman's statement. Most companies also provide an operating and financial review, which explains the financial and trading aspects of the business. Sometimes companies also produce an environmental or community section detailing their environmental and social policies.

Many people wrongly believe that annual reports are important because they state and explain a company's profit. Of course they do state a company's profit but they are not important for just that reason – for example, companies listed on the London Stock Exchange will have normally already released their profit figures to the stock exchange many months earlier in the form of a 'preliminary announcement'. Annual reports are also an important source of other information and offer more specific details about key financial and operating information that are not always provided in a company's preliminary announcements.

Within strict boundaries, annual reports allow readers to examine a packaged version of the company's activities over the past year. The directors use annual reports to explain their actions during the year and how they have looked after the company's assets. Annual reports are therefore a crucial part of the accountability and stewardship process (see Chapter 2, 'Communication, stewardship and accountability').

Limitations

But annual reports are certainly not perfect and most definitely do not provide all the answers. So, often, the annual report leaves the reader wanting to know more. Unfortunately, these limitations are a corporate fact of life. The law, accounting standards and the stock exchange lay down minimum requirements which clearly must be adhered to. Companies can provide additional information if they wish, but few provide any more accounting information than the statutory minimum. In practice, most annual reports frequently fail to provide answers to significant aspects of a company's operating and financial affairs. Users of annual reports frequently need further information to meet their analytical needs. There is no easy way of overcoming these limitations; these weaknesses are largely accepted as a fundamental fact of financial life. Many companies are simply not prepared to provide additional information over and above the regulatory requirements.

Inciting interest

For many recipients, the annual report may not even be opened or, if it is, it may well be aimlessly and rapidly flicked through. But it does not have to be like this. Although, realistically, some sections of the report will never be understood by non-accountants, that is no excuse or justification for producing a document that no layperson would wish to read, either fully or in part. It is a company's responsibility to ensure that the report is written and presented in such a way as to generate at least some degree of interest and foster a relationship between company and reader. The quality and 'readability' of the annual report is entirely the responsibility of the company. The reader is under no obligation to read, yet alone understand, the report. Granted that some complex accounting issues can never be simplified and explained in understandable terms for most readers, nevertheless there are large sections of the annual report that can be made understandable, or at least parts that can be simplified and presented in an attractive and clear manner. In other words, the report can be used as a public relations and informative document. This is your company's annual opportunity to convey the information and the image that you want to portray.

Despite some limitations on the scope and depth of information contained in the annual report, there is another matter that is equally, if not more, important. It concerns messages. As stated earlier, quite simply, but significantly, annual reports give out messages. Your annual report is an ideal opportunity to deliver explicit and also implicit corporate messages to a wider audience. Of course, part of your corporate message will be the delivery of your financial statements and supporting information. In this you have no choice – this information is the centrepiece – an integral component of the report. However, the financial statements are only one part of a very large picture that you should be painting.

Team effort

The complex nature of the economic and trading activities of many companies presents a significant challenge for annual reports which have to reflect the complexity and the diversity of modern corporate life on to a two-dimensional piece of paper. The attempt to portray this economic reality involves the contribution of a number of individuals, experts and professionals in terms of knowledge and skills.

To begin with, your accountants are an extremely important group in preparing your annual report. They will collate all the financial data, select various accounting policies and techniques and attempt to paint an interpretation of what they believe resembles an objective portrait of your company – with the emphasis being on 'objective'. And it is this aspect of objectivity that causes so many problems in the world of accountancy. Of course, conforming to the legal requirements, accounting rules and the Financial Service Authority rules (for stock exchange-listed companies) is important in fulfilling one aspect of presenting some degree of objectivity. However, there is another significant aspect involved. Accountants still have to use their own judgements and opinions in constructing the final accounts. Accounting policies have to be selected, data has to be interpreted and accounting judgements have to be made. These judgements can often cause major difficulties in company accounting. Two accountants can take identical raw financial data and end up with a different reported profit in the final accounts.

An analogy can be made with a painting. A cornfield painted by Constable or Gainsborough will be different in appearance from that portrayed by Van Gogh or Dali. The paintings of Constable or Gainsborough will be often regarded as more 'photographic' whereas those of Van Gogh and Dali will be less clearly defined and more 'impressionist'. But the important point is that, to both groups of painters, their painting does indeed represent a cornfield (*to them*).

Much the same often applies (but perhaps in a less extreme way) to accountants depicting a company's financial affairs. But let us not forget that accountants do not have unfettered judgement or discretion. Once the accounts have been prepared by the company's accountants, external and independent accountants, acting in their capacity of auditors, will state whether, in their opinion, the accounts give a 'true and fair view' and comply with the relevant companies' legislation.

Assistance in preparing the annual report will also be obtained from your company secretary and from your Corporate Affairs or Investor Relations Department. Other professionals will include the graphic designers and photographers who have an influential role in ensuring the design and layout of the report are such that your message is clearly delivered in the form that you wish.

A complete package

Throughout your annual report's preparation it is clearly imperative that the company complies with all other relevant reports and corporate governance recommendations, and produces all the statutory information that, for example, is contained in the directors' report.

Towards the time of printing the report you will need to ensure that all relevant material relating to such issues as the annual general meeting, voting forms and associated procedures are included. Input will also be needed from the chairman's office for the preparation of the traditional chairman's statement, and there is also usually some form of report from the chief executive about the company's progress during the course of the year.

What's your message?

Even during the planning stage of your annual report you should keep one clear point firmly in mind: the theme of your message. It is your overriding objective to decide on the theme(s) of the message that you are trying to convey this year.

Naturally, your annual report will contain the statutory message. You are obliged to incorporate the financial statements and supporting information. It is not only how you deliver this statutory message but also how you deliver other vital messages concerning aspects of your business that really matter.

Preparation and practicalities

Admittedly, you can do little about the content of the financial statements that have been prepared by your accountants. They will have already done their best to put the highest degree of gloss and spin on the accounts – within, of course, the acceptable boundaries of legal and accounting requirements.

It is now down to you to arrange the presentation and layout of the financial statements to achieve maximum impact (see Chapter 13, 'Design, printing and distribution'). More implicitly, your company image can be projected by concentrating on the use of colour, layout, paper size, and creative use of diagrams and photographs to reflect how you wish others to perceive your company.

Do not forget to take account of the cover boards binding your report. This aspect is often overlooked as unimportant, but it can be highly influential. The cover board is the first thing readers see as they take the report out of the envelope. A dull and unimpressive cover board will quickly ensure that your report is thrown into the wastebin. Likewise, the accompanying envelope is also important. An envelope that appears too 'official-looking' or one that resembles 'junk mail' should also be avoided. Many good products have been spoilt through poor packaging. Try to make sure that your packaging looks relatively formal – that it looks important but not too offputting. That said, never choose cheap packaging; it will devalue your report. Your report is worth much more to you than to have it thrown away immediately on receipt (see Chapter 13, 'Design, printing and distribution').

Types of business

In explicit terms, you may wish to concentrate on conveying a theme of, perhaps, an adventurous, exploratory and cutting-edge company on the brink of technological breakthroughs. You may wish to give the impression that you are a fresh, innovative and leading company in your sphere of operations. If this is your aim, then you will need to consider such issues as how you will reflect this innovative and cutting-edge image not only in the presentation of your financial statements but also in the design and presentation of the rest of your report. You also need to consider how you would highlight and discuss aspects of your business in the directors' report and in the operating and financial review (see Chapter 5, 'Major reports, statements and reviews').

Alternatively, you may be an investment or asset management company, or perhaps a banking company, and choose to portray a totally different image. You may wish to appear extremely safe, sound, reliable and, perhaps, even slightly risk-averse. Your aim might be based on projecting a message of integrity, safety and absolute customer confidence. In this case, you will not necessarily wish to use an avant garde presentation with a 'non-conventional' or 'over-artistic' use of colour and presentation. In contrast, an advertising agency might choose to highlight originality, wittiness, new ideas and an ultra-modern approach. A food manufacturing company might wish to emphasize its key products and concentrate on highlighting quality, product innovation and high levels of customer satisfaction. A service or computing software company might wish to place emphasis on service standards or the continuous development and application of software packages. A healthcare company might want to stress a caring and concerned image in its presentation and content.

Overall, it is difficult to generalize – all companies are different. Each company must be examined on a case-by-case basis. Even within companies operating in the same line of business there might be different messages and submessages that need to be portrayed.

Who are you?

At the initial stages of designing each year's annual report, you must ask yourself such questions as:

- What type of company are we?
- How do we see ourselves?
- How do we wish others to see us?
- What key aspects of information do we want to transmit to shareholders (and to the world at large)?
- What is the theme we wish to convey?
- Is our corporate message clearly coming across through our report?
- In short, what is our message?

Developing your message

Once you have decided on your company's particular message, you can then identify a 'running theme' to be the pivotal point in designing your other statements, such as the operating and financial review and the chief executive's and chairman's statements. The continuation and continuity of the corporate theme is important. Do not highlight a theme and then stop. Keep it running throughout the whole of the report. In fact, if you are expressing and projecting a key theme this year, you may wish to keep it running in subsequent years – perhaps for the next two or three years, or even longer.

You might wish to develop and expand themes in subsequent years, or change or modify them as your business changes. But never be satisfied or complacent.

As your business develops, so must your message.

Mission statements: a word of warning

A word of warning is needed here. An increasing number of companies are developing and clearly expressing their own corporate aims, objectives and visions in the form of a 'company mission statement', often boldly printed across the annual report's cover board. Many companies rather meaninglessly state that they 'strive for excellence' or aim to be a 'world leader'. Such (often) pious, smug and even arrogant statements add little value. In many cases, the publication of these mission statements is merely conforming to 'corporate fashions' and has little relevance to most shareholders or other users of the company's services.

It is not the explicit purpose of this book to comment on companies' corporate mission statements except to add a note of caution. If your company is determined to follow this trend of highlighting 'mission statements', then try to ensure that the message you are attempting to portray in your annual report as a whole at least does not contradict the mission statement that you have printed on your cover board. Although the explicit publication of mission statements seems to be on the wane in the US, it still appears to be in popular use in the UK. So, if you are still convinced of the value of displaying your mission statement, synchronize it with your annual report's theme.

Quality and transparency

In recent years, there has been a marked trend for companies to increase the content of their annual reports. In the US this movement towards 'bigger is best' was highlighted during the company reporting season in the spring of 2002. In the previous autumn the US had suffered the collapse of its seventh largest company, the gigantic Enron energy corporation, amid allegations of accounting and auditing fraud and irregularities. There were major congressional investigations into 'hidden' off-balance-sheet debt and claims that the auditors destroyed important working papers relating to Enron's accounting techniques. Many US politicians claimed that corporate financial statements were not as transparent as they should be. The politicians' fears were heightened shortly after the Enron scandal when another major crisis faced corporate reporting. Substantial discrepancies were found in the accounts of WorldCom, the second largest US telecommunications company, which at one time was valued at more than $180 billion. At least $8 billion of revenue expenses were estimated to be wrongly classified as capital expenditure. By misclassifying the expenses as capital items, it was possible to spread the costs over many years (as with other genuine capital transactions). In addition, other leading US companies, including AOL Time Warner, Qwest, Xerox and Tyco, had their accounting policies and disclosures questioned.

Many other US companies were worried. Corporate chairmen were afraid that their companies might receive adverse publicity if there was the slightest hint that their annual reports were not disclosing a full and complete financial picture. Chief executives were worried that even the most trivial omission might cause a negative market reaction. As a result, many large US companies started to produce even more detailed and voluminous annual reports. For example, General Electric's 2002 annual report was almost a third bigger than the previous year's in an attempt to ensure that their annual report and accounts were as transparent and informative as possible, in the post-Enron climate.

The US government also responded to the crisis by initiating discussion as to whether additional information should be placed in annual reports. In addition, it wanted to remove the opaqueness of some companies' financial statements.

In the UK a number of companies are also considering increasing the voluntary disclosure of additional information to improve transparency and confidence in their financial statements (the regulatory position is still under review in the post-Enron environment). However, be warned. Although the Enron affair is still under investigation at the time of writing, you should not necessarily panic and rush into producing vastly extended reports. Bigger reports do not necessarily equate with improved quality. Nevertheless, if your company has become involved in (legal) financial activities such as potentially controversial off-balance-sheet funding schemes, you should be aware that your accounting policies may attract unwanted publicity. You should discuss the matter with your accountants and consider giving some additional information, at least until the upheaval caused by Enron's collapse subsides.

Many companies have no reason to panic – their transactions are often reasonably transparent. But if you are in doubt as to how the market will respond to your transactions, you should provide more information to help your investors understand the company's transactions in a clearer light. But do not just rush in and produce more and more information that hinders, rather than helps, the analysis of your annual report. Quality and clarity are far more important than volume.

2 Communication, stewardship and accountability

Communication

A company's annual report is not just about stewardship and accountability. Certainly, it allows the board of directors to report back and explain their actions and decisions to shareholders, thereby facilitating a degree of accountability to the owners of the business. But there is more to the annual report than just making the directors more accountable for their stewardship of the company's assets; it is a vital means by which a company communicates its corporate message to shareholders, debenture-holders, creditors, the media and the world at large. Essentially, it is your company's voice to the external world. Although all limited companies are legally obliged to produce an annual report, the information contained inside its cover boards does not have to be tediously presented, dull in appearance or lacking in inspiration. A large proportion of the report's contents must, by legal necessity, incorporate masses of detailed and complex financial statements and supporting notes, but this does not prohibit you from presenting the information in the most effective way.

To non-accountants, a considerable proportion of the content of the annual report is often perceived as a mysterious and indecipherable code, most of which they fail to decipher. Accountants and financial analysts can usually extract some information of varying degrees of usefulness, but these groups of specialists are the exception. Some readers of the annual report merely want to know the level of profits earned during the year. But for many readers, even the amount of profit that is disclosed is irrelevant, for many shareholders will already know some of the key information relating to their company since, in practice, profits are disclosed through company announcements and subsequent press comment often many months before the annual report is published.

Stakeholders: your audience

The annual report communicates information to an array of direct or indirect individual and group stakeholders. Stakeholders in a limited company include shareholders (both actual and potential), creditors, banks and lending institutions, employees, investment analysts, the general public and governmental bodies. Some of these groups, such as shareholders and debenture-holders, have a legal right to receive a copy of the annual report but there is no legal obligation to send a copy directly to most of the other user groups.

In the last few years many companies have placed their annual reports on their websites (see Chapter 12, 'The new age: electronic reporting'). You should certainly make use of your website to communicate to your potential readers a priority, if you have not already done so. A website is another important channel of communication.

So whether the annual report is legally required to be sent to some of the user groups is, in some ways, irrelevant. It presents a marvellous opportunity to communicate to all potential users. It is your company, so use this opportunity to convey both the explicit and implicit messages that you want to convey. The annual report is your chance to place your company firmly in the public mind, as well as explaining complex areas and portraying images and impressions to your readers. It can be one of the best public relations opportunities of the year – do not waste it.

Clearly, the required legal information must be included but, at the same time, a wealth of other non-statutory supporting information can be added to enhance user interest.

Legal form

All sole traders, partnerships and companies must produce annual accounts. However, the accounts of sole traders and partnerships are strictly confidential. The financial statements of these two groups need only be legally disclosed to the taxation authorities: it is not possible for the public, creditors or employees to obtain access as a legal right. Therefore, the concept of producing a report and delivering messages is not directly applicable for these categories.

Background: incorporation

There is, however, a major category for which annual reports are highly significant – namely, limited companies. The origins of limited companies can be traced back to the nineteenth century when there was an explosion in the complexity and extent of business activity which necessitated companies raising extensive capital funds. This expansion led to the overwhelming need to 'incorporate'. This incorporation took the form of allowing businesses to register as limited companies. The significance of limited liability status was immense. Legally, the identity of a company would be totally distinct and separate from the owners and providers of share capital. Companies could then raise funds from shareholders for investment and expansion. Companies could also trade, incur debts, buy and sell assets and employ workers in their own legal name. Subsequently, if the company collapsed financially, the shareholder-owners would be protected from the failed business's debts. If a company could not meet its liabilities, then the maximum amount that an investor could forfeit was limited to the extent of their original investment in the company's share capital.

The fact that society in general (through legal provisions) has granted shareholders legal protection from being liable for a business's debts is an immense privilege – one that is so significant that society has insisted that limited companies provide a large concession in return. This concession has taken the form of an obligation on companies to report publicly on their activities and on their financial performance and position. Under the 1985 and 1989 UK Companies Acts, all limited companies are now legally required to produce annual reports and accounts of their activities. (UK company legislation is currently being revised. A new Companies Act is expected to be issued in the near future.)

Stewardship and accountability

Traditionally, annual reports and accounts have been primarily concerned with stewardship and accountability. With the growth of limited companies, it became impractical for the many thousands of shareholders to be involved in managing and operating the companies' business activities.

Accordingly, shareholders elect directors to manage and control the company on their behalf. The company's assets are controlled by the directors on behalf of, and in stewardship for, the shareholder-owners. At the conclusion of every financial year, the managers and directors are required to report back to their shareholders and explain how the company's assets have been used. This process of reporting to shareholders is a key part of director accountability, and a vital means by which this accountability process is implemented is by the publication of an annual report and accounts.

Recipients

Although a company's current shareholders are the principal recipients of annual reports and accounts, there are nevertheless other so-called user groups such as creditors, lending institutions and employees who may also be interested.

Remember, though, that while many of these groups may be seeking to obtain a copy of the annual report and accounts, not all users are legally entitled to directly receive it. There are only two specific categories of users – namely, shareholders and debenture-holders – who, statutorily, must normally receive a copy of the annual report and accounts. However, the remaining user groups can obtain indirect access to the annual report. A copy must also be sent to the Registrar of Companies. Any potential investor, creditor or member of the public can legally obtain access to the financial statements lodged with the Registrar.

Sometimes, some companies do not wish to send copies of the report to members of the public who directly request them. But it is rather pointless not to send a copy of your annual report in these circumstances. A refusal is a largely futile gesture – the potential user will simply obtain a copy from the Registrar of Companies. Anyway, by refusing to supply a copy to non-statutory recipients, the company loses an enormous opportunity to promote itself. Moreover, it will lose significant goodwill and respect from the enquirer and leave a damaging trail of disappointment or suspicion. The unnecessary taint of suspicion of 'just what is this company hiding?' will linger. Every enquiry and opportunity to publicise the company and its corporate messages must be seized.

Since annual reports and accounts are so essential for stewardship, accountability and communication, the whole area is subject to specific and detailed legal, accounting and, sometimes, other regulatory controls – such as for companies listed on the stock exchange.

Legal requirements: filing accounts

In the UK, limited companies are, in effect, split into three categories:

- small
- medium
- large.

The current legal requirements are largely specified in the Companies Acts of 1985 and 1989. Essentially, small and medium-sized companies can file, with the Registrar of Companies, what are termed 'abbreviated accounts'. For small companies, abbreviated accounts means supplying only a simplified balance sheet accompanied by additional supporting notes. A profit and loss account or directors' report is not required. Medium-sized companies have to provide further, and more detailed, information. These companies are required to produce a directors' report, but not a detailed profit and loss account, and provide only modest analysis of some information.

However, there is another complication for small and medium-sized companies. These companies can take advantage of the legislation that allows them to deliver 'modified accounts' to shareholders. Smaller companies can obtain a number of exemptions and produce simplified overall final accounts that are sent to shareholders. Medium-sized companies do not obtain significant concessions.

Companies that do not fall within the definition of 'small' or 'medium' are classified as 'large' and are required to produce full accounts in accordance with legal, accounting and, for stock exchange-listed companies, Financial Services Authority rules.

If you believe that your company falls within the small or medium category, you should discuss with your accountants the precise nature of the accounting information you will have to provide. It is a specialist area and requires specialist advice. However, it is fair to say that the preparation of annual reports is not as critical for some medium- and smaller-sized companies. Most small (and some medium-sized) companies generate far less interest from both actual and potential users. In fact, in many companies, the directors and managers *are* the owner-shareholders – the same people often occupy both roles. Accordingly, the issue of accountability is not such a key issue. But it must be stated that, for other business reasons, there is often still a need for a report and financial statements to be professionally prepared. At some stage, the directors/owners may wish to consider selling the business or perhaps attempt to obtain loans or additional funding. On any criteria, a well-drafted report and accounts will place those businesses in a considerably superior and preferential light.

The actual content of the minimum requirements for the financial statements for large companies is explained in Chapter 4, 'Content of financial statements'.

If your company is listed on the London Stock Exchange you may also wish to consider producing summarized financial statements for shareholders who do not wish to receive the detailed published annual report (see Chapter 7, 'Summary financial statements and interim reports').

Target audience

The principal difficulty in aiming annual reports at an audience is that there is no single target. Annual reports are multipurpose, with a variety of user groups extracting the information that each user requires. Many companies believe that shareholders are the primary targets of their reports. In many respects, of course, current shareholders are a key legal and regulatory target group, but there is also the more commonly forgotten category of the debenture-holders whose primary objective to is to use the report (at least in part) to assess the underlying security of their debenture and whether the company can continue to service the interest on it.

The third category of indirect users is exceptionally vague, imprecise and almost limitless. Once a company has filed a copy of its annual report with the Registrar of Companies, any other user group and any member of the public can obtain a copy of it for whatever reason. Once the report is lodged with the Registrar, it in effect enters into the public domain and hence a virtually unlimited audience. However, this indeterminate audience, ranging from potential shareholders, creditors, employees, financial analysts, the media, government and quasi-governmental organizations, is extremely important. Many of these individual groups of potential users have their own objectives and information needs, so the annual report must accordingly not only be targeted at current shareholders and debenture-holders but also at this cross-section of other potential interested users.

Multipurpose

This array of users causes other practical difficulties. Essentially, annual reports are based on the premise that 'one size fits all' – they must be tailored and aimed at all potential users. And this is where the problems start. Many of the possible users have different needs, yet companies are not compelled by law or other regulations to produce information that is of use or value to all users. For example, the detailed and complex needs of financial analysts may be different in both depth and content from the information required by employees or creditors.

Within the context of statute and regulation, companies must clearly include the minimum disclosures to satisfy these requirements. But the more astute companies will consider the possible interests of the other non-statutory groups. On a voluntary basis, you may wish to consider providing at least some information to some of these groups. In particular, the public at large (usually represented by the media) and financial analysts should be borne in mind. These two groups are often key financial opinion-formers and the effect of their commentary, reporting and analysis of your report in the public arena should not be underestimated. The more sophisticated users, such as financial analysts, will need more information than is contained in the annual report to form a full opinion. But the annual report (combined with the interims and preliminary announcements) is still a worthwhile source of information for a number of users.

Additional information

Remember that the Companies Acts and other accounting requirements are established on a minimum basis. Companies can, and occasionally do, provide information over and above the minimum levels. Companies should certainly consider how they could perhaps provide additional information that might be of at least some value to their wider audience. However, many companies are often loath to provide anything but the absolute minimum legal and accounting requirements for fear of providing more information than their competitors. Nevertheless, the astute company will realize that annual reports are about image and conveying messages. Accordingly, information can be tailored so that it appears to provide useful information and show concern for this wider audience.

Annual reports are much more than the mere fulfilment of legal, accounting and other regulatory requirements. Any company which believes that this is their sole purpose is missing an enormous opportunity to provide additional information to help the company to deliver its message.

Reactions to annual reports

A study of 66 of the UK's financial analysts, undertaken by City analysts Corporate Edge, made an assessment of annual reports and identified what they considered to be their key weaknesses. In particular, they cited the following criticisms:

- too 'gimmicky' (by 45 per cent of respondents)
- overdesigned (38 per cent)
- misleading figures (32 per cent)
- unclear language (30 per cent)

- 'me-too' or 'samey' (29 per cent)
- boring (26 per cent)
- too short (26 per cent)
- confusing design (20 per cent)
- too long (18 per cent)
- failed to show the personality of the company (11 per cent).

The survey revealed that analysts were especially critical of some types of business sector. Telecommunications and information technology companies received the most adverse comments, with over 67 per cent of analysts believing that companies in this line of business produced reports that were too gimmicky, 58 per cent believing that they contained misleading figures, and 42 per cent suggesting that they were overdesigned and boring. More than 60 per cent of analysts believed that reports in the media and advertising business sector were overdesigned and, notably, every analyst indicated that companies in the media sector designed very similar reports.

On a more positive note, the pharmaceutical/chemicals and retail sectors received the most favourable comments.

The survey also highlighted companies' weaknesses in producing their reports. Overall, 59 per cent of analysts believed that companies 'played safe' with their annual reports and did little more than merely publish the basic information. Nearly 41 per cent of analysts believed that companies saw the annual report as a 'necessary evil' and more than 25 per cent of analysts in the food sector thought that companies saw their report as an 'expensive waste of time.'

One of the principal criticisms is that annual reports are 'too gimmicky'. Companies should never produce reports that leave them open to the charge of tackiness, cheapness or pretentiousness.

Some companies in the advertising world seem to believe that their professional skills in devising advertising material for clients can be automatically or instinctively transferred to their own reports. Advertising executives may be brilliant at designing television advertisements and musical jingles for client companies that wish to sell more chocolate bars or new cars, but these same skills are not always so successful when they attempt to design their own annual reports. It is not easy to combine complex technical details into a readable, high-quality and non-gimmicky product. For example, some media and advertising agencies (and, indeed, companies in other business sectors) will add colourful, intricate and clever diagrams, images and cartoons. Too often, these pictures and diagrams do nothing to enhance either the company or its report.

A clear, solid and reliable professional approach is vital. Companies face a difficult balancing act. The report must be serious and informative, yet readable and appealing to the user. It is an exceptionally difficult balance to achieve as complex legal and accounting information must always be combined with any other messages and images that the company wishes to convey.

Image and the message

The annual report reflects the company's whole intrinsic nature. It is a major statement and reflection of a company's image. As this book shows in subsequent chapters, the annual report is not just about how the outside world sees you, but also how you see yourself. This formal and legally required report has to encapsulate the whole feel and ethos of the company. It must highlight the company's individual character and corporate standing. It must reflect the company's role and place in the business world. By reading the report, readers can immediately sense a company's corporate weight and reputation.

This character comes through in many ways: from the report's design, layout and appearance to the use of colour, types of photograph, selection of paper quality, typeface, and so on. As detailed in the following chapters, there are many ways and techniques to make your annual report reflect your corporate identity and convey messages and images to your readership.

3 The regulatory framework of annual reports

Companies' financial statements form a vital component of the annual report. As discussed in Chapter 2, these statements are one of the principal means by which directors account for their actions during the year and communicate with the shareholders. Since these financial statements are so vital, companies must comply with specified legal and accounting requirements. In addition, listed companies must also comply with the rules of the Financial Services Authority which governs companies listed on the London Stock Exchange.

To increase credibility, the financial statements are then subject to independent verification by auditors (see Chapter 6, 'Auditors' reports').

Regulatory sources

There are three major regulatory sources that determine the framework of annual reports in general and financial statements in particular. These are:

- the statutory framework
- the accounting framework
- the stock exchange/Financial Services Authority.

The statutory framework

Historically, the statutory accounting provisions have not been unduly excessive in the UK, compared with many other European countries. Since the nineteenth century, successive UK governments have tended to establish only the basic overall legal framework and, in effect, have delegated considerable sections of the content and technical details of company accounts to the accounting profession. In contrast, many other European countries have a highly formalized and detailed set of rules that are more directly enshrined in statute. Many countries in continental Europe have accounting regulations derived from national state accounting plans that are clearly established by statute. This means that accountants in these countries have far less autonomy in developing and implementing accounting policies.

Background

The European Union has been moving towards greater harmonization between countries of many aspects of company financial statements. In 1977 the European Community 4th Directive attempted to standardize the key aspects of the form and content of company accounting statements. All limited companies in member states were required to publish their profit and loss accounts and balance sheets in a largely standardized and highly regimented fashion. Although a limited degree of choice and options were permitted, the end result was that most published company accounts throughout Europe were broadly similar in content and layout.

The UK initially adopted the requirements of the 4th Directive in the 1981 Companies Act. This 1981 Act was updated and revised in the 1985 Companies Act (with amendments in the 1989 Companies Act).

Under s.226 of the 1985 Companies Act, the directors of every limited company in the UK must prepare annual financial statements. These accounts will predominantly consist of a profit and loss account, a balance sheet and supporting information in the notes.

In addition to these specific accounting statements, companies must legally keep other accounting records which must show, *inter alia*, any sums of money paid and received, stock records and statements identifying all debtors and creditors. These records should be in such detail as to allow the company's financial position to be disclosed, with reasonable accuracy, at any time.

Within the legal framework, there is an overriding legal obligation (s.226; s.227, Companies Act 1985) for all company accounts to provide 'a true and fair view' of its financial statements and comply with the requirements of the 1985 Companies Act (see Chapter 6, 'Auditors' reports').

The accounting framework

The 1985 and 1989 Companies Acts specify the general framework of published accounting statements. However, there is an extensive array of other accounting information that needs to be provided. This detailed and additional information has been primarily laid down by the accounting profession in the form of accounting standards: these comprise Statements of Standard Accounting Practice (SSAPs) and Financial Reporting Standards (FRSs). The SSAPs are gradually being withdrawn, updated and improved and many have been reissued under their new name of FRSs.

Background

The overall accounting regulatory regime is presided over by the Financial Review Council which delegates its authority on day-to-day accounting matters to the Accounting Standards Board (ASB). The ASB currently issues FRSs. Companies should normally ensure that their accounting policies and transactions are in accordance with the comprehensive provisions of these relevant FRSs. These authoritative standards cover such topics as group accounts, leasing, pensions, deferred taxation, intangible assets and many other crucial accounting issues (see Figure 3.1).

Comply or else . . .

The accounting standards are regarded as so important that the 1985 Companies Act requires all large companies to state whether their financial statements have been prepared in accordance with all applicable financial reporting standards. Companies that fail to comply with these standards must provide full details and give the reasons for any departures from compliance.

In themselves, the Financial Reporting Standards do not generally have direct legal authority. However, the ASB has been legally recognized as 'an authorizing body' for issuing standards. Legal advice received by the Accounting Standards Board has indicated that, in most circumstances, it would be expected that companies would need to comply with the Financial Reporting Standards to ensure that their accounts presented 'a true and fair view'. In effect, it is mandatory for companies to comply with accounting standards. In very limited and highly exceptional circumstances, a company can only depart from complying with the standards if the departure is necessary to ensure that its accounts provide 'a true and fair view'.

Another body, the Financial Reporting Review Panel (FRRP) has been established to ensure that companies comply with accounting standards. If

Accounting standards that have been developed by the ASB are contained in 'Financial Reporting Standards' (FRSs).

The ASB has adopted the standards issued by the former Accounting Standards Committee that means that they also fall within the legal definition of accounting standards. These are designated 'Statements of Standard Accounting Practice' (SSAPs). Many of the SSAPs have been superseded by FRSs, but some still remain in force.

The following is a list of FRSs that are currently applicable:

(Most recent listed first.)

- FRS 19 – Deferred Tax
- FRS 18 – Accounting Policies
- FRS 17 – Retirement Benefits
- FRS 16 – Current Tax
- FRS 15 – Tangible Fixed Assets
- FRS 14 – Earnings per Share
- FRS 13 – Derivatives and other Financial Instruments: Disclosures
- FRS 12 – Provisions, Contingent Liabilities and Contingent Assets
- FRS 11 – Impairment of Fixed Assets and Goodwill
- FRS 10 – Goodwill and Intangible Assets
- FRS 9 – Associates and Joint Ventures
- FRS 8 – Related Party Disclosures
- FRS 7 – Fair Values in Acquisition Accounting
- FRS 6 – Acquisitions and Mergers
- FRS 5 – Reporting the Substance of Transactions
- FRS 4 – Capital Instruments
- FRS 3 – Reporting Financial Performance
- FRS 2 – Accounting for Subsidiary Undertakings
- FRS 1 (Revised 1996) – Cash Flow Statements
- FRSSE (Effective March 2000) – Financial Reporting Standard for Smaller Entities

Statements of Standard Accounting Practice (SSAPs)

The following SSAPs are also currently applicable (but may be revised and re-issued as FRSs):

- SSAP 25 – Segmental reporting
- SSAP 24 – Accounting for pension costs
- SSAP 21 – Accounting for leases and hire purchase contracts
- SSAP 20 – Foreign currency translation
- SSAP 19 – Accounting for investment properties
- SSAP 17 – Accounting for post balance sheet events
- SSAP 13 – Accounting for research and development
- SSAP 9 – Stocks and long-term contracts
- SSAP 5 – Accounting for value added tax
- SSAP 4 – Accounting for government grants

Figure 3.1 Financial Reporting Standards (FRSs) issued by the Accounting Standards Board

a company ignores an accounting standard, the FRRP has the legal power to refer the matter to the courts. It will then ask the court to determine whether, by continuing to ignore a standard, a company's accounts provide a true and fair view. Ultimately, the court has the power to require directors to amend defective accounts if they fail to meet this standard.

Recently, an Accounting Foundation Review Board has been established to help ensure that professional accounting organizations and their members are conforming to the highest professional standards. The Urgent Issues Task Force, a subcommittee of the ASB, also occasionally issues pronouncements on accounting matters. These pronouncements, termed 'Abstracts', are rapidly issued statements that, in effect, carry virtually the same status as fully-fledged accounting standards. The Task Force usually issues pronouncements where the interpretation of an accounting matter is required as a matter of urgency.

International Accounting Standards

In 2002, the European Union (EU) agreed to implement greater standardization of accounting standards throughout Europe. All companies listed on a EU stock market will be compelled to prepare their group accounts under IASs – International Accounting Standards (increasingly known as International Financial Reporting Standards) – by the year 2005. The International Accounting Standards Board (IASB) issues the IASs. In some instances, UK standards and IASs are very similar or closely related. In some other accounting cases, the adoption of IASs would result in changes in existing UK practice. It has been recently decided that new IASs will be referred to as International Financial Reporting Standards (IFRSs).

Greater European standardization in accounting policies will provide considerable benefits for listed companies. Common standards will help companies raise funds on European capital markets and also assist in comparing the financial results of companies in different countries. Adoption of the new international standards would mean the creation of a new European accounting regulatory organisation. Initial indications are that the EU will create an Accounting Regulatory Committee, chaired by EU representatives, which will decide which IASs the EU will accept as being applicable to European listed companies.

There are a number of international accounting standards issued by the International Accounting Standards Board. By 2005 any EU company listed on a European stock exchange will be required to prepare its group financial statements in accordance with these international standards (see Figure 3.2).

The currently applicable IASs are:

- IAS 41: Agriculture
- IAS 40: Investment Property
- IAS 39: Financial Instruments: Recognition and Measurement
- IAS 38: Intangible Assets
- IAS 37: Provisions, Contingent Liabilities and Contingent Assets
- IAS 36: Impairment of Assets
- IAS 35: Discontinuing Operations
- IAS 34: Interim Financial Reporting
- IAS 33: Earnings per Share
- IAS 32: Financial Instruments: Disclosure and Presentation
- IAS 31: Financial Reporting of Interests in Joint Ventures
- IAS 30: Disclosures in the Financial Statements of Banks and Similar Financial Institutions
- IAS 29: Financial Reporting in Hyperinflationary Economies
- IAS 28: Investments in Associates
- IAS 27: Consolidated Financial Statements
- IAS 26: Accounting and Reporting by Retirement Benefit Plans
- IAS 24: Related Party Disclosures
- IAS 23: Borrowing Costs
- IAS 22: Business Combinations
- IAS 21: The Effects of Changes in Foreign Exchange Rates
- IAS 20: Accounting for Government Grants and Disclosure of Government Assistance
- IAS 19: Employee Benefits
- IAS 18: Revenue
- IAS 17: Leases
- IAS 16: Property, Plant and Equipment
- IAS 15: Information Reflecting the Effects of Changing Prices
- IAS 14: Segment Reporting
- IAS 12: Income Taxes
- IAS 11: Construction Contracts
- IAS 10: Events After the Balance Sheet Date
- IAS 8: Net Profit or Loss for the Period, Fundamental Errors and Changes in Accounting Policy
- IAS 7: Cash Flow Statements
- IAS 2: Inventories
- IAS 1: Presentation of Financial Statements

Figure 3.2 International Accounting Standards (International Financial Reporting Standards issued by the Accounting Standards Board)

The stock exchange/Financial Services Authority framework

As well as complying with legal and accounting rules, some companies are required to comply with an additional set of regulations. Companies that have been admitted to the Official List of the London Stock Exchange are termed 'listed companies'. The London Stock Exchange has laid down explicit regulations (the 'Listing Rules', sometimes referred to as the 'Yellow Book') that a company must adhere to if it is granted a 'listing'.

Since 2000, the regulation and monitoring of the stock exchange rules has been taken over by the UK Listing Authority, a division of the Financial Services Authority (FSA).

Background

Companies listed on the London Stock Exchange are required to produce an annual report and accounts. If a listed company is UK-registered, these must not only be prepared in accordance with the requirements of the 1985 Companies Act and UK accounting standards, but must also comply with the FSA's rules.

There are also strict time-limits for publishing the accounts. The stock exchange insists that the accounts are published as soon as possible after the accounts have been approved by the directors and, in any case, normally not later than six months after the year-end. Legally, public companies not listed on the stock exchange have longer to issue their annual reports. A UK public company has a time-limit of seven months, which can be extended by three months if the company has overseas interests.

In addition, listed companies must specifically publish further detailed information which should include, *inter alia*:

- a statement by the directors that the company is a going concern with any supporting assumptions or qualifications

- any substantial shareholdings held by investors

- disclosures on directors' remuneration over and above those required by statute; changes in directors' shareholdings after the year-end; shareholders' dividends and directors' emoluments that have been waived

- a commentary on any published forecasts or estimates where the results differ by more than 10 per cent

- various corporate governance statements (see Chapter 8, 'Corporate governance').

No choice

If your company is listed, you have no choice. Your annual report must conform to the legal, accounting and stock exchange requirements – there is no escape. These layers of regulation are so important that the content of your report must contain the relevant information or, ultimately, your listing may be suspended.

Since you cannot change the regulatory rules and content of the accounts, your main chance of improving your report, in terms of these regulatory frameworks, is to concentrate on improving the presentation and clarity of this mandatory information (see Chapter 13, 'Design, printing and distribution').

However, as regards the preparation of the annual financial statements, you will need to take expert advice from your accountants and other advisers. Clearly, the various rules of the regulatory frameworks must not be ignored and, accordingly, there must be no slip-ups in your organization. In the case of larger companies, any minor omissions or breach of the rules will often be picked up by the media. This is publicity that you do not want. Ensure that your technical advice is top-rate; this will allow you to devote your attention to improving the messages that you wish to convey within the confines of the regulatory constraints.

Appendix 3.1: Update on accountancy regulation

After the US corporate accounting scandals in 2001 and 2002, the UK government has recently issued some proposals to improve the regulatory controls over the UK accountancy profession.

A report from the Department of Trade and Industry proposed that:

- The Financial Reporting Council should take on the functions of the Accountancy Foundation and create a new body, provisionally referred to as 'the independent regulator'.
- The independent regulator should have 'clear arrangements for accountability and transparency and should be outward facing in its role'.
- The Auditing Practices Board should take over the professional bodies' responsibilities 'for setting standards for independence, objectivity and integrity for auditors'.
- A new audit inspection unit should report to a board within the Independent Regulator.
- As the successor to the Review Board (of the Accountancy Foundation), a (newly created) Professional Oversight Board should '...retain its wider accountancy remit within a reformed structure'.
- An Investigation and Discipline Board should be brought into being without further delay to provide a 'demonstrably independent forum for hearing significant public interest disciplinary cases'.

Source: *Review of the Regulatory Regime of the Accountancy Profession: Report of the Secretary of State for Trade and Industry*, January 2003, DTI, London.

Part 2
Content and types of report

4 Content of financial statements

In whatever manner your annual report is presented and whatever style is chosen, it must never be forgotten that the accounting content contains substantial information. The financial statements are the major ingredient of the annual report.

At the heart of the annual report lies the critically important 'final' or 'primary' accounting statements. The accountants in your company will be concerned with the technical preparation of the accounts. (Other experts will also be called in once the accounts have been finalized.) The process by which the accountants prepare the final accounts can stretch over many months. In larger companies, which usually have more sophisticated accounting systems, the accounting records and transactions are usually kept continuously up to date. However, at the year-end, there are still often several months of collating, organizing, adjusting and preparing the actual accounting information. Smaller companies, which may have less advanced and less sophisticated accounting systems, will often find that there is proportionately more preparatory work at the year-end.

Even so, accountants in both large and small companies often face a tight deadline to prepare the final accounts.

Any delay incurred by your accountants may well impact on the production timetable of your annual report. Clearly, the report cannot be finalized until your accountants' input is complete.

Types of financial statement: background

There are four final accounting statements ('primary' statements) that have to be prepared. Two of these statements are a legal requirement and two are accounting requirements.

The two statutory statements that must be provided are:

- the profit and loss account (the income statement)
- the balance sheet.

The two professionally required accounting statements are:

- the cash flow statement
- the statement of total recognized gains and losses.

These two latter statements should be given equal prominence in the accounts, along with the profit and loss account and balance sheet.

The 1985 Companies Act (Schedule 4) insists that all companies produce a profit and loss account and balance sheet in a highly prescribed manner. The legal provisions are not only concerned with content but also with the format. This Act allows a choice of four profit and loss account formats and two balance sheet formats.

The profit and loss account

Since the objective of the profit and loss account is to identify the level of profit or losses made over the course of the previous year, it is self-evident that this statement will attract considerable interest. Accordingly, you should ensure that the key components of this statement are clearly highlighted. This does not mean just highlighting the organization's net profit; increasingly, substantial attention is being given to other earnings performance indicators. The current trend is for the profit and loss account to emphasize, perhaps in bold text, not just operating profit and profit before and after taxation but also the company's earnings before deducting interest, taxation, depreciation and amortization of assets – that is, items that are outside the company's direct control, such as taxation, and items that have no direct cash flow implications, such as depreciation.

Multicolumn

A number of companies are also producing multicolumn profit and loss accounts. If there are especially significant costs, such as reorganization or restructuring costs, companies often place these exceptional items in a separate column. Thus, in one column the net earnings will be shown but will exclude the exceptional items; in another column, the exceptional costs will be shown; and in the third column, the first two columns will be totalled (and will thereby net off the exceptional costs) to show the overall net profit. If your company does have substantial exceptional costs it may be worthwhile considering this approach. At least you can hope that shareholders will study the first column (which excludes exceptional items) and see how much more substantial your company's profits would have been but for the 'unfortunate' exceptional items. You could even emphasize the figures in the first column by the judicious use of colour or shading of the columns.

In practice, nowadays the profit and loss account is normally only prepared by adopting one of two 'commonly accepted' vertical formats. The other two formats are almost universally acknowledged to be too old-fashioned because they adopt the now outdated so-called 'horizontal method'.

The two modern, and commonly used, formats are shown in Appendix 4.1 at the end of this chapter. Although there are a number of similarities between the two formats, there are also some differences that can be used to advantage. Format 1 analyses some of the accounting information by function (for example, administrative expenses and distribution costs). In Format 1, companies have to show their gross profit margins, but in Format 2, the gross profit does not legally have to be disclosed. Instead, additional information has to be given concerning changes in stocks of finished goods, work in progress and in own-work capitalized. In practice, the majority of companies adopt Format 1.

Whatever format you adopt, at the very least, you must ensure that the profit and loss account is spaced clearly across the width of the page. Far too many companies attempt to confine the profit statement to an unnecessarily restricted space.

Additional disclosures

In addition to the items shown in Formats 1 and 2 there are three items that must always be shown on the face of the profit and loss account. These are:

- profit on ordinary activities before tax
- dividends paid and proposed
- transfer to or from reserves.

Future developments

The government's 2002 White Paper, *Modernising Company Law,* is considering reforming the layout of the profit and loss account. In future, it is possible that the profit and loss account will form part of a wider performance statement – perhaps by combining part of the Statement of Total Recognized Gains and Losses with the existing profit and loss account.

The balance sheet

The balance sheet should be designed so that it clearly lists your company's assets and liabilities at your financial year-end. As with the profit and loss account, do not restrict the layout of the balance sheet to a small space – it is regarded by many people as too important. Make sure that you clearly show the split of assets into two categories: fixed and current.

The traditional importance attributed to fixed assets, which are used in the business to generate future profits, should not be underestimated. Many financial analysts still examine the historic or current cost values of assets such as land and buildings, plant and machinery, and fixtures and fittings. Some companies also have valuable intangible assets, especially intellectual capital items such as trademarks and brand names, which often form the principal capital base of many technological industrial concerns and heavily branded industries.

In recent years, the value attributed to intangible assets in many companies has been growing in importance. You should certainly discuss the nature and value of these assets in greater detail in the operating and financial review section of your annual report (see Chapter 5, 'Major reports, statements and reviews').

Format

Although the Companies Act allows two formats of balance sheets, virtually all companies use Format 1 in vertical format – the horizontal style is not normally used in the UK (see Appendix 4.1).

It is important to note that financial items in the accounts are preceded either by letters, Roman numerals or Arabic numerals. This identification of items is important: it means that you now have a small degree of choice in preparing your balance sheet.

The presence of a Roman numeral or a letter on the layout indicates those items that must be shown on the face of accounts (see Appendix 4.1 for a model layout). Arabic numerals indicate items that may be totalled and analysed later in the supporting notes to the accounts. It is important to realize that the above information is the statutory minimum level of information that must be provided. Companies can voluntarily provide additional information if they consider it necessary.

Cash flow statements

Companies are also required to produce a cash flow statement (CFS). The CFS is not a legal requirement, but it is required for all companies except those classified as 'small' under the legislation by the professional accounting standard FRS1, *Cash Flow Statements*. This standard requires companies to draft a statement that identifies all the cash movements into and out of the company.

Advantage

A CFS has a considerable advantage over the profit and loss account. The profit statement is prepared under accounting practices and is subject to opinion and interpretation in applying accounting policies, whereas the CFS is solely prepared on the basis of cash received or paid. With a CFS there is little or no judgement required in its preparation or interpretation. It is far more objective and it is not subject to the interpretation of data and events by accountants.

A CFS simply lists all the receipts and payments of cash. These cash movements must be identified under the following major headings:

- operating activities
- returns on investments and servicing of finance
- taxation
- capital expenditure and financial investment
- acquisitions and disposals
- equity dividends paid
- management of liquid resources
- financing.

Formats

A company can choose to produce its CFS in one of two formats. The most common choice is the so-called 'indirect method' (see Appendix 4.2 at the end of this chapter). Under this method, the operating cash flows are calculated by adding back non-cash items (such as depreciation) to the operating profit. The alternative 'direct method' takes as its starting point the cash received from customers and cash paid to suppliers and employees. Only a small minority of companies adopt the direct method, largely because it discloses more detailed information. Although this additional information can often assist in analysis, it has the disadvantage of possibly providing competitors with valuable information.

Your accountants will advise you on the choice of format.

Statement of Total Recognized Gains and Losses (STRGAL)

The preparation of a STRGAL is not a legal necessity, but public companies are normally required, under the accounting standard FRS3, *Reporting Financial Performance*, to publish this statement as part of their financial statements.

This statement is designed to provide support to the profit and loss account. Some transactions, such as a profit on revaluing property or a loss arising from the translation of some forms of foreign currency transactions, are not entered directly in the profit and loss account. These types of transaction are termed unrealized profits or losses, or more colloquially, 'book' or 'paper' profits and losses. Since the profits and losses are not realized – that is, they have not actually been made or lost – the transactions are shown in the STRGAL to provide a full picture of all of a company's gains and losses, both realized and unrealized.

The above four statements should have equal prominence in the financial statements. Although they can be shown anywhere in practice, common sense and practicality usually dictate that they will almost certainly be found at the beginning of your financial statements section.

Reconciliation of movements in shareholders' funds

The financial statements of public limited companies will also contain another statement, a 'Reconciliation of Movements in Shareholders' Funds' which is generally of less importance than the previously discussed four statements. In acknowledgement of its inferior status, it is not referred to as a primary statement.

Shareholders' funds consist of shares and reserves and, essentially, this statement explains how the shareholders' funds have changed over the year. For example, shareholders' funds may have grown because the company has issued additional shares, or its reserves may have increased because of the retention of profits.

In preparing your annual report, you will have no option but to comply with the content and format of the accounting information. Since disclosure of this type of financial information cannot be changed, your overriding objective will be to present this largely mandatory information in the clearest and most informative way (see Appendix 4.2 for extracts of actual published financial statements).

Other contents of financial statements

Notes to the financial statements

In all annual reports, immediately after the financial statements themselves, you will see one or more pages providing supplementary notes which explain many of the accounting policies, practices and other information necessary to provide a more comprehensive understanding of the financial statements.

These notes to the financial statements are extremely important – they are an integral part of the accounts. Some people ignore them because they consider them as irrelevant 'small print'. How wrong they are! These notes are often just as important as the financial numbers – and sometimes more important. They explain the accounting treatment of such key topics as:

- accounting policies
- turnover
- fixed assets

- depreciation
- stocks
- foreign currency
- financial instruments
- taxation
- leases
- pension costs

and many others.

Do not attempt to underplay the significance of these notes by placing them at the back of the annual report or by using a small typeface. This treatment will only attract the attention of financial analysts who will believe that you have something to hide.

Your accountants will draft these technical notes for you. You must then ensure that the information is presented in the best possible way to maximise impact. (See Appendix 4.3 at the end of the chapter for an extract of notes referring to accounting policies.)

Five-year summary

Companies listed on the London Stock Exchange are recommended to produce a five-year summary of the key aspects of their profit and loss account, balance sheet and cash flow statement. Some companies even calculate and show key financial trend ratios to help shareholders understand their company's accounts.

The five-year summary is designed to show the trend of a company's financial data, and sometimes this extract is all that some shareholders examine. So do not waste the opportunity to make another positive impression – this trend information should be laid out clearly and boldly. Some companies attempt to place all this data on a single A4 page and sometimes the page appears overcrowded and cramped as a result. It may well be preferable to extend your summary over two adjacent pages. If you adopt the practice of some companies and use a large typeface with a ten-year trend, then you might certainly need two pages. See the extract of Tate & Lyle PLC's ten-year review in Figure 4.1.

Ten Year Review Financial years to March

Employment of Capital	1992 £ million	1993 £ million	1994 £ million	1995 £ million	1996 £ million	1997 £ million	1998 £ million	1999 £ million	2000 £ million	**2001 £ million**
Fixed assets	1 214	1 383	1 366	1 484	1 718	1 764	1 821	1 892	1 854	**1 807**
Working capital	274	242	324	320	454	326	319	288	211	**307**
Net operating assets	1 488	1 625	1 690	1 804	2 172	2 090	2 140	2 180	2 065	**2 114**
Net borrowings	(705)	(755)	(745)	(743)	(915)	(955)	(1 030)	(986)	(805)	**(963)**
Net (liabilities)/assets for dividends and tax	(47)	(49)	(63)	(66)	(36)	(4)	7	(23)	4	**3**
Total net assets	736	821	882	995	1 221	1 131	1 117	1 171	1 264	**1 154**
Capital Employed										
Called up share capital	115	116	115	115	116	116	117	117	117	**123**
Reserves	532	606	659	736	909	844	846	904	984	**977**
	647	722	774	851	1 025	960	963	1 021	1 101	**1 100**
Minority interests	89	99	108	144	196	171	154	150	163	**54**
	736	821	882	995	1 221	1 131	1 117	1 171	1 264	**1 154**
Profit Summary										
Sales	3 189	3 326	3 715	4 095	4 896	5 047	4 560	4 359	4 090	**4 146**
Operating profit before goodwill amortisation and exceptional items	281	245	278	340	377	253	260	220	237	**156**
Goodwill amortisation	–	–	–	–	–	–	–	–	–	**(5)**
Exceptional items	–	–	–	(13)	(13)	(83)	(9)	(5)	–	**–**
Group operating profit	281	245	278	327	364	170	251	215	237	**151**
Share of profits of joint ventures and associates	6	7	15	17	27	30	30	37	47	**29**
Total operating profit	287	252	293	344	391	200	281	252	284	**180**
Exceptional profit on sale of fixed assets and businesses	–	–	–	–	–	–	–	18	(18)	**(336)**
Profit before interest	287	252	293	344	391	200	281	270	266	**(156)**
Net interest	(57)	(46)	(43)	(43)	(58)	(56)	(65)	(73)	(65)	**(67)**
Net interest of joint ventures and associates	–	(1)	(3)	(5)	(6)	(5)	(10)	(13)	(10)	**(5)**
Profit before taxation	230	205	247	296	327	139	206	184	191	**(228)**
Taxation	(61)	(53)	(65)	(81)	(84)	(39)	(60)	(49)	(63)	**(35)**
Profit after taxation	169	152	182	215	243	100	146	135	128	**(263)**
Minority interests	(23)	(21)	(22)	(29)	(34)	(14)	(7)	4	(17)	**(7)**
Profit for the period	146	131	160	186	209	86	139	139	111	**(270)**
Dividends	(55)	(58)	(62)	(67)	(73)	(83)	(77)	(79)	(99)	**(86)**
Retained profit	91	73	98	119	136	3	62	60	12	**(356)**

Figure 4.1 Tate & Lyle PLC's ten-year review
Reproduced by kind permission of Tate & Lyle PLC.

Preliminary announcements

Although a company may have ascertained its overall profit and other key financial information at, or very shortly after, the year-end it can take many more months to publish and distribute the annual report and accounts.

Normally, in accordance with the FSA/Stock Exchange Listing Rules, a listed company must publish its accounts within six months of the year-end. However, the stock exchange must be informed of a listed company's annual results as soon as possible after the results have received board approval. The actual timing of notification is not prescribed, but the Accounting Standards Board encourages companies to inform the stock exchange of their preliminary announcements within 60 days.

The content of preliminary announcements

As a minimum, the preliminary announcement should include a summarized profit and loss account and other supporting information that is necessary for understanding the accounts being issued. The minimum information to be included in the profit and loss account is:

- net turnover
- profit or loss before tax
- taxation
- dividends paid and proposed
- earnings per share
- comparative figures.

In addition to the above key information, the ASB has recommended that companies provide other information, including the following:

- balance sheet
- cash flow statement
- statement of recognized gains and losses
- management commentary.

It is not always practical to have the results in the preliminary announcement audited. Although the information in the preliminary announcement is expected to be consistent with the audited accounts, waiting for the audit may cause the announcement to be unnecessarily delayed. In practice, many companies issue unaudited announcements. The preliminary announcement must have been agreed with the company's auditors and any uncertainties explained – even if the final accounts have not been formally audited at the time.

Other corporate reporting statements for companies listed on the US stock exchanges

Reconciliation statement

Companies must provide additional accounting information if they are listed on the US stock markets. However there are only a limited number of UK companies – usually large conglomerates – in this position. However, should your company be listed, for example, on the New York Stock Exchange, you will be required to prepare a reconciliation statement which reconciles the financial statements prepared under the UK's generally accepted accounting principles (GAAP) with US accounting practice.

There are some considerable differences in accounting policies, principles and practices between the UK and the US. The reconciliation statement explains the reasons for these differences and their effect on the accounts.

Normally, differences in both profit and shareholders' equity are explained in two separate statements.

In the first statement, the UK profit is adjusted for items that the US treats differently in such areas as goodwill, amortization, deferred taxation, pension costs and redundancy charges. The outcome of this exercise will show the level of profits that would have resulted had the accounts been prepared under US accounting rules.

The other reconciliation statement shows the amount of capital and reserves in the UK and explains what the comparative US figure would be if US accounting rules were used.

A brief explanation of the differences between specific UK and US accounting principles is also usually provided.

Generally, this information is aimed at the professional analysts and more technical readers – and, even then, these groups of people will want more information than is normally supplied. To most readers, the technical information will convey no messages, and the professional analysts will produce their own UK/US adjustments, so most companies regard the preparation of this information as something of an irritation. In terms of preparing your annual report, you should not normally devote excessive effort to presenting this particular item – allow two or three pages and simply publish the technical information provided by your accountants. Most companies merely state the information towards the end of their report – without embellishment or ceremony (see Appendix 4.4).

Form 20-F

The small number of UK companies seeking a US listing will also need to provide further information known as 'Form 20-F'. The US financial regulator, the Securities and Exchange Commission, requires companies to provide even more technical and legal information than that required in a UK/US GAAP reconciliation statement. The technical information required consists of facts and figures, including: the company's history and development; operating results; liquidity and capital resources; details of directors; major shareholders' share capital; and taxation information.

Some companies put the additional information required in a separate section at the end of the annual report or sometimes in a separate booklet. But since most UK companies do not trade their shares on the US market this will only usually concern a small number of UK multinational corporations.

Since it is a regulatory requirement you must obviously provide the information but, as with reconciliation statements, the vast majority of readers will not be interested. So if you have to prepare this information, just take the details from your accountants and include it in the Form 20-F. The information is almost always used only by a few financial analysts and they will take and adapt the information for their own complex and intricate purposes. Do not devote effort to preparing 20-F information; you will not reap large rewards.

Appendix 4.1: Balance sheet and profit and loss account formats

The balance sheet and profit and loss account formats are set out in Schedule 4 to the Companies Act 1985. The formats, with certain amendments, apply to both group accounts and the accounts of individual companies. Small and medium-sized companies may modify the profit and loss account and balance sheet formats. These precise modifications are outside the scope of this book.

Balance sheet Format 1
Note: Balance sheet Format 2 is not supplied. This form of balance sheet would be in 'horizontal' format and is not normally adopted in the UK.

A Called-up share capital not paid

B Fixed assets

I Intangible assets

1 Development costs
2 Concessions, patents, licences, trade marks and similar rights and assets
3 Goodwill
4 Payments on account

II Tangible assets

1 Land and buildings
2 Plant and machinery
3 Fixtures, fittings, tools and equipment
4 Payments on account and assets in course of construction

III Investments

1 Shares in group undertakings
2 Loans to group undertakings
3 Participating interests (excluding group undertakings) (see note 1)
4 Loans to undertakings in which the company has a participating interest

5 Other investments other than loans
6 Other loans
7 Own shares

C Current assets

I Stocks

1 Raw materials and consumables
2 Work in progress
3 Finished goods and goods for resale
4 Payments on account

II Debtors

1 Trade debtors
2 Amounts owed by group undertakings
3 Amounts owed by undertakings in which the company has a participating interest
4 Other debtors
5 Called-up share capital not paid
6 Prepayments and accrued income

III Investments

1 Shares in group undertakings
2 Own shares
3 Other investments

Cash at bank and in hand

D Prepayments and accrued income

E Creditors: amounts falling due within one year

1 Debenture loans
2 Bank loans and overdrafts
3 Payments received on account
4 Trade creditors
5 Bills of exchange payable
6 Amounts owed to group undertakings

7 Amounts owed to undertakings in which the company has a participating interest
8 Other creditors including taxation and social security
9 Accruals and deferred income

F Net current assets (liabilities)

G Total assets less current liabilities

H Creditors: amounts falling due after more than one year

1 Debenture loans
2 Bank loans and overdrafts
3 Payments received on account
4 Trade creditors
5 Bills of exchange payable
6 Amounts owed to group undertakings
7 Amounts owed to undertakings in which the company has a participating interest
8 Other creditors including taxation and social security
9 Accruals and deferred income

I Provisions for liabilities and charges

1 Pensions and similar obligations
2 Taxation, including deferred taxation
3 Other provisions

J Accruals and deferred income

Minority interests

K Capital and reserves

1 Called-up share capital
2 Share premium account
3 Revaluation reserve

IV Other reserves

1 Capital redemption reserve
2 Reserve for own shares

3 Reserves provided by articles of association
4 Other reserves

V Profit and loss account

Minority interests

Profit and loss account Format 1

1 Turnover
2 Cost of sales
3 Gross profit or loss
4 Distribution costs
5 Administrative expenses
6 Other operating income
7 Income from shares in group undertakings
8 Income from participating interests (excluding group undertakings)
9 Income from other fixed asset investments
10 Other interest receivable and similar income
11 Amounts written off investments
12 Interest payable and similar charges
13 Tax on profit or loss on ordinary activities
14 Profit or loss on ordinary activities after taxation
Minority interests
15 Extraordinary income
16 Extraordinary charges
17 Extraordinary profit or loss
18 Tax on extraordinary profit or loss
Minority interests
19 Other taxes not shown under the above items
20 Profit or loss for the financial year

Profit and loss account Format 2

1 Turnover
2 Change in stocks of finished goods and work in progress
3 Own work capitalized
4 Other operating income
5 (a) Raw materials and consumables
(b) Other external charges
6 Staff costs

7 (a) Depreciation and other amounts written off tangible and intangible fixed assets
(b) Exceptional amounts written off current assets
8 Other operating charges
9 Income from shares in group undertakings
10 Income from participating interests (excluding group undertakings)
11 Income from other fixed asset investments
12 Other interest receivable and similar income
13 Amounts written off investments
14 Interest payable and similar charges
15 Tax on profit or loss on ordinary activities
16 Profit or loss on ordinary activities after taxation
Minority interests
17 Extraordinary income
18 Extraordinary charges
19 Extraordinary profit or loss
Minority interests
20 Tax on extraordinary profit or loss
21 Other taxes not shown under the above items
22 Profit or loss for the financial year

Note: Formats 1 and 2 of the profit and loss account can also each be expressed in 'horizontal' format. However, this is rarely used.

Appendix 4.2: Extracts from Allied Domecq PLC's financial statements

The extracts from the financial statements of a public limited company set out on the following pages are reproduced by kind permission of Allied Domecq PLC.

Group profit and loss account

Year to 31 August 2001

	Note	Year to 31 August 2001 Before goodwill and exceptional items £m	Goodwill and exceptional items £m	Total £m	Year to 31 August 2000 Before goodwill and exceptional items £m	Goodwill and exceptional items £m	Total £m
Continuing operations		**2,879**	**–**	**2,879**	2,602	–	2,602
Discontinued operations		**–**	**–**	**–**	18	–	18
Turnover	1	**2,879**	**–**	**2,879**	2,620	–	2,620
Operating costs – goodwill amortisation		**–**	**(12)**	**(12)**	–	(3)	(3)
– other	6	**(2,311)**	**(9)**	**(2,320)**	(2,143)	(54)	(2,197)
Continuing operations		**568**	**(21)**	**547**	473	(57)	416
Discontinued operations		**–**	**–**	**–**	4	–	4
Operating profit		**568**	**(21)**	**547**	477	(57)	420
Share of profits of associated undertakings							
– continuing operations	15	**22**	**–**	**22**	14	–	14
– discontinued operations	15	**–**	**–**	**–**	9	–	9
Trading profit	1	**590**	**(21)**	**569**	500	(57)	443
Profit on sale of businesses in continuing and discontinued operations	7	**–**	**6**	**6**	–	13	13
Profit on disposal of fixed assets in continuing operations	7	**–**	**–**	**–**	–	46	46
Profit on ordinary activities before finance charges		**590**	**(15)**	**575**	500	2	502
Finance charges	8	**(90)**	**–**	**(90)**	(83)	–	(83)
Profit on ordinary activities before taxation		**500**	**(15)**	**485**	417	2	419
Taxation	9	**(130)**	**2**	**(128)**	(108)	15	(93)
Profit on ordinary activities after taxation		**370**	**(13)**	**357**	309	17	326
Minority interests – equity and non-equity	24	**(13)**	**–**	**(13)**	(9)	–	(9)
Profit earned for ordinary shareholders for the year		**357**	**(13)**	**344**	300	17	317
Ordinary dividends	11			**(127)**			(116)
Retained profit	23			**217**			201
Earnings per ordinary share:							
– basic	10			**32.6p**			29.9p
– diluted	10			**32.6p**			29.9p
– normalised	10	**33.9p**			27.4p		
– normalised (excluding Mexican excise rebate)	10	**31.0p**			27.4p		

Group balance sheet

At 31 August 2001

	Note	31 August 2001 £m	31 August 2000 £m
Fixed assets			
Intangible assets	12	**618**	108
Tangible assets	13	**767**	517
Investments and loans	14	**87**	67
Associated undertakings	15	**82**	77
Total fixed assets		**1,554**	769
Current assets			
Stocks	16	**1,203**	947
Debtors due within one year	17	**679**	646
Debtors due after more than one year	17	**316**	260
Cash at bank and in hand		**111**	112
Total current assets		**2,309**	1,965
Creditors (due within one year)			
Short term borrowings	20	**(770)**	(558)
Other creditors	18	**(1,189)**	(864)
Total current liabilities		**(1,959)**	(1,422)
Net current assets		**350**	543
Total assets less current liabilities		**1,904**	1,312
Creditors (due after more than one year)			
Loan capital	20	**(1,195)**	(806)
Other creditors	18	**(48)**	(37)
Total creditors due after more than one year		**(1,243)**	(843)
Provisions for liabilities and charges	19	**(199)**	(213)
Net assets		**462**	256
Capital and reserves			
Called up share capital	22	**267**	267
Share premium account	23	**26**	26
Merger reserve	23	**(823)**	(823)
Profit and loss account	23	**924**	720
Shareholders' funds – equity		**394**	190
Minority interests – equity and non-equity	24	**68**	66
		462	256

Approved by the board on 29 October 2001 and signed on its behalf by:

Chris Hogg

Sir Christopher Hogg
Chairman

Graham Hetherington

Graham Hetherington
Director

Group cash flow information

Year to 31 August 2001

Reconciliation of operating profit to net cash inflow from operating activities	Note	**Year to 31 August 2001 £m**	Year to 31 August 2000 £m
Operating profit		**547**	420
Exceptional operating costs		**9**	54
Goodwill amortisation		**12**	3
Depreciation		**56**	51
Increase in stocks		**(72)**	(43)
Increase in debtors		**(55)**	(97)
(Decrease)/increase in creditors		**(43)**	39
Expenditure against provisions for reorganisation and restructuring costs		**(34)**	(54)
Other items		**3**	(1)
Net cash inflow from operating activities		**423**	372

Group cash flow statement			
Net cash inflow from operating activities		**423**	372
Dividends received from associated undertakings		**9**	8
Returns on investments and servicing of finance	26	**(76)**	(81)
Taxation paid	26	**(34)**	21
Capital expenditure and financial investment	26	**(118)**	(11)
Acquisitions and disposals	26	**(635)**	(217)
Equity dividends paid		**(163)**	–
Cash (outflow)/inflow before use of liquid resources and financing		**(594)**	92
Management of liquid resources		**(6)**	52
Financing	26	**488**	(68)
(Decrease)/increase in cash in the year		**(112)**	76

Reconciliation of net cash flow to movement in net debt			
(Decrease)/increase in cash in the year		**(112)**	76
Increase/(decrease) in liquid resources		**6**	(52)
(Increase)/decrease in loan capital		**(488)**	68
Movement in net debt resulting from cash flows		**(594)**	92
Exchange adjustments		**(8)**	(29)
Movement in net debt during the year		**(602)**	63
Opening net debt		**(1,252)**	(1,315)
Closing net debt	28	**(1,854)**	(1,252)

Group statement of total recognised gains and losses

Year to 31 August 2001

	Year to 31 August 2001 £m	Year to 31 August 2000 £m
Profit earned for ordinary shareholders for the year	**344**	317
Currency translation differences on foreign currency net investments	**(16)**	7
Total recognised gains and losses for the year	**328**	324

Group note of historical cost profits and losses

Year to 31 August 2001

	Year to 31 August 2001 £m	Year to 31 August 2000 £m
Profit on ordinary activities before taxation	**485**	419
Realisation of property revaluation gains of prior years	**–**	2
Historical cost profit on ordinary activities before taxation	**485**	421
Historical cost retained profit	**217**	203

Group reconciliation of movements in shareholders' funds

Year to 31 August 2001

	Year to 31 August 2001 £m	Year to 31 August 2000 £m
Shareholders' funds at the beginning of the year	**190**	2,273
Total recognised gains and losses for the year	**328**	324
Ordinary dividends	**(127)**	(116)
Capital reduction due to disposal of UK Retail business	**–**	(2,294)
Goodwill written back on disposals	**3**	3
Net movement in shareholders' funds	**204**	(2,083)
Shareholders' funds at the end of the year	**394**	190

Appendix 4.3: Accounting policies

The extracts of information relating to the accounting policies of a listed public limited company set out below are reproduced by kind permission of Tate & Lyle PLC.

Notes to the financial statements: Tate & Lyle 2001

Basis of accounting

These accounts cover the 53-week financial period from 26 March 2000 to 31 March 2001, with comparative figures for the 78 weeks ended 25 March 2000.

These financial statements are prepared under the historical cost convention, as modified by the revaluation of certain tangible fixed assets, and in accordance with the Companies Act 1985 and applicable UK accounting standards.

New accounting standard

The accounting standard FRS18 'Accounting Policies' has been adopted in these financial statements for the first time but has not led to any change in accounting policy.

Basis of consolidation

The accounts of all subsidiary undertakings are consolidated from the date of their acquisition up to the date of sale. At acquisition, fair values are attributed to the assets and liabilities of the company acquired. Any excess of consideration given over these fair values is described as goodwill. In accordance with the transitional provisions of FRS10, goodwill arising on acquisitions after 26 September 1998 is included within intangible fixed assets and amortised over its useful economic life of 20 years. Goodwill relating to acquisitions on or before 26 September 1998 was transferred to the profit and loss reserve. As permitted by Section 230 of the Companies Act 1985, a profit and loss account is not presented for Tate & Lyle PLC.

Associates are accounted for by the equity method and joint ventures by the gross equity method from the date of their acquisition up to the date of sale. The investment is recognised initially at cost: a fair value is attributed to the investment acquired and any excess of consideration given over this fair value is described as goodwill and included as a separate component of the carrying value.

Foreign currencies

Assets and liabilities in foreign currencies are translated into sterling at the rates of exchange ruling on the last day of the financial period (the closing rate) except when they are hedged by an open foreign exchange contract, in which case the rate of exchange specified in the contract is used.

The profits of overseas companies are translated at the annual average of daily exchange rates and the difference when compared with that arising from the use of closing rates, together with differences on exchange arising from the translation of the opening balance sheets of overseas companies at year end rates are taken directly to distributable reserves. Other profits and losses on exchange are credited or charged to operating profit.

Sales

Sales comprise the amount receivable in the ordinary course of business, net of value added and sales taxes, for goods and services provided. By-product revenues are credited to the cost of raw materials.

Stock

Stock is valued at the lower of direct cost together with attributable overheads and net realisable value and is transferred to the profit and loss account on a 'first in, first out' basis.

Tangible fixed assets

Certain tangible fixed assets are carried at amounts based upon valuations recognised before the publication of FRS15 'Tangible Fixed Assets'. As is permitted by the transitional provisions of FRS15, these revaluations have not been updated. Finance costs directly attributable to the construction of tangible fixed assets are capitalised as part of the cost of those assets.

The depreciation charge is calculated so as to allocate the cost or revalued amount of tangible fixed assets systematically over their remaining useful economic lives using the straight-line method. These asset lives are reviewed at the end of each financial year.

The following asset lives are used:

Freehold land: No depreciation
Freehold buildings: 20 to 50 years
Leasehold property: Period of the lease
Bulk liquid storage tanks: 12 to 20 years
Plant and machinery: 3 to 28 years

Tangible fixed assets held under finance leases are capitalised and depreciated in accordance with the Group's depreciation policy.

Operating lease charges are charged to profit as incurred.

Research and development

All expenditure on research and development is charged to profit as incurred.

Advertising

Advertising costs are charged to profit when the advertising first takes place.

Post-retirement benefits

The Group operates a number of defined benefit pension schemes and, in North America, some post-retirement healthcare and life assurance schemes. The expected cost of post-retirement benefits is charged to the profit and loss account, on the advice of our actuary, so as to accrue the cost over the service lives of employees on the basis of a constant percentage of earnings. Variations from the regular cost are spread over the expected remaining service lives of current employees in the scheme.

Deferred taxation

Deferred taxation is recognised at the anticipated tax rate using the liability method on differences arising from the inclusion of income expenditure in taxation computations in periods different from those in which they are included in the financial statements, to the extent it is probable that a liability or asset will crystallise. Deferred tax on post-retirement benefits is recognised in full.

Financial instruments and their derivatives

Financial instruments and their derivatives are categorised as held for trading or held as hedges.

Financial instruments held for trading

The fair value of all instruments held for trading is recognised in the balance sheet and all unrealised profits and losses are taken to operating profit.

Financial instruments held as hedges

All hedging instruments are matched with their underlying hedged item. Each instrument's gain or loss is brought into the profit and loss account and its fair value into the balance sheet, at the same time and in the same place as is the matched underlying asset, liability, income or cost. For foreign exchange and commodity instruments this will be in operating profit matched against the relevant purchase, or sale, and for interest rate instruments within interest payable or receivable over the life of the instrument or relevant interest period.

The profit or loss on an instrument may be deferred if the hedged transaction is expected to take place or would normally be accounted for in a future period.

The finance costs of debt instruments are charged to the profit and loss account over the term of the debt at a constant rate on the carrying amount. Such costs include the costs on maturity or issue and any discount to face value arising on issue, or any premium payable.

Differences arising from the movement in exchange rates during the year from the translation to sterling of the foreign currency borrowings and similar instruments used to finance long-term foreign equity investments are taken direct to distributable reserves and reported in the statement of total recognised gains and losses. Changes in the fair value of most financial instruments or the underlying hedged item are not usually recognised in the profit and loss account. However, if unrealised changes in the fair value of the hedged item are included in the profit and loss account, changes in the value of the instrument are also included.

Initial margin deposits and variation margin deposits and receipts for futures contracts are included in current assets or current liabilities while the position is open. Unamortised premiums are also held in similar accounts.

All premiums or fees, paid or received, in respect of a financial instrument are accounted for over the life of the matched underlying asset, liability, income or cost, even if the instrument has been sold. If the matched underlying asset, liability, income or cost ceases to exist, or is no longer considered likely to exist in the future, the hedging instrument is sold. Any profit or loss on the sale is recognised in the profit and loss account as part of operating profit.

Appendix 4.4: Extract from the UK/US reconciliation statement of AstraZeneca plc

A typical statement that reconciles the financial statements prepared under UK and under US accounting principles is reproduced on the following pages by kind permission of AstraZeneca plc.

Additional information for US investors

Differences between UK and US accounting principles

The accompanying consolidated financial statements included in this report are prepared in accordance with UK GAAP. Certain significant differences between UK GAAP and US GAAP which affect AstraZeneca's net income and shareholders' equity are set out below.

Purchase accounting adjustments
Under UK GAAP the merger of Astra and Zeneca was accounted for as a 'merger of equals' (pooling-of-interests). Under US GAAP the merger was accounted for as the acquisition of Astra by Zeneca using 'purchase accounting'. Under purchase accounting, the cost of the investment is calculated at the market value of the shares issued together with other incidental costs and the assets and liabilities of the acquired entity are recorded at fair value. As a result of the fair value exercise, increases in the values of Astra's tangible fixed assets and inventory were recognised and values attributed to their in-process research and development, existing products and assembled work force, together with appropriate deferred taxation effects. The difference between the cost of investment and the fair value of the assets and liabilities of Astra has been recorded as goodwill. The amount allocated to in-process research and development is required, by US GAAP, to be expensed immediately in the first reporting period after the business combination. Fair value adjustments to the recorded amount of inventory have been expensed in the period the inventory was utilised and additional amortisation and depreciation have also been recorded in respect of the fair value adjustments to tangible and intangible assets and the resulting goodwill. Pre-acquisition results are excluded from US GAAP net income.

In the consolidated financial statements prepared under UK GAAP, goodwill arising on acquisitions made prior to 1 January 1998 accounted for under the purchase method has been eliminated against shareholders' equity, whilst under US GAAP this goodwill (after allocations to the fair value of tangible and intangible assets) is required to be capitalised and amortised. Under the requirements of UK Financial Reporting Standard 10 'Goodwill and Intangible Assets', goodwill on acquisitions made after 1 January 1998 is capitalised and amortised over its estimated useful life which is generally presumed not to exceed 20 years. UK GAAP requires that on subsequent disposal or termination of a previously acquired business, any goodwill previously taken directly to shareholders' equity is then charged in the income statement against the profit or loss on disposal or termination.

For the purpose of the adjustments to US GAAP included below, goodwill (including that capitalised under UK GAAP) is being amortised through the income statement over the estimated useful lives assigned to each individual acquisition. At 31 December 2000, these lives varied between 5 years and 40 years with a weighted average life of approximately 27 years. Identifiable intangible assets, which principally include patents, 'know-how' and product registrations, are amortised over their estimated useful lives which vary between 4 years and 40 years with a weighted average life of approximately 16 years.

At 31 December 2000 and 1999, shareholders' equity includes capitalised goodwill of $13,500m and $15,793m respectively (net of amortisation and impairment of $1,503m and $1,945m) and capitalised identifiable intangible assets of $11,611m and $13,825m respectively (net of amortisation and impairment of $2,402m and $1,439m). The carrying value of goodwill is reviewed for impairment whenever events or changes in circumstances indicate that the carrying amount may not be recoverable. Provision is made where there is a permanent impairment to the carrying value of capitalised goodwill and intangible assets. Goodwill on businesses disposed of is charged to the gain or loss on disposal.

On disposal of a business, the gain or loss under US GAAP may differ from that under UK GAAP due principally to goodwill capitalised and amortised, together with the appropriate share of other differences between UK and US accounting principles recognised previously.

Capitalisation of interest
AstraZeneca does not capitalise interest in its financial statements. US GAAP requires interest incurred as part of the cost of constructing fixed assets to be capitalised and amortised over the life of the asset.

Dividends
Under UK GAAP Ordinary Share dividends proposed are provided for in the year in respect of which they are recommended by the Board of Directors for approval by the shareholders. Under US GAAP such dividends are not provided for until declared by the Board.

Deferred taxation
Deferred taxation is provided on a full liability basis under US GAAP, which permits deferred tax assets to be recognised if their realisation is considered to be more likely than not; under UK GAAP, provision is made for deferred taxation only if there is reasonable evidence that such deferred taxation will be payable in the foreseeable future.

Pension and post-retirement benefits
There are three main differences between UK GAAP and US GAAP in accounting for pension costs:

(i) US GAAP requires measurements of plan assets and obligations to be made as at the date of the financial statements or a date not more than three months prior to that date. Under UK GAAP, calculations may be based on the results of the latest actuarial valuation;

Differences between UK and US accounting principles (continued)

(ii) US GAAP mandates a particular actuarial method – the projected unit credit method – and requires that each significant assumption necessary to determine annual pension cost reflects best estimates solely with regard to that individual assumption. UK GAAP does not mandate a particular method, but requires that the method and assumptions taken as a whole should be compatible and lead to the actuary's best estimate of the cost of providing the benefits promised; and

(iii) under US GAAP, a negative pension cost may arise where a significant unrecognised net asset or gain exists at the time of implementation. This is required to be amortised on a straight-line basis over the average remaining service period of employees. Under UK GAAP, AstraZeneca's policy is not to recognise pension credits in its financial statements unless a refund of, or reduction in, contributions is likely.

Restructuring costs
Under UK GAAP, provisions are made for restructuring costs once a detailed formal plan is in place and valid expectations have been raised in those affected that the restructuring will be carried out. US GAAP requires a number of specific criteria to be met before such costs can be recognised as an expense. Among these are the requirements that the costs incurred are incremental to other costs incurred by the company, or represent amounts to be incurred under contractual obligations which are not associated with or do not benefit activities that will be continued. Also, all significant actions arising from a restructuring and their completion dates must be identified by the balance sheet date. To the extent that restructuring costs are related to the activities of the acquired company, US GAAP allows them to be recognised as a liability upon acquisition.

Software costs
Under UK GAAP, AstraZeneca expenses all software costs. Under US GAAP, with effect from 1 January 1999, certain of these costs are required to be capitalised and amortised over three years.

Foreign exchange
Under UK GAAP, unrealised gains and losses on foreign currency transactions to hedge anticipated, but not firmly committed, foreign currency transactions may be deferred and accounted for at the same time as the anticipated transactions. Under US GAAP such deferral is not permitted except in certain defined circumstances.

Current assets and liabilities
Current assets under UK GAAP include amounts which fall due after more than one year. Under US GAAP such assets would be reclassified as non-current assets. Borrowings under UK GAAP are classified according to the maturity of the financial instrument, while under US GAAP, certain borrowings would be classified according to the maturity of the available back-up facility. Provisions for liabilities and charges under UK GAAP include amounts due within one year which would be reclassified to current liabilities under US GAAP. In addition, provisions would be shown as part of amounts payable and accrued liabilities due after one year.

Statement of cash flows: Basis of preparation
AstraZeneca's Statement of Group Cash Flow is prepared in accordance with United Kingdom Financial Reporting Standard 1 (Revised 1996) ('FRS 1'), whose objective and principles are similar to those set out in SFAS No. 95, 'Statement of Cash Flows'. The principal differences between the standards relate to classification and also that the UK GAAP cash flow statement combines the cash flow statements of Astra and Zeneca for all periods whilst the US GAAP cash flow statements includes the cash flows of Astra only from the date of acquisition, 6 April 1999. Under FRS 1, the Company presents its cash flows for (a) operating activities; (b) dividends received from joint ventures and associates; (c) returns on investments and servicing of finance; (d) tax paid; (e) capital expenditure and financial investment; (f) acquisitions and disposals; (g) dividends paid to shareholders; (h) management of liquid resources; and (i) financing. SFAS No. 95 requires only three categories of cash flow activity being (a) operating; (b) investing; and (c) financing.

Cash flows from taxation, returns on investments and servicing of finance and dividends received from joint ventures and associates under FRS 1 would be included as operating activities under SFAS No. 95; capital expenditure and financial investment and acquisitions and disposals would be included as investing activities; and distributions would be included as a financing activity under SFAS No. 95. Under FRS 1 cash comprises cash in hand and deposits repayable on demand, less overdrafts repayable on demand; and liquid resources comprise current asset investments held as readily disposable stores of value. Under SFAS No. 95 cash equivalents, comprising short-term highly liquid investments, generally with original maturities of three months or less, are grouped together with cash; short-term borrowings repayable on demand would not be included within cash and cash equivalents and movements on those borrowings would be included in financing activities.

New accounting standards not yet adopted
Statement of Financial Accounting Standards (SFAS) No. 133 – 'Accounting for Derivative Instruments and Hedging Activities' as amended by SFAS No. 137, 'Accounting for Derivative Instruments and Hedging Activities – Deferral of the Effective Date of FASB Statement No. 133', and SFAS No. 138, 'Accounting for Certain Derivative Instruments and Certain Hedging Activities', is effective for the Company as of 1 January 2001. SFAS No. 133 requires that an entity recognise all derivatives as either assets or liabilities measured at fair value. The accounting for changes in the fair value of a derivative depends on the use of the derivative. Adoption of these new accounting standards will result in a cumulative after tax increase in net income of approximately $32m. Adoption will also impact assets and liabilities recorded on the balance sheet, and may have a material effect on future results.

Additional information for US investors

Differences between UK and US accounting principles (continued)

Introduction
As a result of the significant difference between the UK GAAP and US GAAP treatment of the combination of Astra and Zeneca in the year of acquisition, and in the results of preceding periods, condensed statements of operations and cash flow under US GAAP have been prepared for the benefit of US investors. In particular, under US GAAP, results and cash flow of Astra are excluded from the consolidated results and cash flows respectively for all periods prior to 6 April 1999.

The following is a summary of the material adjustments to net income and shareholders' equity which would have been required if US GAAP had been applied instead of UK GAAP.

Net income

	2000 $m	1999 $m	1998 $m
Net income, as shown in the consolidated statements of income before exceptional items	**3,119**	2,730	2,553
Exceptional items after tax	**(581)**	(1,587)	58
Net income for the period under UK GAAP	**2,538**	1,143	2,611
Pre-acquisition results of Astra	**–**	(413)	(1,427)
	2,538	730	1,184
Adjustments to conform to US GAAP			
Purchase accounting adjustments (including goodwill and intangibles)			
Deemed acquisition of Astra			
In-process research and development	**–**	(3,315)	–
Inventory step-up	**–**	(826)	–
Amortisation and other acquisition adjustments	**(1,756)**	(759)	–
Others	**(20)**	(61)	(80)
Divestment of Specialties business	**–**	284	–
Impairment of Salick Health Care goodwill	**–**	(308)	–
Capitalisation, less disposals and amortisation of interest	**45**	5	8
Deferred taxation			
On fair values of Astra	**284**	547	–
Others	**(146)**	117	(28)
Pension expense	**(50)**	(103)	(53)
Post-retirement benefits/plan amendment	**4**	4	5
Software costs	**98**	29	–
Restructuring costs	**(97)**	119	–
Unrealised losses on foreign exchange and others	**(35)**	(2)	–
Net income/(loss) in accordance with US GAAP	**865**	(3,539)	1,036

Differences between UK and US accounting principles (continued)

US GAAP Condensed Consolidated Statement of Operations

For the years ended 31 December	2000 $m	1999 $m	1998 $m
Sales	**15,804**	12,789	4,971
Cost of sales	**(4,181)**	(4,278)	(1,169)
Distribution costs	**(210)**	(200)	(97)
Research and development	**(2,620)**	(2,178)	(806)
Selling, general and administrative expenses	**(4,861)**	(4,323)	(1,700)
Acquisition related costs	**(419)**	(4,562)	–
Amortisation of intangibles and goodwill	**(2,043)**	(1,601)	(67)
Other income	**223**	115	115
Operating income/(loss)	**1,693**	(4,238)	1,247
Net interest income/(expense)	**183**	(23)	(54)
Income/(loss) from continuing operations before taxation	**1,876**	(4,261)	1,193
Taxes on income from continuing operations	**(969)**	190	(397)
Net income/(loss) from continuing operations	**907**	(4,071)	796
Discontinued operations:			
Net (loss)/income from discontinued operations	**(42)**	108	240
Gain on disposal of Specialties business, net of income taxes	**–**	424	–
Net income/(loss) for the year	**865**	(3,539)	1,036
Weighted average number of $0.25 Ordinary Shares in issue (millions of shares)	**1,768**	1,569	950
Dilutive impact of share options outstanding (millions of shares)	**2**	3	4
Diluted weighted average number of $0.25 Ordinary Shares in accordance with US GAAP (millions of shares)	**1,770**	1,572	954
Net (loss)/income per $0.25 Ordinary Share and ADS in accordance with US GAAP – basic and diluted ($)	**0.49**	(2.26)	1.09

	2000	1999	1998
Net income/(loss) from continuing operations per $0.25 Ordinary Share and ADS in accordance with US GAAP – basic and diluted ($)	**0.51**	(2.60)	0.84
Gain on disposal of Specialties business, net of income taxes – basic and diluted ($)	**–**	0.27	–
Net (loss)/income from discontinued operations per $0.25 Ordinary Share and ADS in accordance with US GAAP – basic and diluted ($)	**(0.02)**	0.07	0.25

The dividend in specie in respect of the demerger of Zeneca Agrochemicals under US GAAP amounted to $836m, after exchange on the translation of foreign currency financial statements realised of $297m.

Additional information for US investors

Differences between UK and US accounting principles (continued)

US GAAP Statement of Comprehensive Income

For the years ended 31 December	2000 $m	1999 $m	1998 $m
Net income/(loss) for the year	**865**	(3,539)	1,036
Exchange gains/(losses) net of tax	**(2,184)**	(437)	90
Exchange realised on demerger of Zeneca Agrochemicals	**(297)**	–	–
Other movements	**(2)**	64	(7)
Total Comprehensive Income	**(1,618)**	(3,912)	1,119

The cumulative exchange gains and losses (net of tax) on the translation of foreign currency financial statements under US GAAP are set out in the following note:

For the years ended 31 December	2000 $m	1999 $m	1998 $m
Balance at 1 January	**(364)**	73	(17)
Movement in year	**(2,481)**	(437)	90
Balance at 31 December	**(2,845)**	(364)	73

Stock compensation
In the Group's financial statements prepared under UK GAAP, no cost is accrued for the share options awarded to employees under the Zeneca 1994 Executive Share Option Scheme, the AstraZeneca Share Option Plan, and the AstraZeneca Savings-Related Share Option Scheme as the exercise price is equivalent to the market value at the date of grant. Under US GAAP the cost is calculated as the difference between the option price and the market price at the date of grant or, for variable plans, at the end of the reporting period (until measurement date). Under the requirements of APB Opinion No. 25 any compensation cost would be amortised over the period from the date the options are granted to the date they are first exercisable. SFAS No.123 sets out an alternative methodology for recognising the compensation cost based on the fair value at grant date. Had the Group adopted this methodology, the effect on net income under US GAAP is shown below:

	2000 $m	1999 $m	1998 $m
Net (loss)/income under US GAAP as reported	**865**	(3,539)	1,036
Compensation cost	**(46)**	(16)	(13)
Pro forma net income	**819**	(3,555)	1,023
Net income per $0.25 Ordinary Share and ADS under US GAAP (basic):			
As reported ($)	**$0.49**	($2.26)	$1.09
Pro forma ($)	**$0.46**	($2.27)	$1.08

Differences between UK and US accounting principles (continued)

The fair value of options granted is estimated, based on the stock price at the grant date, using the Black-Scholes option pricing model with the following assumptions:

	2000	1999	1998
Dividend yield	**2.0%**	3.0%	2.0%
Expected volatility	**20.0%**	20.0%	20.0%
Risk-free interest rate	**5.9%**	5.1%	5.1%
Expected lives: 1994 Scheme	**6.0 years**	6.0 years	6.0 years
Expected lives: AstraZeneca Share Option Plan	**6.0 years**	n/a	n/a
Expected lives: SAYE Scheme	**4.6 years**	4.4 years	4.6 years

The options are based on existing AstraZeneca shares and therefore have no dilution effect as the Company would be buying shares in the open market rather than issuing new shares. Subsequent to the effective date of the merger no share options have been awarded under the Astra Shareholder Value Incentive Plan.

In the initial phase-in period, the effects of applying SFAS No.123 for disclosing compensation cost may not be representative of the effects on pro forma net income and earnings per share for future years.

Shareholders' equity	**2000 $m**	1999 $m
Total shareholders' equity under UK GAAP	**9,521**	10,302
Adjustments to conform to US GAAP		
Purchase accounting adjustments (including goodwill and intangibles)		
Deemed acquisition of Astra		
Goodwill	**12,610**	14,202
Tangible and intangible fixed assets	**9,510**	11,174
Others	**31**	490
Capitalisation, less disposals and amortisation of interest	**135**	151
Deferred taxation		
On fair value of Astra	**(2,702)**	(3,172)
Others	**(278)**	(247)
Dividend	**830**	834
Pension expense	**(129)**	(172)
Post-retirement benefits/plan amendment	**(32)**	(31)
Software costs capitalised	**120**	29
Restructuring costs	**22**	119
Others	**69**	56
Shareholders' equity in accordance with US GAAP	**29,707**	33,735

5 Major reports, statements and reviews

This chapter is predominantly concerned with the information provided in the following:

- operating and financial review
- directors' report
- chairman's statement
- chief executive's review.

It is many years since company reports consisted largely of accounting figures and just a few pages of brief supporting notes. Over the last two decades there has been a marked increase in the volume of material that supports the technical accounting information.

This additional material has largely been the product of a general movement to bring about greater understanding and enlightenment for the reader who has little or no knowledge of accounting. Much of this expansion has been provided in the form of narrative explanation and some of the impetus behind it has been initiated by professional requirements and recommendations, as opposed to legislation.

Operating and financial review

The first significant narrative statement is the operating and financial review (OFR).

In an attempt to improve corporate accountability, the Cadbury Report suggested that listed companies should attempt to clarify and explain some of the technical accounting details (see also Chapter 8, 'Corporate governance'). Supporting the Cadbury recommendations, in 1993, the Accounting Standards Board (ASB) recommended that listed companies produce a statement called an operating and financial review which is defined as '... a framework for the directors to disclose and analyse the business's performance ... and ... to assist users to assess for themselves the future potential of the business'. Companies were not legally required to publish an OFR – it was regarded as an example of 'best practice'. Since then, the OFR has proved beneficial to many users – so much so that the government, in its 2001 Company Law Review, indicated that the publication of this review might become a legal requirement.

The OFR provides an ideal opportunity to impart your company's attributes and character. The fact that the OFR framework is not too prescriptive works to your advantage in that you can prepare the OFR in a way that allows expression and a degree of corporate character formation. At the moment, the ASB only suggests an overall structure and typical content. The detail, presentation and underlying theme are down to you. Remember that the whole point of an OFR is to discuss key trading and financial matters in a form that that all general users of your annual report can understand.

It is often advisable to ensure that your draft OFR is read by non-accounting staff before approval of the final version. Accountants can be their own worst enemies in that they are so often wound up in the financial jargon and concepts of their own discipline that they fail to appreciate that the general user does not always understand terms that, to them, appear so obvious.

With all this in mind, you should pay particular attention to writing style, the use of colour and the selection of appropriate photographs to convey your corporate aims. For example, as with the rest of your annual report, you should never just include photographs of the chairman, directors or senior executives. This status-driven approach is unnecessary, outdated and unwarranted. Corporate life has moved on. Your OFR must reflect the fact that companies need and value all categories of employees. Photographs of all levels of staff are essential – and do not select static passport-type photographs. More dynamic and 'action-packed' photographs offer a far more interesting reflection of your whole company.

Key features

An OFR should contain a number of key features. It should:

- be written in a clear and succinct style, be readily understandable by the general reader and generally only contain information that is likely to be of significant value to investors

- be balanced and objective and discuss both positive and negative aspects of the business

- concentrate on providing analytical discussion, rather than mere numerical analysis

- discuss the reasons for, and the effect of, any changes in accounting policies

- make reference to comments in previous statements, if these have not been borne out by events

- make clear how any financial ratios or other numerical information provided relate to the financial statements

- include a discussion of trends and factors underlying the business that have affected the results, as well as any known events, trends and uncertainties that are expected to have an impact on the business in the future

- follow a 'top-down' structure and discuss individual aspects of the business in the context of a discussion of the business as a whole.

It is a good idea to ensure that your OFR includes all, or certainly most, of these sections. The majority of your users will view most of the pages that comprise your financial statements as complex, highly technical and largely indecipherable information. Accordingly, the OFR is your major opportunity to communicate your financial performance and trading position to the lay reader in a form and language that they should understand. Do not waste this opportunity.

Sections

As its name implies, an OFR is, in practice, split into two sections: an operating section and a review section.

The operating section will include a discussion on topics such as factors affecting future results, capital expenditure and the likely resulting benefits, any uncertainties affecting the business, dependency on major suppliers and any skills or labour shortages.

The financial section is intended to explain the capital structure of the business, its treasury policy and the dynamics of its financial position. As part of this discussion, it will cover the business's liquidity and future financing requirements. This section may also discuss a company's risk management and highlight such issues as: treasury risk management; finance and interest rate risk; currency and commodity risks; and credit exposure risks.

An OFR builds upon experience in the US where companies produce an equivalent OFR, termed a 'management discussion and analysis'. Do not fall into the habit of some US (and indeed some UK) companies which sometimes produce unbalanced reports by unjustly highlighting their positive achievements and playing down any negative implications. An open and honest assessment of your business is essential – anything less than this will eventually be found out.

Presentation

How you present your OFR is important. Some companies show their OFR under separate headings (an operating and a financing section) and, in effect, produce two statements. There are no hard and fast rules. Provided that the content and style of both sections is clearly thought out, then it matters little whether the operating and financial sections are combined in one section or shown separately under individual headings. An OFR may be a stand-alone statement or included as part of another section such as the chief executive's report. The ASB encourages companies to experiment and be innovative in the design and presentation of the OFR. Take advantage of this flexibility. Keep clearly in mind at all times just how you can maintain the reader's attention and interest in the document.

What is important is that the OFR sections are written in a clear, confident and authoritative style. Always remember your intended audience. Do not be tempted to write and produce the OFR in a similar technical style as the rest of the financial statements. The underlying theme throughout the OFR must be clarity and understanding for the general reader.

Usually the OFR will be written by a senior person in a company's finance department. Many accountants believe that they are writing for the general reader, but still tend to use inappropriate terms, poor explanations and even meaningless technical abbreviations so that the finished product is anything but understandable.

Once the OFR has been written, it is useful to obtain a 'second opinion'. Ask a non-accounting colleague (or colleagues) to read it. Can a human resources manager, engineer, software designer, administrator or marketing specialist (or anyone else without an accounting background) understand the finished product? If there is any doubt or confusion, redraft the statement.

Business risks

Some analysts believe that some companies' OFRs could be improved by more in-depth disclosure and discussion of the risks faced by the business. The identification of business risk is becoming one of the fashionable areas for corporate reports, and there is nothing to prohibit your company from considering and discussing all the key issues of risk that it faces. The stock exchange also requires listed companies to report risks which may have a material impact on a company's profits and which may not have been anticipated by the public. Furthermore, the accounting profession is encouraging companies to make a more meaningful disclosure of the risks that face their business activities. However, these risks (and, indeed, other risks) may not necessarily be shown in the OFR. It is worth projecting your OFR in a more enlightened fashion and taking the disclosures further. Your company should benefit if the nature of all significant risks are comprehensively explained – whether there is an OFR recommendation or not. So rather than wait for the imposition of more detailed and regulatory risk disclosure requirements, it may be a sound idea to begin now to incorporate more risk information.

The nature of these risks can be wide-ranging. They can encompass both specific business risks faced by the company and the impact of more general economic risks on the business.

Specific examples of risk can incorporate those factors that may impinge on corporate earnings, risks to supplies and labour and threats to the company's intellectual capital. More general risks may be related to the economic impact of changes in interest rates, changes in foreign currency rates and overseas trading conditions. It is a good idea to always devote a section of your OFR to discussing the major risks.

A slight word of warning – when you are discussing risks, do not do it in a threatening or exaggerated fashion. There is no point in unnecessarily worrying or provoking undue alarm or concern in shareholders and other interested parties. By all means identify the key risk factors, but do not dwell on, or overexaggerate, their importance. Instead, highlight the risk factors and then explain how these risks can be incorporated into your business strategy. Discuss how you may possibly minimize some of these risks and their impact on your business. Figure 5.1 gives an example.

A note of caution – take care not to release commercially sensitive information in the OFR. The ASB advises directors to weigh the benefits of

Risk factors and additional information

Risk factors

Risk of loss or expiration of patents or trademarks
Scientific and technological innovation is critical to the long-term success of AstraZeneca's business. In the pharmaceutical market, a drug, diagnostic or medical device is normally only subject to competition from alternative products during the period of patent protection, but thereafter it will also be open to competition from generic copy products. AstraZeneca believes that it has patent or trademark protection for many of its most important products, although certain important patents will expire in the near future.

For example, patents covering the compound, omeprazole, the active substance in *Losec* (*Prilosec* in the US), which in 2000 accounted for 40% of AstraZeneca's sales for continuing operations, have now expired in all major markets but patent term extensions extend substance patent protection until April 2001 in the US and 2004 in Japan, and supplementary protection certificates ('SPCs') extend substance patent protection until 2002-2005 in most of Europe. Patents protecting the salt in *Losec* MUPS expire in Europe in 2004 and in the US in 2005. Formulation patents relating to *Losec* remain until 2007 in most major markets. *Zestril* patent protection in the US expires in December 2001 but a further six months' marketing exclusivity may be granted by the FDA if data from AstraZeneca's ongoing paediatric trial programme are accepted.

The expiration or loss of certain patents or trademarks could have an adverse effect on the pricing and sales with respect to these products and, consequently, could result in a material adverse effect on AstraZeneca's financial condition, liquidity and results of operations.

Difficulty of integrating large and complex businesses and realising synergies
The merger of Astra AB with Zeneca Group PLC in 1999 involved the integration of two large and complex businesses that previously operated independently. AstraZeneca expects to realise significant cost savings and other synergies from the merger, but for various reasons, it may not be able to achieve all of these synergies or may not be able to achieve them within the expected timescale.

Impact of fluctuations in exchange rates
The results of operations of AstraZeneca are accounted for in US dollars. Approximately 56% of AstraZeneca's 2000 sales were in the Americas (comprised of the US, Canada and Latin America) with a significant proportion of that figure being in respect of US sales. The US is, and is expected to remain, AstraZeneca's largest and potentially fastest growing major market. Sales in certain other countries are also in US dollars, or in currencies whose exchange rates are linked to the US dollar. Major components of AstraZeneca's cost base are however located in Europe, where an aggregate of approximately 60% of the combined Group's employees are based. Movements in the exchange rates used to translate foreign currencies into US dollars may therefore have a significant impact on AstraZeneca's reported results of operations from year to year. Therefore, we cannot ensure that AstraZeneca's reported financial results will not fluctuate significantly from year to year as a result of changes in exchange rates.

Certain subsidiaries of AstraZeneca import and export goods and services in currencies other than their own functional currency, although AstraZeneca minimises this practice. The results of such subsidiaries could, therefore, be affected by currency fluctuations arising between the transaction dates and the settlement dates for those transactions. AstraZeneca hedges these exposures through financial instruments in the form of forward contracts and currency swaps. The notional principal amount of AstraZeneca's financial instruments used to hedge these exposures, principally forward foreign exchange contracts and purchased currency options, at 31 December 2000 was $2,427 million. The policies of AstraZeneca seek to mitigate the effect of exchange rate fluctuations on the value of foreign currency cash flows and in turn their effects on the results of the various subsidiaries, but do not seek to remove all such risks. In general, a unilateral strengthening of the US dollar adversely affects the results of AstraZeneca whereas a weakening of the US dollar is generally favourable. AstraZeneca cannot ensure that exchange rate fluctuations will not have a material adverse effect on its business, financial condition or results of operations in the future.

Risk that R&D will not yield new products that achieve commercial success
Like other pharmaceutical companies, AstraZeneca devotes substantial resources to R&D. In the pharmaceutical industry, R&D is expensive, prolonged and entails considerable uncertainty. The process of developing a new pharmaceutical product, from the start of development to the submission of an application for registration, typically takes between five and seven years, but this period varies considerably from case to case and country to country. Because of the complexities and uncertainties associated with pharmaceutical research, we cannot ensure that compounds currently under development by AstraZeneca will survive the development process and ultimately obtain the regulatory approvals needed to market such products successfully. For example, in 2000 AstraZeneca stopped the development of Zendra (clomethiazole) for the treatment of stroke after clinical trials showed no efficacy benefits for patients suffering acute cases of stroke. There can be no assurances regarding the development of and commercial success of any of the products in the current pipeline. The commercial success of products in the current pipeline will be particularly important to AstraZeneca because several current key products will lose patent protection in major markets in the 2001-2002 period.

Figure 5.1 Extract from a discussion on risk assessment. Reproduced by kind permission of AstraZeneca plc.

disclosing certain types of information. If the dangers of disclosing too much detail threaten your commercial strategy, then consider ways to 'water down' the information, or perhaps omit the information entirely.

Mandatory requirement?
Over the next few years the preparation of an OFR will probably become mandatory for many companies. The DTI's review of company law (2001) proposes that 'all companies of significant economic size' should be legally required to produce an OFR as part of their annual report and accounts. So if you have not done so already, you should start to consider how you could improve and emphasize the themed messages of your OFR (see Appendix 5.2 at the end of this chapter).

Directors' report

Under the 1985 and 1989 Companies Act it is a legal requirement that the directors' report be laid before a company's annual general meeting and filed with the Registrar of Companies.

A directors' report must, *inter alia*, include:

- the principal activities of the company
- a business review.

Essentially, these requirements mean that your company must describe its key trading operations and then review the development of the business during the year. An indication of likely future developments should also be discussed.

Do not exaggerate or to be too over-optimistic about the future. The directors' report is subject to review by the statutory auditors who are legally required to comment in their report if any information given in the directors' report is inconsistent with the other information contained in the financial statements.

Other areas that must be included are: the names of directors and details of their shareholdings; any material differences in trading results from published forecasts; any significant departures from accounting standards; analysis of geographical areas of turnover and their contribution to trading profits; amounts of dividends recommended by directors; significant changes in fixed assets and any post-balance sheet events. (Post-balance sheet events are important events that have occurred between the year-end and the date when the directors approve the accounts.) A statement of outstanding bank loans and overdrafts must also be included.

With these items there is very little you can do to enhance either the content or presentation. Most of the above information is largely factual and the requirements are predominantly dictated by legislation. As with other factual statements, look at how you could improve the presentation of the information and concentrate on the design and layout of the pages containing this section.

Disabled employees

There are other legal requirements that need to be discussed in a directors' report that can certainly be clarified and improved.

The directors' report must contain information about disabled employees. If a company's average number of UK employees exceeds 250, the directors are legally required to state their company's policies with regard to:

- the employment of disabled persons
- employment and training opportunities for those who become disabled whilst employees of the company
- the training, career development and promotion opportunities of disabled employees.

Quite properly, the treatment of disabled employees should be an important area of concern for all companies. Unfortunately, some companies fail to take the opportunity to explain their policies fully – for example, merely stating that their policy is '... to provide where possible employment opportunities and training for disabled people, to care for employees who become disabled and to make the best possible use of their skills and potential' (Annual Report of Rolls Royce plc, 2000). Such statements are of limited value and convey little information to users – they could be vastly improved and made more informative.

In the contemporary social and political climate it is essential to provide far more meaningful information, such as the numbers of disabled employees in your company, the numbers of employees who become disabled in the course of their work, the nature and extent of retraining programmes and so on. In short, be informative and perhaps support your statements with real-life case studies of individual (possibly named and photographed) employees who may have overcome disability to achieve successful careers.

Employee involvement
In addition, companies are required to provide information on employee involvement. If companies, on average, employ more than 250 people, the directors must explain how they introduce, maintain and develop arrangements for:

- systematically providing information of concern to employees
- consultative practices with employees
- encouraging employee involvement in the company's performance.

Equal opportunities
Many companies include a statement concerning their equal opportunity programmes in the directors' report. As with the section on disabled employees, this is an important political and social commentary. Do not follow the example of so many companies and produce a bland statement that merely states that your company 'supports equal opportunities for all sections of staff'; these types of statement convey little useful information and some border on being useless. Instead, comprehensively explain what your company is doing to open up opportunities to everyone. Give examples of recruitment policies, training and promotional initiatives and provide explicit examples of how jobs, promotion and training are open to all sections of the workforce. If possible, support your comments with hard facts and figures, perhaps even providing a case-study example of employees in your company. Also explain any reviews and measures implemented to ensure that all your company's anti-discrimination policies are operating properly. It might be a useful idea to ask the Human Resources Department, well in advance of the production of the annual report, to be prepared to supply this information for this section.

As with the information relating to disabled employees, many companies give brief, vague and often very restricted information about these other employee-related areas. Do not make this mistake. Too many companies blatantly (and quite properly) state that employees are their greatest asset and then fail to provide evidence to help substantiate these assertions. In the directors' report you should provide examples of consultative staff committees in your company; assess the strengths and weaknesses of current employee participation and involvement; and suggest ways (on a self-critical basis) in which you may improve existing structures. It is also a good idea to identify individual employees who have made a particularly valuable contribution. If you are providing a detailed discussion about employees, you might wish to have a separate section in the annual report to highlight their importance. But whatever you do, do not fall into the trap of only highlighting the names and significance of directors and senior employees at the expense of other junior employees. If you display photographs of more junior staff undertaking their company duties, always remember to give their names and *never* use patronizing language or facile comments to describe their activities. Such actions are demeaning, unbecoming and totally removed from progressive employment practice.

Political and charitable donations

You are also legally required, in this section, to state any contributions your company makes to political and charitable donations if, together, they exceed £200. For individual political contributions exceeding £200 the names of the recipients must also be provided. Political donations are always a sensitive area and are clearly a matter for directors and their shareholders. However, be warned that this information will be filed with the Registrar of Companies and, consequently, you may be required to explain your donations in a wider political and social arena. An increasing number of companies are now ceasing to make political donations. However, if you are determined to make such donations it may be prudent to explain, in the directors' report, why you are making a donation to a particular political party and just how your company and shareholders will benefit.

The directors

The directors' report will also contain considerable detail about the directors themselves. You are required, amongst other things, to provide the directors' names and details of their interests in the company's shares and debentures. Other information such as directors' emoluments, pensions and compensation payments are normally shown in the supporting notes to the profit and loss account.

Creditor payment policy

Since 1996, directors of public companies are required to state their creditor payment policy. In response to criticism that some large companies were deliberately delaying paying their suppliers, legislation was implemented to require companies to disclose their payment policy more explicitly. In practice, many companies merely issue a rather bland and simple statement that their policy is to pay all invoices from suppliers within (say) 45 days. To be more informative and helpful, it would be far more useful to provide more details not only about your policy but also about your practice. You could explain how the creditor payment time has changed over the last couple of years and even explain how you might attempt to improve the speed of your payments (if, indeed, that is your aim).

Additional voluntary information

In addition to the above legal requirements, a directors' report should also include information required by the stock exchange. As an option, some companies include additional voluntary information, such as further details on the year's trading events and, perhaps, future developments. Nowadays, many companies place much of their voluntary information either in the OFR or in the chairman's statement.

When drafting your directors' report, you may prefer to follow recent trends and place most of the additional voluntary information in the OFR. After all, the OFR tends to attract more attention, and this approach may be a more effective way of putting your message across (see Appendix 5.3.)

Future developments

The government's White Paper, *Modernising Company Law* (2002), is considering reforming the content of the directors' report as a supplementary statement to the financial statements. Further details are awaited

Chairman's statement

Traditionally, all annual reports contain a statement by the company's chairman, placed at the very beginning. This statement is not legally required but, invariably, companies will produce two or three pages of the chairman's comments.

Content

The chairman's statement will normally refer to such matters as:

- a summary of the general trading conditions over the financial year, usually placing the company's trading position in the context of the national and global economies
- particularly good or bad trading performances by individual subsidiaries or divisions
- the contribution of employees

- events of a special nature – for example, the opening or closing of factories or offices, staff redundancies and new business ventures

- overall company strategy and plans for the future

The chairman's statement comes with a warning. As these statements are not directly audited as such, sometimes they can display a rather cavalier disregard for all the facts. Many chairmen are eternal optimists and nearly always view the trading climate in a most enthusiastic manner. In some ways, this often false optimism is understandable. Even under the most severe economic and trading conditions it is part of the chairman's task to 'rally the troops'. Confidence in the company's future must be matched by a company commitment to achieve better results next year. Encouraging and praising employees is an essential attribute of a chairman. Likewise, it is important to pacify shareholders when results are poor and persuade investors that trading circumstances will improve. Such themes are expected in an annual report – the field marshal must always exude enthusiasm to all ranks. These themes have traditionally appeared in chairmen's statements so it is perhaps not a sound idea to deviate too much from convention. Most investors and analysts expect to find this information in the same place, so do not disappoint them. But convention should not prevent you from being more innovative and imaginative.

Practicalities

The practicalities of preparing a chairman's statement can produce problems. Many chairmen of blue-chip companies still prefer to be actively involved in producing their own statement. Many prefer to personally write at least part of their statement, because it gives them a sense of involvement and a feeling of relating to their company.

Some chairmen do not always take kindly to other employees lower down the corporate hierarchy offering ideas and even suggestions about improving their statement. It takes considerable diplomatic skills to persuade the chairman to change his or her ways and approach, and such changes may be better attempted on an incremental basis. Try suggesting to the chairman or his or her office that other progressive blue-chip companies are now producing their chairman's statement by such and such a method. Explain that corporate fashion is changing and the company needs to keep up with 'best practice'. The alternative is to appear old-fashioned and backward.

Improvements

A chairman's statement is not part of the legal framework; it neither has to be written in formal terms nor conform to a detailed checklist of items that must be included. In some ways, this lack of regulatory control can work to your advantage. So how can the chairman's statement be improved?

The first tip is to improve the style of presentation. Far too many chairmen's statements predominantly consist of narrative, often rather rambling and disjointed in places and spread over two or three pages. Invariably, a photograph of the chairman will be prominently placed at the beginning of the statement. At least try to avoid the stereotyped bland 'passport-type' photograph that is so often used.

The chairman's message must make an initial impact. A strong headline-type statement in bold heavy typeface on the first page sets the scene – for example, 'Earnings Soar 20% – Another Highly Successful Year' or 'Heroic Efforts of Staff Ensure Merger Success'.

It is important to have a succinct headline on which the chairman can build and hang the rest of his or her statement. Unfortunately, some chairmen will replicate parts of the more complex commentary more suitably found in the OFR or directors' report. Do not fall into this trap. Keep the chairman's message clear, authoritative, strong and targeted at the audience. Do not try to add gravitas to the statement by referring to excessive technical accounting details.

If parts of the company have not performed satisfactorily, then say so, but be sure to discuss, clearly and concisely, how you intend to ensure that the company will remedy these deficiencies in the future. Readers do not want excuses and pious assertions of a better tomorrow; they need an objective and open explanation as to why matters went astray and the procedures being introduced to stop mistakes happening again.

A clear and honest report and appraisal is far preferable to the over-glossy, over-optimistic and rather syrupy statements that are written by some chairmen. Most City analysts 'see through' the thick coating of gloss found in some chairmen's statements. Professional analysts have always ignored large chunks of chairmen's statements. Large financial institutions, investment analysts and the accounting profession already treat this statement with a large degree of scepticism. It is these large-scale investors in particular that can have such an influential impact on a company's share price. To these groups of professional investors, chairmen's statements do not carry much weight for the very good reason that very little value can be gained from them in their current form.

This lack of interest needs to be overcome. Taking the readership as a whole, it makes far more sense to produce a honest, open and balanced assessment of the company. Business failings and trading disappointments should be equally discussed along with success stories: *always* give realistic and open reasons for lower-than-expected earnings and disappointments. Never hide beneath a cloak of over-optimism about the future.

Better-quality information can be delivered in the chairman's statement by relegating some of the narrative to other sections of the annual report. A more comprehensive report on, for example, changes in turnover in an overseas subsidiary or changes in financing policy may be better placed in the OFR. The chairman's statement needs only to refer to very broad and general issues. The chairman can always refer the reader to the OFR for further details if the need arises. However, do not leave readers having to search through the report themselves for more details: fully cross-reference any further information.

Many chairmen's statements acknowledge the value of their employees' work, but often in rather bland and repetitive ways. The statement should give the appearance of being genuine, sincere and heartfelt. Beware, however, of being patronizing – a trap that is all too easy to fall into. Provide some brief, but key, statistics about commitment to staff in the form of investment in career development schemes or equal opportunities programmes, and highlight some outstanding achievements of employees. The message can be conveyed even more effectively by including photographs of the chairman meeting other named employees in the work environment.

You will also need to be careful about the typeface, background colour and the use of photographs (see Chapter 13, 'Design, printing and distribution'). Since the chairman's statement is normally found at the beginning of the annual report it is important to create a solid presence. Do not encourage the potential reader to ignore other information by a poorly designed, badly presented and unduly technical and 'jargon-ridden' chairman's statement.

The presentation of the chairman's statement comes with an implicit warning. Many statements are personally written by the chairmen themselves – although often with some help from staff in their offices. By virtue of the chairman's status and position in the organization it can often be difficult to broach the topic if revisions to his or her statement are necessary. If you want to highlight a particular theme in the chairman's statement, it might be best to approach the issue upwards through the finance director's department. The finance director can then, perhaps in conjunction with the chief executive or managing director, approach the chairman's office to discuss matters.

Once the chairman's statement has been added into the annual report's preparatory processes it is a good idea to check how the comments fit in with the context of the overall annual report. Further amendments might still be necessary. If so, the chairman's office will need to be diplomatically approached again.

Never underestimate the significance of the chairman's statement. For some readers of the annual report, this section is, understandably, attractive quite simply because it is often a short and optimistic statement and lacks the technically confusing detail often found elsewhere in the report. For many, its attraction lies in its relative brevity.

Therefore, do not dismiss the importance of this statement. It has a considerable role to play in communicating your corporate message (see Appendix 5.4).

Chief executive's review

In addition to the chairman's statement, some companies include a review by the company's chief executive. In some companies, this review replaces all, or parts, of an OFR. By all means, include a chief executive's review but do not use it to replace the OFR, either fully or partially. Also, take care not to duplicate the information contained in the chairman's statement in the chief executive's review. Many chief executives' reviews take up, and enlarge, some of the themes highlighted by the chairman. However, many chief executive's reviews concentrate, in particular, on key strategic issues of the business components and divisions and on the impact of major decisions on shareholders.

Strategic marketing issues also form a significant feature of most reviews. Any corrective trading action by management and details of expansion plans can also be discussed. But heed a few words of warning. The demarcation lines between an OFR, chairman's statement and chief executive's review must be clearly established. The biggest danger is of either duplication or omission. When the annual report is being prepared, you need to consider carefully where sections and issues are to be placed.

Also, do not make the chief executive's review too complex and over-technical. It needs to be authoritative, clear and confident yet without arrogance, irrelevancies or complex explanations.

Since the OFR is becoming a key section of the annual report, do not devalue or undermine its importance by moving parts of the text that should more properly be found in the OFR into the chief executive's review.

The chief executive's review does have a point in its favour. It allows the company's most senior employee and the users to communicate directly with, and perhaps relate more closely to, each other (see Appendix 5.5).

Appendix 5.1: Operating and financial review (OFR)

In January 2003, the Accounting Standards Board issued a statement on operating and financial reviews. (This Statement was issued as '. . . a formulation and development of best practice; it is intended to have persuasive rather mandatory force and is not an accounting standard'.)

The ASB recommended that the OFR should:

- Highlight accounting policies that have required the exercise of judgement in their application and to those issues for which the results are particularly sensitive.
- Identify any information from the financial statements that has been adjusted for inclusion in the OFR; and also provide a reconciliation.
- Highlight and comment on the measures that are used by directors as being 'key performance indicators in managing the business'.

Source: *Operating and Financial Review*, 2003, ASB, London.

Appendix 5.2: Extract from Tate & Lyle PLC's OFR

The extract from an operating and financial review (OFR) for a listed company, as shown below, is reproduced by kind permission of Tate & Lyle PLC.

Operating and financial review: Tate & Lyle 2001

Summary of Financial Results

Change of Year End
Last year's change in financial year end from September to March means that these results cover the 53-week period ended 31 March 2001, and are compared with those in the previous Annual Report, for the 78-week period ended 25 March 2000.

In order to assist shareholders, unaudited results for the 52 weeks ended 25 March 2000 are also included. This Operating and Financial Review principally compares trading for the year ended 31 March 2001 with this unaudited comparative period.

Trading
Sales increased by £56 million. Disposals of businesses reduced sales by £406 million and exchange rate movements increased sales by £133 million. Group profit before interest, exceptional items and goodwill amortisation fell by £99 million from £284 million to £185 million.

Exchange rate movements increased profits before interest by £7 million.

Exceptional Items and Goodwill Amortisation
Profits and losses on disposal have been classified as exceptional due to their size producing a net total loss of £336 million, which includes £193 million of goodwill previously written off to reserves. After a tax charge of £3 million on these exceptional items the effect of the exceptional profits and losses on shareholders' funds is a reduction of £146 million. The exceptional profit on sale of businesses was £9 million. The exceptional write-down in recognition of the planned sale of businesses

was £345 million. The write-down comprises £111 million in respect of Western, of which £75 million was charged at the half-year, £227 million in respect of Domino and £7 million in respect of other businesses. The write-down includes goodwill of £25 million relating to Western, and £149 million relating to Domino.

The goodwill of £153 million arising on the acquisition of the Amylum and Staley minorities was capitalised. £5 million of capitalised goodwill was amortised in the year.

Segmental Analysis of Profit before Interest

Sweeteners and Starches – Americas
Profits before exceptional items and interest from continuing businesses fell by 38% from £156 million to £96 million. IMASA, the Argentinian starch and cereal sweetener business, made £5 million before it was sold in the previous year. Exchange rate movements increased profits by £14 million.

Staley and Tate & Lyle Citric Acid
Although Staley's starch business began the year strongly this was not sustained. The strong dollar had a major impact on the sales of the US paper industry, Staley's largest starch market, and the general economic slowdown in the US became increasingly felt as the year progressed.

The sweetener market was weak due to low demand and low pricing. However, there were signs of improvement during January to March 2001. Double digit percentage increases in average selling prices were achieved, consistent with industry trends. Corn gluten meal pricing and corn oil pricing remain at depressed levels in spite of some recovery in the former. Whilst the cost of corn per bushel is at reasonable levels, net corn costs were higher due to the low co-product values. Consolidation in the industry continued. Customers continued to grow in size through merger and acquisition but, for the first time in many years, combinations also occurred among our competitors. In August an agreement was reached with DuPont for the joint development of the production of 1,3-propanediol for the textile industry using a corn-based fermentation medium. Both a pilot and a demonstration plant were successfully commissioned.

Energy costs at Staley rose following substantial increases in natural gas and electricity prices. The impact of these increases was moderated somewhat by Staley's reliance at its larger facilities on coal, which is protected from similar upward price pressures. Projects with excellent paybacks are under way to reduce energy usage further and also recycle steam and heat. A debottlenecking project at Loudon was completed and new drying facilities are being installed at Decatur.

In Mexico the Almex joint venture performed well, increasing sales, but higher corn costs reduced margins, and results were below last year's excellent performance.

The market for citric acid was competitive during the year. Profit declined slightly, with lower selling prices but higher volumes.

The creation of a global citric business continued. The Tate & Lyle Citric Acid brand is becoming recognised globally and product standards have been established among all the citric plants to ensure quality products for our customers, regardless of the plant from which the product is sourced. The citric plants were included in the global Tate & Lyle purchasing network, enabling the citric plants to obtain the best pricing available in the Group. We completed expansions to plants in the US, UK and Brazil and the full benefit of increased volumes will be seen next year. The global market for citric acid continues to grow at 5% annually.

Profit before Tax

Loss before tax was £228 million. Before goodwill amortisation and exceptional items, profit before tax was £113 million, a reduction of £96 million or 46% on the prior year. Exchange rate movements increased profit by £5 million.

Taxation

The Group taxation charge was £35 million. The underlying rate of tax on profit, before goodwill amortisation and exceptional items, was 28.3% (2000 – 26.7%). The increase was due to lower profits in low tax jurisdictions.

Dividend

A final dividend of 12.3p will be recommended as an ordinary dividend to be paid on 8 August 2001 to shareholders on the register on 13 July 2001. An interim dividend of 5.5p was paid on 16 January 2001. Dividend cover is 0.9 times before goodwill amortisation and exceptional items.

Cash Flow and Balance Sheet

Cash Flow and Debt

Operating cash flow totalled £219 million (2000 – £450 million). £125 million (2000 – £191 million) was paid to providers of finance as dividends and interest. Taxation paid was £36 million (2000 – £44 million). Plant replacement, improvement and expansion expenditure of £124 million was below depreciation of £132 million. Investment expenditure was £224 million, of which £212 million related to the cash element of the purchase of Amylum and Staley minorities. Disposals of fixed assets and investments generated cash of £186 million. Focus on these issues was assisted by Economic Value Added (EVA) techniques. Exchange translation, and other non-cash movements, increased debt by £54 million. The Group's net borrowing rose from £805 million to £963 million.

The gearing ratio rose to 83% at 31 March 2001 (2000 – 64%). The average debt for the year was £885 million (2000 – £926 million). Net debt peaked at £982 million in January 2001 (June 1999 during the 12 months ended March 2000 – £1 ,016 million). Interest cover before exceptional items and goodwill amortisation decreased to 2.3 times (2000 – 3.6 times).

Funding

In March 2001, Tate & Lyle completed a £280 million three-year syndicated facility. The proceeds of this facility were used to refinance existing debt obligations. At March 2001 the long-term credit ratings from Moody's and Standard and Poor's were Baa2 and BBB+ respectively.

At the year end the Group held cash and current asset investments of £117 million (2000 – £261 million) and had undrawn committed multicurrency facilities of £569 million (2000 – £378 million). These resources are maintained to meet the projected maximum cash outflow from debt repayment and seasonal working capital needs foreseen until the end of the next calendar year. Group policy is to ensure that, after subtracting the total of undrawn committed facilities, no more than 30% of gross debt matures within 12 months and at least 50% has a maturity of more than two and a half years. The maturity profile of the Group's debt has lengthened so that at the year end the results of these calculations were 0% (so that the debt maturing within 12 months was fully backed by undrawn committed facilities) and 64% respectively (2000 – 10% and 61%).

Euro borrowings were increased to match the increased exposure to euro assets following the purchase of the Amylum minority. The proceeds were converted into sterling and US dollars to reduce borrowings. The proportion of Group net debt denominated in US dollars and Canadian dollars fell from 69% on 25 March 2000 to 53% on 31 March 2001. Following the sale of Bundaberg the Group has no debt denominated in Australian dollars. Debt in euros rose from 13% to 32%.

Share Issue

24,083,913 new ordinary shares valued at £69 million were issued as part consideration for the acquisition of the Amylum and Staley minorities in August 2000.

Disposals

The major disposal was Bundaberg, the Australian sugar and rum group, which was completed in July. Proceeds were £160 million, £6 million higher than assumed when the loss on sale was provided for in last year's accounts. Disposals in the Animal Feed segment involved the Grains business and the Sweetlix blocks business in the US and Rumenco (animal feed), UMT (feed mill engineering) and ABS (dry storage) in Europe.

In the Other segment, we sold our joint venture agribusinesses Fletcher Smith and Booker Tate, and a charcoal business.

Total proceeds from disposals were £180 million.

Pensions
The valuation of the UK pension fund at 31 March 2001 will be completed in late summer.

The results are likely to indicate a need for the resumption of contributions to the fund at an annual rate of around £10 million. This will impact cash flow but not profit.

Post-Balance Sheet Event
Zambia Sugar, in the Rest of the World segment, was sold for £8 million in April 2001, after the year end.

In June 2001 a conditional agreement was entered into for the disposal of Western Sugar for £68 million.

Control & Governance

Management of Financial Risk
The major financial risks faced by the Group are funding risk, interest rate risk, currency risk and certain commodity price risks. The Board of Tate & Lyle PLC regularly reviews these risks and approves written policies covering the use of financial instruments to manage risk, and overall risk limits. The last review was in March 2001. All the Group's material financial instruments are categorised as being held either for trading or risk management. Trading of financial instruments within the Group is severely limited, confined only to tightly controlled areas within the sugar and maize pricing operations.

Control and Direction of Treasury
Group financing, including debt, interest costs and foreign exchange matters, is directed by the Group treasury company, Tate & Lyle International Finance PLC, whose operations are controlled by its Board. The treasury company is chaired by the Group Finance Director.

Appendix 5.3: Extract from Allied Domecq PLC's directors' report

The extract from a directors' report for a listed company, as shown on the following pages, is reproduced by kind permission of Allied Domecq PLC.

Directors' report
The directors are pleased to present their annual report and accounts for the year ended 31 August 2001.

Business review and future developments
The Chairman's statement and the Operating and financial review on page 3 and pages 16 to 25 provide a review of the business and likely future developments.

Acquisitions
Details of the acquisitions during the year are shown in note 25 of the accounts on pages 59 and 60.

Main trading activities
The group's main trading activities are the production, marketing and sale of spirits and wine and the franchising of quick service restaurants.

Post balance sheet events
Details of events since the balance sheet date are shown in note 33 of the accounts on page 63.

Dividends
An interim dividend of 4.5p per share was paid on 27 July 2001 and the directors are pleased to recommend a final ordinary dividend of 7.6p per share, making a total for the year of 12.1p. The final dividend will be paid on 5 February 2002 to shareholders on the register on 4 January 2002.

Annual General Meeting
The AGM will be held on 31 January 2002 at Le Meridien Grosvenor House Hotel, Park Lane, London W1K 7TN. Details of the business to be considered at the AGM and the notice of meeting are included in the accompanying chairman's letter.

Share capital
Details of the company's share capital and options over the company's shares under the group's employee share plans are given in note 22 of the accounts on page 58. As at 31 August 2001 the company had authority to purchase up to 10% of its ordinary shares. Shareholders' approval is being sought for the renewal of this authority and for an increase in the authorised share capital of the company at the AGM.

Substantial interests
The company has been notified of the following disclosable interests in Allied Domecq ordinary shares:

Suntory Limited	3.54%
AXA Sun Life Investment Management Limited	3.87%

Employees
Allied Domecq operates a policy of equal opportunity and continues to give full and fair consideration to applications for employment made by disabled persons. Employees who become disabled will, wherever possible and practicable, be retained in employment and, where necessary, appropriate training will be provided.

Employees are encouraged to become shareholders in the company. Grants of options over a total of 6,159,984 shares were made to eligible employees under the company's employee share option plans during the year and rights were granted to employees under the company's share appreciation rights plan. The company continues to extend its SAYE plan to new countries and is intending to launch a new All Employee Share Ownership Plan in the UK in February 2002.

Communications and involvement
Considerable emphasis is placed by the group on communications with its employees. In addition to obtaining a comprehensive range of attitudes and views from employees through employee opinion surveys, group companies involve and consult them with regard to the activities and performance of their businesses and any matters of concern to them. It is normal practice to use formal joint consultative bodies locally for one-to-one and group meetings. Allied Domecq has a European Council which acts as a forum for Pan-European consultation and discussion.

Health, safety and welfare
The group has achieved its goal of global co-ordination of health and safety matters based on strategically based steering groups and health and safety champions. This year the group again benchmarked its environmental, health and safety (EHS) performance across a broad range of EHS business processes. Global operating units are also working towards certification of their health and safety management systems based on Occupational Health & Safety Assessment Series 18001. For the first time the group's forthcoming environmental report will also include our health and safety performance and plans, becoming a full EHS document.

Research and development
The amount spent by the group on research and development during the period was £1m but this does not include the full cost of new product development.

Creditor payment policy
The company's policy, in relation to all of its suppliers, is to settle the terms of payment when agreeing the terms of the transaction, to ensure that suppliers are aware of the terms of payment and to abide by those terms provided it is satisfied that the goods or services were supplied in accordance with the agreed terms and conditions. The company does not follow any particular code or standard on payment practice. Creditor days have not been calculated as the company had no trade creditors at 31 August 2001. The company's invoices for goods and services are settled by subsidiaries acting as agents for the company.

Directors
The names and brief biographical details of the directors as at 29 October 2001 are given on page 28. All of whom served throughout the year. In accordance with the articles of association, Graham Hetherington, Sir Christopher Hogg and David Scotland retire at the forthcoming AGM and offer themselves for re-election.

Political and charitable contributions
No political donations were made to EU political parties or organisations during the year. Charitable contributions in the UK totalled £71,000. In addition the Allied Domecq Trust gave £6,000 to charitable causes.

Auditor
KPMG Audit Plc, has expressed its willingness to continue in office as auditor of the company. A resolution for the re-appointment of the auditor, at a rate of remuneration to be determined by the directors, will be proposed at the AGM.

By order of the board

Leonard A Quaranto
Secretary
29 October 2001

Appendix 5.4: Extract from Kingfisher plc's chairman's statement

The extract from a chairman's statement for a listed company, as shown below, is reproduced by kind permission of Kingfisher plc.

Kingfisher plc: Chairman's Statement 2001

Kingfisher is one of very few global retailers to focus on the high-growth home improvement and electricals markets which, as Chief Executive Sir Geoffrey Mulcahy describes in his report, makes the company's future growth prospects very attractive.

But the exciting expansion opportunities which lie ahead for 'new' Kingfisher cannot be allowed to disguise the fact that this has been a most difficult year. The strong sales growth and important strategic progress made did not translate satisfactorily into growth in earnings.

However, overall the most significant feature of the year was the decision we announced in September 2000 to separate the UK General Merchandise companies (Woolworths, Superdrug and our entertainment businesses) from the internationally-focused Home Improvement and Electrical and Furniture businesses – 'new' Kingfisher. This will benefit both groups of businesses.

'New' Kingfisher will be able to concentrate its international management skills and finances on accelerating its growth record. The General Merchandise growth strategy will focus on the development of its customer propositions through destination stores, and stores offering convenience 'everyday' shopping, as it exploits its strong positions in a range of growth markets.

When we announced the demerger, we said it would be completed in the second quarter of 2001, and we remain on schedule. Demerger remains the main plank of our approach, but because shareholder value is a prime consideration we are looking at alternatives and will report progress in due course.

By the high standards we have set ourselves, 2000/01 was a disappointing year: record profits from B&Q, Brico Depot, NOMI,

F Darty, Comet and BUT were offset by disappointing performances in some of our other businesses. We also made important strategic progress which will serve shareholders well in the future.

A strong top-line growth resulted in record sales of more than £12.1 billion. Home Improvement and Electrical and Furniture achieved an increase in sales revenue of 15 per cent or more in local currency terms – more than respectable in a deflationary environment.

B&Q further strengthened its leading UK position during a year in which all its principal UK competitors changed hands. Our Electrical and Furniture sector sales were up 16.7 per cent in local currency terms which, combined with an increased cash margin, was a notable achievement

Following the separation, 'new' Kingfisher will be an attractive international retail group with strong positions in home-making markets which are expected to experience rapid growth across the globe:

- Number one French and UK positions in home improvement, with growing businesses in other international markets.
- Number one position in French electricals, number two position in the UK with a growing presence in emerging markets, particularly central Europe.
- Important growth potential in furniture and soft furnishings, building on BUT's success in France.

The achievements of the past and potential for the future would not have been possible without the hard work and dedication to serving customers demonstrated by all our 134,000 employees worldwide. I would like to take this opportunity to place on record our gratitude to all of them for a job well done in intensely competitive circumstances.

Two directors stood down from the Board during the year: The Lady Howe and Philippe Frances have both made major contributions to Kingfisher and will be much missed. We wish them every happiness with their respective futures.

Sir John Banham *Chairman*
Kingfisher plc Annual Report and Accounts 2001

Appendix 5.5: Extract from Tate & Lyle PLC's chief executive's review

The extract from a chief executive's review for a listed company is reproduced on the following pages by kind permission of Tate & Lyle PLC.

Chief Executive's Review from Larry Pillard

Change of Year End

In order to provide meaningful comparisons in the review that follows, the audited results for the 53 weeks to 31 March 2001 are compared with the unaudited results for the 52 weeks to 25 March 2000.

Group Performance

Results for the year were disappointing, with profit before tax, exceptional items and goodwill amortisation falling from £209 million to £113 million.

The tough conditions faced in the US sugar market towards the end of the prior year have persisted throughout the year ended March 2001 and show no signs of improving. Our US sugar operations incurred a £20 million loss before interest. Increased energy costs across the Group, especially in the second half, have also squeezed margins by £45 million. Our sweetener and starch businesses on both sides of the Atlantic faced very competitive markets, with lower margins. Although energy costs remain high, there was good news in the pricing rounds for the 2001 calendar year, with Staley reporting double digit price rises for sweeteners and Amylum securing price rises of around 10% on most product lines. These price improvements will mainly benefit the financial year ending March 2002.

Rising to these challenges, we have been focused on executing our strategy. We have delivered efficiency gains through reorganisation and consolidation and have continued to dispose of smaller businesses in non-core markets and those businesses from which we did not expect to achieve acceptable returns.

Profit before interest
£ million
Before exceptional items and goodwill amortisation
Years ended March

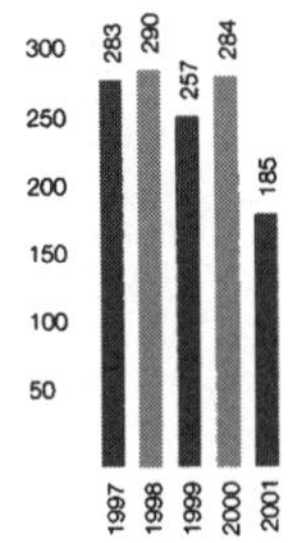

Focus on Key Activities

Good progress has been made to capture the full benefits from the acquisition of the Staley and Amylum minorities last August. We are already delivering benefits and are confident that we will achieve the target of £50 million benefit per annum by 2003/04.

We completed the disposal of Bundaberg, our Australian sugar milling and related activity group, in July 2000. This disposal, coupled with the sale of ten smaller businesses in the Animal Feed and Other segments, will reduce overheads and provides a cash inflow of £180 million. The other disposals include animal feed and agribusiness companies. After the year end, we also sold Zambia Sugar.

As you will have seen from the Chairman's Statement, we have also entered into an agreement

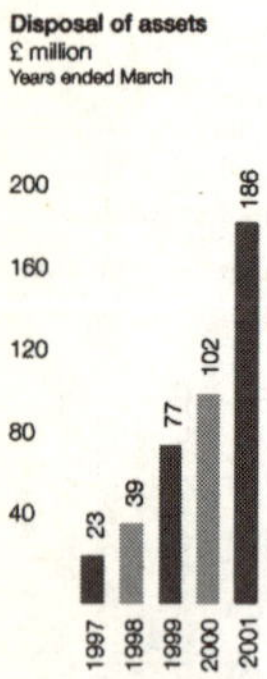

that should lead to the disposal of Western and are in advanced negotiations for the sale of Domino.

We announced last year that we were looking for a strategic solution for these underperforming businesses that continue to incur losses, this year totalling £20 million before interest. This is an industry-wide issue, a result of a dysfunctional US sugar regime and an oversupply of beet and cane sugar in the market. These problems require a political solution that also addresses the disputes between Mexico and the US over NAFTA access for Mexican sugar to the US market, and US high fructose corn syrup to the Mexican market. We cannot be certain of any significant improvement to the US market in the near future.

We have explored many alternatives for these businesses, from outright divestment to various forms of industry rationalisation. We are convinced that, provided this can be concluded on satisfactory terms, the sale of Western and Domino offers the best way forward for the Group.

The completion of these disposals will be an important step in the delivery of our strategy to refocus our portfolio of assets on those that are core, and that we can expect to deliver an acceptable level of return.

Performance of Main Businesses

Increased energy costs reduced margins at all our main business units. Staley and Amylum profits were below those of the previous year, impacted also by lower sweetener and starch margins. The high fructose corn syrup market in the US showed little growth last year, reflecting reduced growth in carbonated soft drink sales. The industry did not bring any significant additional capacity on line and supply and demand moved more closely in balance due to some capacity being diverted to other higher margin products such as ethanol.

The market for industrial starches, especially to the paper industry, was very competitive due to the strength of the US dollar and consolidation within the industry. Speciality food starches were resilient in difficult market conditions. Citric profitability declined slightly, with lower selling prices but higher volumes.

Our announcement in August 2000 that we had signed a joint development agreement for bio-based polymers with DuPont provides a glimpse of the future for Tate & Lyle. This project will provide a significant step towards manufacturing advanced polymers from renewable resources, replacing products now made from petroleum. Producing products from carbohydrates will have a role in how the world manages carbon dioxide emissions in the future. This is an excellent fit with our global carbohydrates business and our proven Research & Development capabilities, and presents an important opportunity to advance our strategy of growing through the development of new value-added products.

Our cane refineries in the UK, Canada and Portugal continued to perform well. In our North American sugar businesses losses increased as the oversupply of beet and cane sugar continued to squeeze margins to uneconomic levels, sending the largest US producer to seek 'Chapter 11' protection from its creditors. More positively, we have arrived at a settlement of the long-running labour dispute at Domino's Brooklyn refinery. The new barge was commissioned in September, enabling the more cost-effective transfer of sugar syrup from Baltimore to Brooklyn.

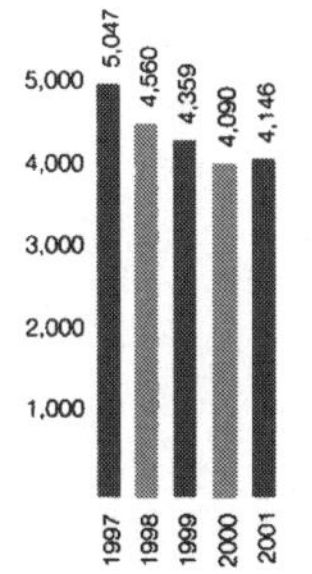

Performance of Other Businesses

Many of the businesses in this category were sold during the year. Of the remaining businesses, both sugar and starch joint ventures in Central Europe performed well despite drought conditions, cutting costs and increasing profits as sugar regimes were introduced in preparation for entry to the European Union.

Molasses trading had a difficult year, with demand impacted by problems in the farming sector. Sugar trading activity remained profitable, with Brazil and Thailand being the key suppliers.

Demand for sucralose continues to grow, especially in Japan and the US. Plans for the development of this business globally await completion of the commissioning period of the new Johnson & Johnson production facility. New issues related to dietary guidelines recently developed by a number of governments and increasing concern with obesity will create many new opportunities for this product.

Safety

Safety continues to be a central concern and the past year has seen an improvement across the whole Group. We have a history as the leader in safety in the US corn wet-milling industry statistics and have undertaken to transfer this expertise worldwide. Each business has been set safety targets and we publish a quarterly Safety Index in the employee magazine *Tate & Lyle World*. This is an invaluable tool for measuring, reporting and improving the Company's record on health and safety throughout its operations. The full Board reviews health and safety performance annually and supports the drive for continuous improvement.

Energy

We are committed to reducing energy consumption on both economic and environmental grounds. All businesses have been set a target to reduce energy consumption on a per unit basis by 3% per year. In December 2000, the Group published an Energy Index for each of our major plants which tracks energy consumption across the Group and is being used to focus conservation efforts.

6 Auditors' reports

As discussed in Chapter 2, a company's shareholders elect directors to control and manage the company on a day-to-day basis and take responsibility for the company's assets. At the end of the financial year, the directors have to report back to the owners – the shareholders – and explain their stewardship of the company's assets. It is this whole concept of accountability of the directors to their shareholders that forms an essential function of the annual report.

Verification

Since the annual report is, in effect, produced by the directors on behalf of the shareholders, it is important that a degree of verification is established. Checks and balances need to be imposed to ensure that the annual report is independently examined so that shareholders and other users can have, at least in theory, some degree of faith and confidence in the accounting process. Independent accountants, who act in their capacity as auditors, conduct this impartial and objective verification process. In their report, the auditors will clearly explain what they have done and what accounting statements have been audited. The report will also highlight the respective responsibilities of the directors and auditors.

Every listed company is required to appoint the auditors at the company's annual general meeting, and the selected auditors will hold this position until the conclusion of the next AGM.

In an attempt to reduce administrative cost burdens on smaller companies, the government has progressively increased the audit exemption threshold. Currently, companies with an annual turnover of under £1 million do not need to have their accounts audited, and consideration is being given to increasing this sales threshold to £4.8 million.

In practice, although the directors select the auditors, the auditors' appointment needs to be ratified by the shareholders at their annual general meeting. It should be noted that auditors report to the members of the company – namely, the shareholders – and not to the directors. At the conclusion of their audit, the auditors will produce a report which is always included in the company's annual report. Obviously, a company will aim to ensure that its accounts receive its auditors' approval in the form of a so-called 'unqualified' or 'clean' auditors' report, rather than a 'qualified' or even an 'adverse' report in which the auditors highlight areas where legal or accounting requirements have not been observed, either fully or partially. A 'qualified' or 'adverse' report can have serious, and sometimes fatal, consequences for a company. The nature and full implications of qualified and unqualified reports are discussed later in this chapter.

Audit failures

However, over the past two decades in particular, some auditors' reports have received adverse publicity from some quarters with regard to some auditors' failure to highlight areas of potential concern. Indeed, a number of leading 'blue-chip' companies, such as Polly Peck, Maxwell Communications, BCCI, Queen's Moat and Barings Bank, have collapsed shortly after the publication of a 'clean' or unqualified report. In all these cases, the auditors did not highlight any financial difficulties or find any evidence that these companies were not a 'going concern'. Auditors do not always get it right. They may sometimes be negligent, too rushed or simply apply poor-quality audit tests or risk management assessment techniques. The crash of the energy conglomerate Enron, America's seventh largest company, in the winter of 2001 brought the role of the auditors into sharp focus. There was evidence that Andersens, Enron's auditors, did not operate to the high standards expected of a professional firm of auditors. Subsequent allegations of poor auditing standards and the destruction of audit and accounting evidence led to the demise of Andersens as a reputable firm.

The inclusion of an auditors' report is not only a legal requirement but is also subject to the requirements of professional auditing standards in terms of its form and content. Just as accountants have to comply with professional accounting standards, accountants acting in their auditing capacity have to comply with professional auditing standards called Statements of Auditing Standards (SASs).

Wording

You will not be able to alter the wording or influence the content of an auditors' report. It is their report, not yours! Legislation and the professional auditing standards have laid down strict requirements that auditors need to adhere to when producing their report. Most auditors will only significantly qualify the accounts after they have conducted the most searching investigations. A seriously qualified auditors' report may well cause a company to experience major difficulties and even its failure.

In fact, there is very little work for you or your finance department to perform. The auditors themselves will write, sign and date the report. Admittedly, they will normally discuss their report with your company's finance director and some other key executives (and your audit committee, in the case of most large companies) before it is finalized. Only in the case of contentious auditing issues, where the auditors are considering issuing a qualified report, may there be some limited scope for your accountants to discuss with the auditors why they believe that other wording is more appropriate.

Auditors' reports have changed considerably in content in recent years. The most significant change has been their expansion, and they now define more clearly the nature and extent of an auditor's duties and responsibilities. In particular, auditors have attempted to dispel some of the myths surrounding their work by providing more detailed explanation.

This explanation dispels the commonly held view that the purpose of the statutory audit of a limited company is to guarantee that no fraud is taking place. Auditors merely report that the accounts are 'true and fair' and comply with legislation. Part of the auditors' work in ensuring that the accounts are true and fair will entail carrying out test-checking on some of the company's transactions. If there is material fraud in the company, these tests may pick up some incidences of this. However, the statutory audit is not set up primarily to detect fraud; the principal aim is to ensure that the accounts are 'true and fair'.

In an attempt to improve corporate governance, many companies have established audit committees comprised of non-executive directors. These committees are involved in all matters of appointing and dismissing auditors and in discussing contentious accounting and auditing issues.

Form

The auditors' report should be attached to the accounts and include the following:

- a title identifying to whom the report is addressed – for the purposes of the 1985 Companies Act, this audience will be the shareholders
- a short paragraph which clearly identifies the accounts that have been audited
- a separate section that explains:
  - the respective responsibilities of the directors and auditors
  - the basis of the auditors' opinion, which should include a statement of compliance or otherwise with auditing standards, and any reasons for departure from these standards
  - whether, in the auditors' opinion, the accounts give a true and fair view and have been properly prepared in accordance with the Companies Act 1985
  - the signature of the auditors with the accounts
  - the date.

Appendix 6.1, at the end of this chapter, gives an example of an auditors' report.

Content

An auditors' report will normally contain three key sections:

- statement of directors' and auditors' responsibilities
- basis of audit opinion
- opinion.

Statement of directors' and auditors' responsibilities
This section identifies the principal responsibilities of the directors and auditors. Many of the areas in the expanded auditors' report originally arose from direct and indirect responses to high levels of litigation against

auditors in the US. In the UK, the Auditing Practices Board has attempted to import some of these US measures to highlight clearly the responsibilities of the parties involved.

The auditors will include a statement that their responsibilities are to report whether, in their opinion, the financial statements give a true and fair view and are properly prepared in accordance with the Companies Act 1985. They are also required to report if the directors' report is not consistent with the financial statements and also, where applicable, whether the corporate governance statements reflect compliance with the 'Combined Code' (see Chapter 8, 'Corporate governance'). The auditors will 'read the other information contained in the Annual Report...' and consider whether it is consistent with the audited accounts. If they become aware of any apparent misstatements or material inconsistencies with the accounts, the auditors will also consider the implications for their report.

Basis of audit opinion

This section attempts to minimize misunderstandings of the auditor's duties and responsibilities. It states that the audit has been conducted in accordance with professional auditing standards. It will stress that an audit includes examination, on a test basis, of evidence relevant to the amounts and disclosures in the accounts. It includes an assessment of the significant estimates and judgements made by the directors in the preparation of the accounts, whether the accounting policies are appropriate to the company's circumstances and whether they have been applied and adequately disclosed.

It will also be explained that the audit has been performed so as to obtain all the information and explanations that the auditors consider necessary in order to obtain 'reasonable assurances' that the accounts are free from material misstatement.

Opinion

This section contains one of the most important statements of the auditors' report – namely the auditors' opinion as to whether the accounts give a 'true and fair view' and have been properly prepared in accordance with the Companies Act 1985. Professional auditing regulations require the auditors to report circumstances where accounting standards are not disclosed in the accounts.

The auditors' duties will also ensure that:

- proper returns have been received from branches

- proper accounting records have been kept
- the accounts are in agreement with the underlying records and returns
- they have obtained all the information and explanations they consider necessary
- the information contained in the directors' report is not inconsistent with the accounts.

The auditors should also refer to any significant departures from the requirements of applicable accounting standards. Professional auditing regulations require auditors to report circumstances where departure from accounting standards is not disclosed in the accounts.

Statement of directors' responsibilities

Essentially, the directors' responsibility statement will discuss the extent of their responsibilities as regards preparing the accounts (see Appendix 6.2). The statement will highlight that, legally, the directors are responsible for ensuring that the financial statements give a true and fair view, and will also point out that, in preparing these accounts, they are required to:

- select suitable accounting policies and apply them consistently
- make judgements and estimates that are reasonable and prudent
- state whether applicable accounting standards have been followed and, if not, give full reasons and explanations
- prepare the financial statements on a 'going concern' basis – unless it is inappropriate to do so.

The directors are also required to state that it is their responsibility to keep proper accounting records which disclose, with reasonable accuracy, the company's financial position and to ensure that the financial statements comply with the Companies Act 1985.

The statement should also state that the directors are responsible for the company's system of internal control, for safeguarding the company's assets and hence for taking reasonable precautions to prevent and detect fraud and other irregularities.

Improvements

Any company intent on changing the content or wording of the directors' statement of responsibilities will be disappointed. These statements have been formally standardized leaving little or no scope for improvements on these specific issues. However, all is not lost. Even if the wording cannot be changed, there are other areas of potential improvement – notably presentation. Try not to squeeze this statement into a small confined space. Most statements, however technical and seemingly dull, can be made more acceptable by allocating sufficient space. Many of the points raised in the directors' statement of responsibilities are important and highlight significant aspects of their responsibilities. So do your utmost to convey their significance and meaning and investigate how you can improve the layout.

A useful way of improving the standing of statements is to allocate each statement a new page in the annual report. It does not matter if the directors' statement only uses half a page – leave the rest of the page blank. Allocation of space is seldom a limiting factor here, so there is no need to squeeze as much information as possible onto each page. In addition, you could 'box' the statement in order to convey a degree of authority and standing. Do not necessarily limit yourself to a black outline – for example, dark red often works well in conveying a sense of authority and importance. Consider using an imaginative selection of other colours as well. The actual statement could, for example, be shaded a lighter colour (such as pale yellow or pale blue) and overlaid on a white page background. The presentation will also be improved by a bold, clear heading at the top of the page.

Use a typeface that is clear and, most importantly, not too small. Give the statement a sporting chance – if the typeface is too small, the statement will largely be ignored.

Qualified report

The vast majority of auditors' reports will be termed 'unqualified'. Of course, contrary to what is sometimes believed, this does not mean that the auditors are unqualified in terms of experience or technical knowledge, but rather that the auditors have not qualified their opinion – that is, their report is 'clean' of adverse comment and that the company's accounts, in their opinion, provide 'a true and fair view' and comply with the legislation. Clearly, an unqualified report is always the desired objective of companies.

However, there may sometimes be circumstances where auditors do not believe that the accounts are true and fair or comply with legislation and, in these instances, they are compelled to issue a qualified report. Depending on the nature and extent of the qualification, an auditor's opinion that is qualified is extremely serious for any company. In effect, it means the whole system and relationship between the directors and the company's shareholders have broken down and, depending on the nature of the qualification, that shareholders and other interested parties cannot have full confidence in the company's accounts.

The wording of a qualified auditors' report is important. Just as accountants are subject to detailed accounting rules, such as the Financial Reporting Standards, auditors also have their own regulations. These regulations, in the form of the Statement of Auditing Standard (SAS) 600, clearly spell out the precise wording that must be used in the audit report.

A qualified opinion is usually issued when there is some limitation as to the scope of an auditors' examination or when the auditors disagree with the treatment of disclosures in the financial statements. If the auditors decide that an item, transaction or omission is material to the accounts, and therefore affects the true and fair requirement of the accounts, then they must qualify their report.

In practice, there are two major qualified opinions that can be given:

- adverse opinion
- disclaimer of opinion.

Adverse opinion

An adverse opinion is issued when the effect of a disagreement is so material or persuasive that the auditors conclude that your financial statements are seriously misleading. As a consequence, the auditors will state that, in their opinion, your accounts are *not* 'true and fair'. This is the most devastating qualification you can have appended to your accounts. The almost certain consequence will be that no one will trust your accounts anymore. With a qualification as severe as this, there will be little future prospect for your company.

However, if the auditors believe that the effect of a disagreement is not sufficient to require an adverse opinion, they will express an opinion that is qualified by stating that the financial statements give a true and fair view, *except* for the effects of the matter that gave rise to the disagreement.

Disclaimer of opinion

Auditors also have the option of disclaiming to give an opinion. If the scope of an audit is so limited that the auditors have been unable to obtain sufficient evidence to support an opinion, this will be recorded – for example, by simply stating that they are 'unable to form an opinion'. However, if the auditors believe that the possible effect of the limitation is not so significant as to require a disclaimer, they will state that the accounts are true and fair, except for the effects of any adjustments that might be necessary.

Either way, if your company faces having a disclaimer of opinion attached to its accounts, it will still face extremely serious repercussions affecting its whole viability in terms of trading. Quite simply, everyone – banks, suppliers, shareholders and employees – will immediately be mistrustful of your company as a result of such a damning indictment.

A message to avoid

In many ways, there is little that you can do to improve the situation – normally the damage has been done already. A qualified auditors' report is one message that you certainly do not want to be delivered. Admittedly, as far as qualifications go, it is preferable to have a 'watered-down' qualification that states that the accounts are true and fair *except* for the area causing contention between you and the auditors.

At all costs, you do not want an auditors' report that states your accounts are *not* true and fair. In some circumstances, your company's accountants, in discussion with the auditors, may be able to persuade the auditors that the qualification should be 'downgraded' from an adverse report (that is, the accounts are not true and fair) to a qualification that indicates accounts are true and fair except for the areas of contention.

Nevertheless, ultimately the decision rests with your auditors – not you.

Facing disaster

If your auditors insist, on very rare occasions, that your accounts are not true and fair, there is very little you can do to put a positive 'spin' or gloss on the message. The battle has been lost and, in all probability, so is your company. And by the way, it is no use suggesting that your company dismisses the auditors and replaces them with another firm of auditors who may be more amenable to your viewpoint. Dismissing an auditor is fraught with legal and professional auditing difficulties – for example, a dismissed auditor has the legal right to turn up at the AGM and to put his or her side of the story. In addition, a new replacement auditor is professionally bound to contact the previous auditors to establish that there are no accounting or auditing issues of which he or she should be aware before taking up the new appointment.

If your auditors' report uses a less disastrous or watered-down version that states your accounts are true and fair except for certain specified areas, then hope remains. You must immediately set about implementing a damage limitation process. For the moment, time is on your side. The fact that the auditors are considering qualifying your accounts should become apparent internally before the outside world knows of your problems. Act methodically but quickly.

From discussions with your company accountants, you should know why this qualification has arisen and just what is the financial and trading significance for your company. The chairman's office, chief executive, managing director or their representative will also have to be brought in on the discussions – if they have not been already. This matter is of direct concern to the most senior figures of the company – after all, the full board will rapidly become aware of the situation anyway. A qualification is a matter of the utmost seriousness and could have major implications on your share price. Once your discussions in the company have formed a common approach, and all parties are agreed on the response to the qualification, it is time to face the outside world. Members of your audit committee should be advised immediately – assuming that they do not know already.

Go on the offensive and take the fight to the media and financial markets. Urgent press releases must be issued to key outlets. Briefing notes to journalists will help soften the blow. Unfortunately, you must expect significant (and sometimes fatal) damage to your company. Be prepared to explain why there is a qualification and why you believe it to be inappropriate.

You are advised to consult Chapter 14, 'Problems and challenges', on delivering bad news.

Presentation of the auditors' report

As indicated earlier, in terms of the auditors' report's form and content there is little you can do. The wording is strictly laid down by legislation and by detailed auditing standards. Nevertheless, in the public's eyes, the auditors' statement carries considerable importance. Rather simplistically, and sometimes naïvely, many shareholders and other users often attribute great significance to the auditors' report in terms of conveying confidence in the company's directors and management. So do not disappoint them.

Since you cannot change the wording of an auditors' report, concentrate on presentation.

Do not tuck your auditors' report away as a technical auditing formality. Place it on the page before the accounts actually start, perhaps on the page before the profit and loss account, and give it the status that some shareholders and lenders think it deserves. Allocate a complete and separate page for the report. Make a 'big deal' of it; boast about it. Refer to its 'unqualified' nature – if that is the case in your company. Glowingly mention its nature in your operating and financial review. Give the report a bold heading to make sure that it cannot be missed. Avoid using a small size typeface and do not include photographs on the same page. Nothing should detract from its significance and standing.

If you have a qualified report, you may wish to think again. You certainly do not want to draw attention to the situation, and the more cynical adviser might suggest that the report is moved to the end of the mass of accounting notes at the end of the accounts. Reduce its conspicuousness through a smaller typeface and a less prominent position. Of course, these tactics may not be that useful because your qualification will be already known to the markets, but there is still no need to display the limitations of your report prominently.

Generally, if and when you receive your 'clean' or unqualified auditors' report, you can breathe a sigh of relief – at least for this year. So, remember, there is no need to hide 'the good news'. Since you cannot change the formal wording of an auditors' report, you should make the best of it. Concentrate on prominence, clarity and visibility.

Appendix 6.1: Extract from Kingfisher plc's 2001 auditors' report and statement of directors' responsibilities

The extract below is reproduced by kind permission of Kingfisher plc.

Independent auditors' report to the members of Kingfisher plc

We have audited the financial statements which comprise the profit and loss account, the balance sheet, the cash flow statement, the statement of total recognised gains and losses and the related notes, which have been prepared under the historical cost convention (as modified by the revaluation of certain fixed assets) and the accounting policies set out in the statement of accounting policies.

Respective responsibilities of directors and auditors
The directors' responsibilities for preparing the annual report and the financial statements in accordance with applicable United Kingdom law and accounting standards are set out in the statement of directors' responsibilities.

Our responsibility is to audit the financial statements in accordance with relevant legal and regulatory requirements, United Kingdom Auditing Standards issued by the Auditing Practices Board and the Listing Rules of the Financial Services Authority.

We report to you our opinion as to whether the financial statements give a true and fair view and are properly prepared in accordance with the Companies Act 1985. We also report to you if, in our opinion, the directors' report is not consistent with the financial statements, if the Company has not kept proper accounting records, if we have not received all the information and explanations we require for our audit, or if information specified by law or the Listing Rules regarding directors' remuneration and transactions is not disclosed.

We read the other information contained in the annual report and consider the implications for our report if we become aware of any apparent misstatements or material inconsistencies with the financial statements. The other information comprises only the directors' report, the Chairman's statement, the operating and financial review and the corporate governance statement.

We review whether the corporate governance statement reflects the Company's compliance with the seven provisions of the Combined Code specified for our review by the Listing Rules, and we report if it does not. We are not required to consider whether the Board's statements on internal control cover all risks and controls, or to form an opinion on the effectiveness of the Company's or Group's corporate governance procedures or its risk and control procedures.

Basis of audit opinion

We conducted our audit in accordance with auditing standards issued by the Auditing Practices Board. An audit includes examination, on a test basis, of evidence relevant to the amounts and disclosures in the financial statements. It also includes an assessment of the significant estimates and judgements made by the directors in the preparation of the financial statements, and of whether the accounting policies appropriate to the Company's circumstances are consistently applied and adequately disclosed. We planned and performed our audit so as to obtain all the information and explanations which we considered necessary in order to provide us with sufficient evidence to give reasonable assurance that the financial statements are free from material misstatement, whether caused by fraud or other irregularity or error. In forming our opinion we also evaluated the overall adequacy of the presentation of information in the financial statements.

Opinion

In our opinion the financial statements give a true and fair view of the state of affairs of the Company and the Group at 3 February 2001 and of the profit and cash flows of the Group for the year then ended and have been properly prepared in accordance with the Companies Act 1985.

PricewaterhouseCoopers
Chartered Accountants and Registered Auditors
London
13 March 2001

Appendix 6.2: Example of information found in a statement of directors' responsibilities

The extract below is reproduced by kind permission of Kingfisher plc.

Statement of the Directors' Responsibilities

The following statement is made with a view to distinguishing for shareholders the respective responsibilities of the directors and the auditors in relation to the financial statements.

The directors are required by company law to prepare financial statements for each financial year which give a true and fair view of the state of affairs of the Company and Group as at the end of the financial year and of the profit for the year to that date. In preparing the financial statements the directors are required:

- to ensure that the Company keeps accounting records which disclose with reasonable accuracy the financial position of the Company and which enable them to ensure that the financial statements comply with the Companies Act 1985;
- to take such steps as are reasonably open to them to safeguard the assets of the Company and Group and to prevent and detect fraud and other irregularities;
- to apply suitable accounting policies in a consistent manner, supported by reasonable and prudent judgements and estimates where necessary;
- to comply with all applicable accounting standards (except where any departures from this requirement are explained in the notes to the financial statements); and
- to ensure the maintenance and integrity of the Company's corporate website where used for the electronic publication of financial statements.

7 Summary financial statements and interim reports

Summary financial statements

For many shareholders, the full and detailed set of financial statements is too overwhelming in terms of both quantity and complexity. The mass of technical detail in large companies is just too intricate for the majority of readers. Much of the key information is often hidden amongst many pages of what is, to many readers, a highly complex and indecipherable financial code. For most readers, the accounting, legal and stock exchange regulations make no sense – incomprehensible to everyone except accountants and financial analysts. To make matters worse, their actual volume seems totally indigestible. Essentially, the vast majority of shareholders do not want, and do not understand, the full set of accounts contained in the annual report.

Background

Until the legislation was amended in 1985, companies had no choice about the content and detail in their annual report; they were legally compelled to send the full and detailed financial statements to every shareholder on the shareholders' register. In practice, this was usually a pointless activity. Many shareholders merely disposed of the reports – often without opening them.

The situation deteriorated during the 1980s. With the creation of millions of smaller shareholders as a result of massive privatization and demutalization schemes, the costs of printing annual reports soared. The flotation of companies such as British Telecommunications, British Gas and the Trustee Savings Bank created millions of small private shareholders new to the stock market. For many of these new shareholders, annual reports were a total mystery. Bluntly, many of these shareholders had no interested in a large annual report – they were only interested in two essential matters. First, at what price were their shares quoted on the stock market? And, second, how much dividend income were they to receive? Other matters were not regarded as being very significant as far as their personal circumstances were concerned.

In response, these privatized companies believed that it was pointless to send a full annual report and accounts to millions of shareholders who had no real interest in the masses of technical detail, so they petitioned the government to change the law to allow the sending of only a reduced version of the annual report.

The government acknowledged that many shareholders would be more satisfied with receiving a considerably simplified set of accounts which was thought to be of far more value to them. The reduced version of the annual report was termed 'summary' or 'summarized' accounts. These condensed accounts would only include and make reference to key figures and vital extracts in the financial statements.

Legal provisions

The 1985 Companies Act relaxed the legal requirement that all limited companies must send a copy of the full accounts to all parties entitled to receive them. Instead, *listed* companies were permitted to send to their shareholders summary (or summarized) financial statements. (Do note however, that if a company is prohibited by its memorandum or articles of association from sending out summary financial statements, then full accounts must continue to be sent to all persons entitled to receive them.) Then in 1992, (in addition to shareholders) debenture-holders and other people entitled to receive notice of general meetings (termed 'entitled persons') were permitted to be sent summary financial statements – if that was their wish. To encourage even greater use of summary accounts, the regulations were further amended in 1995 to make it as easy and convenient as possible for companies to establish the wishes of entitled persons.

An entitled person grants consent to receiving the summary accounts if, *inter alia*:

- he or she notifies the company in writing that he or she wishes to receive the summary accounts in the future, or

- he or she fails to respond to a relevant consultation notice from the company giving the opportunity for him or her to elect to receive the summary accounts.

More cynical commentators will argue that it is a waste of money and resources to even produce summary accounts as many shareholders do not even want these. Nevertheless, legally they must be sent a copy if they do not wish to receive the full accounts and have not taken advantage of electronic reporting (see Chapter 12, 'The new age: electronic reporting'). Also, on grounds of accountability, there is a strong argument that shareholders should receive at least some record of what their directors have achieved with the shareholders' invested funds.

Content

The summary financial statements primarily consist of:

- a summary (or brief) profit and loss account (with an accompanying note of the directors' total remuneration)
- a summary (or brief) balance sheet
- information about the company's earnings per share
- extracts from the directors' report
- last year's comparative figures
- a statement from the company's auditors confirming whether, in their opinion, the summary financial statements are 'consistent' with the full detailed accounts and comply with the Companies Act 1985.

Obtaining detailed accounts

These summary statements must also contain a warning that they do not contain sufficient information to permit a full understanding of the accounts. The full accounts must be used if a comprehensive analysis of the company is to be conducted. There must therefore be a clearly displayed statement on the summary accounts indicating that a copy of the full accounts can be obtained for that year if shareholders and debenture-holders so wish. There should also be a statement that an entitled party can elect to receive a full set of accounts in all future years.

Ascertaining choice

Before 1995 companies were required to ascertain the wishes of users entitled to receive the full accounts in order to establish whether they wished to continue to receive these detailed accounts. Companies were required to send a postage-paid card, in advance, to entitled persons asking whether they wished to receive the full accounts in the future and spelling out the consequences if no response was made. Alternatively, companies could send out, to entitled persons, a notice explaining the content of summarized financial statements and enclose a postage-paid card by which such entitled persons could state their wish to receive the full accounts. Normally, in both cases, if there were no reply, companies would state that that they would only send summary financial statements in future.

However, since 1995 it is no longer necessary to send entitled persons a reply-paid card allowing them to request the full report and accounts. Instead, you must now include a clear and conspicuous statement in the summary accounts explaining how shareholders and debenture-holders can obtain a free copy of the full report and accounts and also permit the automatic receipt of the full accounts in future years.

Types of summary accounts

Some companies produce the summary financial statements and an annual review of the business in one booklet and the (full and detailed) financial statements, minus the annual review, in a second, separate annual report. Shareholders who opt for the full annual financial statements will receive both. The provision of two booklets is not strictly necessary, because the financial statements will then be provided both in summary and in full. Since the shareholders who want the full accounts will need an annual review, they are also sent a booklet containing both the summary and the annual review. This process is sometimes cheaper and more convenient than separating out the annual review and summary financial statements into separate booklets. Some companies put the annual review within the full financial statements and only send out the summary financial statements and a very brief review in a separate booklet.

In practice, it makes little difference which course of action you choose. However, on balance, it is perhaps marginally preferable not to send out the full accounts *and* the summarized accounts to those shareholders who request the full annual report. Overall, you should send out the summary accounts in accordance with the legislation, but perhaps also insert a brief review of the business for the shareholders' benefit. The shareholders who select to receive all the detailed accounts can also receive a full annual review. The practical implication is that you may have to précis the full annual review of the business to construct a shortened version for inclusion in the summary financial statements.

Finally, it is a good idea to include a financial calendar highlighting key dates in the company's financial year. These events include: the date and location of the AGM; the date that the interim results will be announced; and dates when the final and interim dividends will be paid.

Increasing understanding

Currently only about a third of the leading FTSE 100 companies produce summary accounts. Many companies believe that producing a simpler set of accounts is not worth the time, effort and cost.

However, producing a simplified and more readable set of financial statements can be significant in encouraging shareholder understanding.

Since the introduction of summary financial statements, the vast majority of shareholders now choose not to receive the full accounts. For example, in some of the now privatized (former state-owned) utility companies, up to 98 per cent of small shareholders are apparently content to receive just the summary financial statements.

You are advised not to neglect the use of summary accounts to help ensure that you convey your message to potentially large groups of shareholders who otherwise would probably not even glance at the full annual report and accounts.

Presentation

It is important to stress that you must comply with the legislation concerning summary financial statements. However, you can improve upon the legal minimum requirements by concentrating on their content and presentation to deliver your message, just as you would with the full detailed financial statements.

Remember, with summarized financial statements you have a different audience. Financial analysts, accountants and large-scale investors will demand their right to receive the full financial statements and will have no interest in these summary accounts. By definition, the shareholders who receive summary financial statements are those who did not ask for the full accounts and will thus not want detailed and technical explanations.

The content should reflect the interests of this mass of shareholders. Much of the information contained in this book about conveying the message in the annual report also applies to summary financial statements. Keep summary statements brief, clear, non-technical, informative and, above all, interesting. And never descend into a patronizing tone of writing. You must keep your intended audience on your side at all times.

Do bear in mind the impact of presentation. A bright and breezy cover will attract the reader's attention the moment the summary accounts are withdrawn from their envelope. When preparing summary financial statements you must always remember that your readers will not necessarily be accounting experts or even particularly interested in technical accounting detail. Their choice not to receive the full annual report in effect tells you this.

Accordingly, the onus is on you to plan carefully how the statutory information (as well as other information that you choose to voluntarily provide) should be reflected in the summary statements. Always bear in mind that it is your responsibility to try to make the summary statements interesting and appealing to your readers – they are under no obligation whatsoever to devote effort to deciphering just what you are trying to say.

Also bear in mind what message or theme you wish to convey this year, albeit in summary form. If it has been a difficult trading year you may wish to stress briefly how you are going to remedy the situation. In such cases, you may wish to explain how you are going to improve matters. Stick to two or three key remedial courses of action. Do not confuse readers by laboriously reciting tedious management reorganization details or explaining how complex new management systems will improve your business. Keep to the vital issues – for example, identifying a new market, launching new products or closing uneconomic factories. Whatever you do, highlight no more than two or three essential themes, again bearing in mind that your readers do not want or need comprehensive details (which can, if necessary, be discussed in the full annual report and accounts). At all times keep the needs and interests of your intended audience in mind.

In addition, you should start with a welcome note and brief discussion of the year's trading results by the chairman. Do not forget to provide interesting and eye-catching photographs that highlight some of the company's activities.

Future changes

There may well be changes in summary accounts in the future. A Discussion Paper from the Accounting Standards Board (published in February 2000) proposed that the minimum content of summary financial statements should be the same as that for preliminary announcements – which would mean an increase in the content of summary accounts. These summary accounts would be sent automatically to all shareholders. The full report and accounts would be filed with the Registrar of Companies and would be available to all shareholders on request.

The ASB is concerned that increasing the content of the summary accounts (to match the preliminary announcement) might confuse some shareholders and defeat the very purpose of summary accounts, so it is considering giving shareholders the option of receiving a 'simplified financial review' instead.

Some of the ASB's proposals were also supported by the 2001 Company Law Review, which may eventually make preliminary announcements a statutory requirement, thus removing the need for summary financial statements.

Appendix 7.1, at the end of this chapter, gives examples of summary financial statements.

Interim reports

Listed companies are required under stock exchange/Financial Service Authority regulations to prepare an interim report on their activities and profits for the first six months of each financial year. This report must be sent to shareholders or published in at least one national newspaper not later than four months after the period end.

In addition, the stock exchange requires interim reports to include an explanatory statement, which allows investors to make an informed assessment of the companies' activities and results.

The Cadbury committee (see also Chapter 8, 'Corporate governance') called for an improvement in the content of interim reports by suggesting the inclusion of a balance sheet. It also suggested that the interim report should be reviewed, rather than audited, by the company's auditors. If the figures in the interim report have been audited, the full report of the auditors should be produced in its entirety.

In 1997 the ASB issued a Statement on Interim Reports, which set down 'best practice'. The Statement suggested that interim reports should:

- be produced using the same principles and practices that were adopted in the annual reporting process

- provide more information, namely:
  - a more detailed commentary
  - a summarized profit and loss account
  - summarized balance sheet
  - a cash flow statement
  - a statement of total recognized gains and losses, where applicable

- contain other information including details of acquisitions, segmental information and comparative figures for the corresponding interim period.

In addition to sending the interim report to all holders of listed securities, there is nothing to prohibit you from also placing advertisements in newspapers in order to disseminate your company's results to a much wider audience than just your shareholders.

Provided that the advertisement meets the minimum requirements of the stock exchange you can use it to broadcast your company's successes. The advertisement should preferably be placed in the financial pages of a quality newspaper and perhaps also in a more mass-market 'middle of the road' newspaper. By using two newspapers, you will capture different markets and transmit your financial news to both business opinion-formers and a wider mass market. Use a pertinent and succinct headline to capture newspaper readers' attention.

In addition, it is useful to send shareholders a personal copy. This not only cements the company–shareholder relationship, but also highlights the perceived importance of shareholders and shows that they are not forgotten.

A short explanatory letter from the company's chairman accompanying the interim report adds weight. The advertisements and also a personal copy of the interim report sent to shareholders are well worth the cost. However, with the development of Internet communications, some companies are now using electronic communications to convey the message in their interim report (see Chapter 12, 'The new age: electronic reporting').

Most companies that choose to send out interim reports to their shareholders usually print the reports, comprising around 8–12 A5 pages. The report should commence with a brief summary of the key points so far during the year (see Appendix 7.2).

Many companies are now recognizing the importance of interim reports, and many investors are increasingly requiring more and better-quality interim reporting information. Most listed US companies already produce quarterly reports and it seems that, in future, this trend will become more pronounced in the UK. The European Union is currently considering making quarterly reporting a mandatory corporate requirement. If your company has not devoted many resources to interim or quarterly reporting in the past, then it might be time to start considering how you can improve your company's interim and quarterly statements.

Appendix 7.1: Summary financial statements

Example 1 Summary financial statements: Marks and Spencer plc
Marks and Spencer's 2001 summary annual review of its activities and financial statements take up eight full A4 pages at the beginning of its statements.

The summary review of the summary financial statements includes the chairman's statement, spread over two pages. However, be warned that you do not fall into the presentational traps that have befallen Marks and Spencer. The chairman's statement is written and superimposed over an ill-defined background picture of the company's stores, which causes some loss of impact. Do not make the same mistake. Always have text superimposed onto a plain or pale coloured background. Do not cause difficulties for the reader.

Apart from this point, the summary financial statements are clear, informative and effective.

The extract on the following pages has been reproduced by kind permission of Marks and Spencer plc.

Summary reports

The Summary Financial Statement on pages 22 to 26, the Summary Remuneration Report on page 27 and the Summary Directors' Report on this page are summaries of information contained in the Annual Report and Financial Statements. The aim is to provide shareholders with the key financial information in a clear and concise manner. For this reason the Summary Financial Statement does not contain sufficient information to give a full understanding of the results of the Group and state of affairs of the Company and the Group.

The Directors' Report, the full accounts and the Auditors' Report on those accounts, which is unqualified, are contained in a separate publication entitled Annual Report and Financial Statements 2001. Copies may be obtained free of charge from the Company as noted on page 28.

Summary Directors' report

Principal activities

The principal activities of the Group are Retailing in the UK and overseas and Financial Services.

Financial Services includes the operations of the Group's Retail Financial Services companies, which provide account cards, personal loans, unit trust management, life assurance, personal insurance and pensions.

Review of activities and future performance

A review of the Group's activities and of the future development of the Group is contained in the reviews of financial and operating performance on pages 10 to 19.

Dividends

The directors have declared dividends as follows:

	£m
Ordinary shares	
Interim paid, 3.7p per share (last year 3.7p)	106.3
Proposed final, 5.3p per share (last year 5.3p)	152.0
Total ordinary dividends, 9.0p per share (last year 9.0p)	**258.3**

The final dividend will be paid on 20 July 2001 to shareholders whose names are on the Register of Members at the close of business on 1 June 2001.

Directors

Current members of the Board are shown on page 20, with details of membership of principal Board committees.

David Norgrove and Roger Holmes were appointed executive directors on 18 September 2000 and 1 January 2001 respectively.

Tony Ball and Kevin Lomax were appointed non-executive directors on 1 September 2000.

Roger Aldridge, Sir Martin Jacomb, Barry Morris and Joe Rowe resigned from the Board on 19 July 2000.

Clara Freeman, Guy McCracken and Peter Salsbury resigned from the Board on 18 September 2000.

Alison Reed will be appointed to the Board as Finance Director and Sir Michael Perry, Sir Ralph Robins and Sir David Sieff will be retiring from the Board on 11 July 2001.

Summary Corporate Governance

The Company is committed to high standards of Corporate Governance and complies with all the provisions of the Combined Code. A detailed statement of how the Company applies the principles is set out in the Annual Report and Financial Statements.

Annual General Meeting

The AGM will be held at 11.00 am on 11 July 2001 at the Royal Festival Hall in London. The Notice of Meeting (together with explanatory notes) is given in the booklet which accompanies this report.

Auditors' report

Auditors' report to the members of Marks and Spencer p.l.c.

We have examined the Summary Financial Statement set out on pages 22 to 26 and the amounts disclosed relating to directors' remuneration on page 27.

Respective responsibilities of directors and auditors

The directors are responsible for preparing the Annual Review and Summary Financial Statement in accordance with applicable law. Our responsibility is to report to you our opinion on the consistency of the Summary Financial Statement within the Annual Review with the Annual Report and Financial Statements and its compliance with the relevant requirements of section 251 of the United Kingdom Companies Act 1985 and the regulations made thereunder. We also read the other information contained in the Annual Review and consider the implications for our report if we become aware of any apparent misstatements or material inconsistencies with the Summary Financial Statement.

Basis of opinion

We conducted our work in accordance with Bulletin 1999/6 'The Auditors' Statement on the Summary Financial Statement', issued by the Auditing Practices Board.

Opinion

In our opinion the Summary Financial Statement is consistent with the Annual Report and Financial Statements and Directors' Report of Marks and Spencer p.l.c. for the year ended 31 March 2001 and complies with the requirements of section 251 of the Companies Act 1985 and the regulations made thereunder.

PricewaterhouseCoopers
Chartered Accountants and Registered Auditors
London
21 May 2001

Summary profit and loss account

	52 weeks ending 31 March 2001 Before exceptional items £m	Exceptional items £m	After exceptional items £m	53 weeks ending 1 April 2000 Before exceptional items £m	Exceptional items £m	After exceptional items £m
Turnover	**8,075.7**	**–**	**8,075.7**	8,195.5	–	8,195.5
Operating profit	**467.0**	**(26.5)**	**440.5**	543.0	(72.0)	471.0
Loss on sale of property and other fixed assets	**–**	**(83.2)**	**(83.2)**	–	(22.3)	(22.3)
Loss on sale/termination of operations	**–**	**(1.7)**	**(1.7)**	–	(45.4)	(45.4)
Provision for loss on operations to be discontinued	**–**	**(224.0)**	**(224.0)**	–	–	–
Net interest income	**13.9**	**–**	**13.9**	14.2	–	14.2
Profit on ordinary activities before taxation	**480.9**	**(335.4)**	**145.5**	557.2	(139.7)	417.5
Taxation on ordinary activities	**(151.2)**	**8.5**	**(142.7)**	(177.2)	19.0	(158.2)
Profit on ordinary activities after taxation	**329.7**	**(326.9)**	**2.8**	380.0	(120.7)	259.3
Minority interests (all equity)	**(1.5)**	**–**	**(1.5)**	(0.6)	–	(0.6)
Profit attributable to shareholders	**328.2**	**(326.9)**	**1.3**	379.4	(120.7)	258.7
Dividends	**(258.3)**	**–**	**(258.3)**	(258.6)	–	(258.6)
Retained profit/(loss) for the period	**69.9**	**(326.9)**	**(257.0)**	120.8	(120.7)	0.1
Basic earnings per share			**0.0p**			9.0p
Adjusted earnings per share			**11.4p**			13.2p
Dividend per share			**9.0p**			9.0p

All results in both the current and preceding financial year are derived from continuing operations.

Notes to summary profit and loss account

Turnover	52 weeks 2000/2001 £m	52 weeks 1999/2000 £m	53 weeks 1999/2000 £m
UK Retail	**6,293.0**	6,351.1	6,482.7
International Retail:			
Europe	**548.3**	545.2	555.6
North America (excl. Canada)	**761.2**	658.7	669.2
Far East	**110.1**	99.1	101.2
Canada	**–**	22.2	22.2
Total International	**1,419.6**	1,325.2	1,348.2
Financial Services	**363.1**	364.6	364.6
Total	**8,075.7**	8,040.9	8,195.5

Operating profit before exceptional charges	52 weeks 2000/2001 £m	52 weeks 1999/2000 £m	53 weeks 1999/2000 £m
UK Retail	**334.8**	386.8	420.1
International Retail:			
Europe	**(11.4)**	(9.4)	(6.1)
North America (excl. Canada)	**32.0**	14.0	16.4
Far East	**7.4**	(4.3)	(3.3)
Canada	**–**	–	–
Total International	**28.0**	0.3	7.0
Financial Services	**96.3**	115.9	115.9
Excess interest charged within Financial Services	**7.9**	–	–
Total	**467.0**	503.0	543.0

The reporting period this year covers a 52-week period compared to a 53-week period last year. We have therefore included a 52-week pro-forma analysis for last year to aid comparison between the two periods.

Commentary

The layout of the profit and loss account shows the exceptional items for this year and last year separately. The left hand column for each year, which shows the results excluding the effect of exceptional items, gives a clearer understanding of the underlying trading performance of the Group.

Turnover

UK Retail sales (including VAT of £638.2m) for the 52 weeks comprise clothing, footwear and gifts £3.6bn (last year £3.9bn); home £0.4bn (last year £0.3bn); and foods £2.9bn (last year £2.9bn).

A summary of the sales performance (including VAT) for the year is given below. Like-for-like sales, which are estimated by comparing total sales with new and developed stores excluded, are also given:

	Actual sales % on 52 weeks	Like-for-like sales % on 52 weeks
Clothing, footwear & gifts	–5.5	n/a
Home	+11.5	n/a
General	–4.2	–6.3
Foods	+3.7	+2.6
Total	**–1.0**	**–2.6**

Within **International Retail**, sales for Europe can be analysed further as follows:

	52 weeks 2000/2001 £m	52 weeks 1999/2000 £m	53 weeks 1999/2000 £m
Continental European subsidiaries	**285.0**	289.2	294.3
Other European operations	**263.3**	256.0	261.3
Total	**548.3**	545.2	555.6

Operating Profit

The fall in **UK Retail** operating profit results from the 1.0% decline in sales including VAT (on a 52-week basis) and a 3.2% increase in operating costs, partly offset by an improvement in the gross margin as a result of better buying practices. The increase in operating costs arises largely as a result of:

- higher property related costs as a result of the concept store rollout (£13.0m);
- charges for merchant service fees payable on both third party credit cards (£9.0m) and the Marks & Spencer Chargecard (£16.2m).

The charge of £16.2m in respect of the Marks & Spencer Chargecard is treated as income within the Financial Services division.

International Retail increased operating profits before exceptional items by £28m overall on a 52-week basis, driven by increases in operating profits in North America and the Far East.

European operating profits before exceptional items can be analysed further as follows:

	52 weeks 2000/2001 £m	52 weeks 1999/2000 £m	53 weeks 1999/2000 £m
Continental European subsidiaries	**(34.0)**	(26.9)	(24.8)
Other European operations	**22.6**	17.5	18.7
Total	**(11.4)**	(9.4)	(6.1)

Financial Services operating profits decreased by £19.6m largely as a result of lower margins on chargecard and personal lending.

Exceptional charges

Exceptional charges of £335.4m are presented in the second column of the profit and loss account. These charges cover the following:

- £224.0m for the closure of our Continental European subsidiaries. This charge includes a provision for future trading losses, together with provisions for the loss on disposal of assets and estimated redundancy costs;
- £35.5m for the closure of the 'Direct' catalogue business. This charge includes a provision for the loss on disposal of assets of £19m which is included within the charge for loss on sale of property and other fixed assets;
- £64.2m for the closure of UK stores, including six satellite stores;
- £10.0m for the elimination of roles at the Group's head office; and
- a loss of £1.7m on the sale of the Group's interest in Splendour.com Ltd.

Taxation

The charge for taxation of £142.7m represents 98.1% of the profit before tax. This effective tax rate is distorted by the magnitude of the exceptional charges, the majority of which will not attract tax relief. Excluding the effect of exceptional items, the Group tax charge for the year is £151.2m giving an effective rate of 31.4% (last year 31.8%).

Earnings per share

An adjusted earnings per share figure of 11.4p (last year 13.2p) has also been calculated, which excludes the effect of all the exceptional items shown above. The adjusted earnings per share for the 52-week period last year was 12.2p.

Summary balance sheet

AT 31 MARCH 2001

	2001 £m	2000 £m
Fixed assets		
Intangible assets	–	1.3
Tangible assets	**4,118.9**	4,242.1
Investments	**58.3**	55.0
	4,177.2	4,298.4
Current assets		
Stocks	**472.5**	474.4
Debtors	**2,629.3**	2,555.2
Cash and investments	**414.4**	687.5
	3,516.2	3,717.1
Current liabilities		
Creditors: amounts falling due within one year	**(1,981.6)**	(2,162.8)
Net current assets	**1,534.6**	1,554.3
Total assets less current liabilities	**5,711.8**	5,852.7
Creditors: amounts falling due after more than one year	**(735.1)**	(804.3)
Provisions for liabilities and charges	**(315.7)**	(126.6)
Net assets	**4,661.0**	4,921.8
Shareholders' funds (all equity)	**4,645.4**	4,905.3
Minority interests (all equity)	**15.6**	16.5
Total capital employed	**4,661.0**	4,921.8

Approved by the Board 21 May 2001
Luc Vandevelde, Chairman and Chief Executive
Robert Colvill, Group Finance Director

Commentary

Tangible fixed assets relate mainly to our properties and their fitting out, and also to equipment and computers.

The decrease in net book value of £123.2m since March 2000 reflects the following:

- additions relating to our capital investment programme of £255.7m of which £211.8m arises within our UK Retail business;
- depreciation charges for the year of £275.9m;
- a provision for the loss on disposal of fixed assets of £111.2m to cover the anticipated losses on the closure of UK and European stores and the 'Direct' catalogue assets; and
- the disposal of properties and assets during the year.

Debtors have increased by £74.1m reflecting further growth in customer advances within the Financial Services business of £117.8m, offset by a reduction in other debtor balances.

Cash and investments have decreased by £273.1m. Last year's balance included the proceeds from the sale, immediately prior to the year end, of our investment properties at The Gyle in Edinburgh and in Newcastle. These proceeds have subsequently been used to repay borrowings.

Total creditors due within and after more than one year have decreased by £250.4m. This largely reflects a £235.6m decrease in borrowings linked to the decrease in cash and investments referred to above.

Provisions for liabilities and charges have increased by £189.1m largely as a result of:

- provisions established during the year for the anticipated cost of closing the Continental European subsidiaries and the 'Direct' catalogue business; offset by
- utilisation of prior year provisions in respect of redundancy costs within the UK Retail business.

Shareholders' funds have decreased by £259.9m reflecting the fact that this year's dividend is not covered by profit after tax and minority interests and will therefore be paid out of earnings retained in prior years. In addition, shareholders' funds were also reduced further by the purchase of own shares during the year at a cost of £20.3m.

Summary cash flow information

FOR THE YEAR ENDED 31 MARCH 2001

	2001 £m	2000 £m
Operating activities		
Received from customers	**7,967.8**	7,989.9
Payments to suppliers	**(5,240.7)**	(5,357.1)
Payments to and on behalf of employees	**(1,089.8)**	(1,138.3)
Other payments	**(930.6)**	(803.8)
Exceptional operating cash flows	**(30.3)**	(49.2)
Cash inflow from operating activities	**676.4**	641.5
Returns on investments and servicing of finance	**12.6**	15.2
Taxation	**(164.6)**	(145.7)
Capital expenditure and financial investment	**(258.2)**	(167.0)
Acquisitions and disposals	**5.9**	(21.1)
Equity dividends paid	**(258.6)**	(413.5)
Cash inflow/(outflow) before funding	**13.5**	(90.6)

Commentary

Cash inflow from operating activities of £676.4m can be split between Retailing cash inflows of £654.2m (last year £728.4m) and Financial Services cash inflows of £22.2m (last year outflow £86.9m).

Taxation is largely paid in arrears and the outflow therefore reflects the payment of the tax due for the previous year.

Capital expenditure and financial investment of £258.2m largely reflect our payments to acquire fixed assets of £269.8m, offset by sales proceeds of £18.9m.

Equity dividends paid of £258.6m represent the previous year's final dividend and this year's interim dividend. The reduction in the amount paid compared to last year reflects the reduction in the final dividend at the end of last year.

Cash inflow before funding of £13.5m has been financed by an overall increase in the net debt of the Group to £1,277.8m (last year £1,251.4m). Within this, a reduction in cash and investments has been used to repay borrowings and fund the purchase of Marks & Spencer shares. The net debt breaks down into net funds within Retailing of £369.4m (last year £364.5m) and net debt within Financial Services of £1,647.2m (last year £1,615.9m).

Example 2 Summary financial statement: Abbey National plc

However you prepare your summary financial statements, you must accept the fact that the vast majority of the shareholders will not be interested. And why should they? They are not accountants or analysts. It is up to you to make the statements more appealing – as the banking group, Abbey National plc, appears to have achieved.

Abbey National places its summary accounts at the end of its annual review – produced in a six-page, A4-size glossy magazine-type format. A short and snappy review of the company's business activities is heavily interspersed with photographs, largely depicting staff and customers. Imaginative use of print colour and different coloured paper provides a lively impact. The review also highlights the importance of its business in the 'Community and Environment' and explains progress that the company is making in its social reporting. It concludes with a brief summary of the directors' career backgrounds. The end result is an annual review that gives the appearance of wanting to inform, and communicate with, its readers.

The summary financial report extract on the following page is reproduced with permission from Abbey National plc. Copyright 2002 Abbey National Plc. All rights reserved.

Summary

Summary consolidated profit and loss account

for the year ended 31 December 2000

	2000 Total £m	1999 Total (restated) £m
Net interest income	2,680	2,661
Commissions, fees and other income	1,614	1,141
Operating expenses excluding depreciation on operating lease assets	(1,815)	(1,615)
Depreciation on operating lease assets	(178)	(52)
Provisions for bad and doubtful debts	(273)	(303)
Provisions for contingent liabilities and commitments	(21)	(23)
Amounts written off fixed asset investments	(32)	(26)
Profit on ordinary activities before tax	1,975	1,783
Tax on profit on ordinary activities	(559)	(522)
Profit on ordinary activities after tax	1,416	1,261
Minority interests - non-equity	(51)	-
Profit attributable to the shareholders of Abbey National plc	1,365	1,261
Transfer to non-distributable reserve	(156)	(13)
Dividends including amounts attributable to non-equity interests	(687)	(610)
Profit retained for the financial year	522	638
Earnings per ordinary share - basic (pence)	93.4p	86.2p
Earnings per ordinary share - diluted (pence)	92.8p	85.5p

Change in accounting presentation Depreciation on operating lease assets is reported within operating expenses. This represents a change in presentation from previous years, where operating lease depreciation was reported as a charge against income on operating lease assets within commissions, fees and other income. This change results from the application of FRS15, 'Tangible fixed assets', which applies to the accounts for the year ended 31 December 2000.

Note 1999 includes a £27m charge before tax (£19m after tax) for exceptional items relating to costs incurred in preparing the Group for Year 2000 and the introduction of the euro.

Aggregate directors' emoluments The total emoluments for the directors of the year ended 31 December 2000 were £4,828,617 (£3,615,167). In addition, gains made during the year by directors on the exercise of share options were £100,948 (£899,853).

Glossary of terms

1 Net interest income
The difference between the interest and similar income received on loans and investments and the interest paid on liabilities in the year.

2 Operating expenses
Running costs of the business, such as salaries, wages, bought-in services, depreciation and other overheads.

3 Provisions for bad and doubtful debts
Amounts set aside to cover situations where customers fail to repay money owed to us.

4 Provisions for contingent liabilities and commitments
Amounts set aside to meet likely future claims and liabilities.

5 Amounts written off fixed asset investments
The reduction in value of long term investments which is not expected to be recovered.

6 Earnings per ordinary share
Earnings for the year divided by the average number of ordinary shares in issue during the year.

7 Directors' emoluments
The total of all salaries and other benefits earned by the Board of Directors during the period.

Important note: This summary financial statement does not contain sufficient information to allow a full understanding of the results and state of affairs of the Group. For further information, the Directors' Report and Accounts, which includes the full annual financial statements, should be consulted. The Directors' Report and Accounts is available on the internet at www.abbeynational.plc.uk, or a free copy of the Directors' Report and Accounts is available on request from Shareholder Services by calling the shareholder enquiries number on the back of this Review. If, in addition, you would like to receive the Directors' Report and Accounts of Abbey National plc in future years, please write to Shareholder Services giving your full name, address and your shareholder account number (which can be obtained from your dividend tax voucher).

Summary consolidated balance sheet

as at 31 December 2000

	2000 £m	1999 £m
Assets		
Cash, treasury bills and other eligible bills	1,596	1,815
Loans and advances to banks	12,168	11,472
Loans and advances to customers	81,752	75,221
Loans and advances to customers subject to securitisation	7,927	1,930
less: non-returnable finance	(4,629)	(1,379)
	3,298	551
Net investment in finance leases	5,192	5,441
Securities and investments	69,573	59,740
Long term assurance business	1,538	1,042
Intangible fixed assets	245	203
Tangible fixed assets excluding operating lease assets	389	759
Operating lease assets	1,963	358
Other assets	7,594	6,703
Assets of long term assurance funds	19,083	17,439
Total assets	204,391	180,744
Liabilities		
Deposits by banks	34,996	29,824
Customer accounts	66,795	59,911
Debt securities in issue	57,078	51,407
Other liabilities	13,074	11,444
Subordinated liabilities including convertible debt	5,871	4,641
Liabilities of long term assurance funds	19,083	17,439
	196,897	174,666
Minority interests - non-equity	664	-
Non-equity shareholders' funds	450	450
Equity shareholders' funds	6,380	5,628
Total liabilities, minority interests and shareholders' funds	204,391	180,744
Memorandum items		
Contingent liabilities	2,433	2,691
Commitments	27,810	23,259

The summary financial statement set out on pages 10 and 11 was approved by the Board on 13 February 2001 and signed on its behalf by:

Lord Tugendhat Chairman **Ian Harley** Chief Executive **Mark Pain** Finance Director

Shareholder analysis

2000 figures as at 31 December 2000

	Ordinary shares of 10p		Preference shares of £1	
Size of shareholding	Shareholders	Shares	Shareholders	Shares
1-100	1,227,241	118,750,633	1	100
101-1,000	748,434	300,720,294	23	17,345
1,001+	34,043	1,012,202,663	1,117	324,982,555
Total	2,009,718	1,431,673,590	1,141	325,000,000

HECK OUT 04/01/2011
:23:

- -

ss Xiaofei Wang

- -

counting in a business context
rcode:055145801X
e date:25/01/2011

- -

counting and finance for non-
ecialis
rcode:0460328013
e date:25/01/2011

- -

ual reports : delivering your
pora
rcode:0522440010
date:25/01/2011

- -

nk you for using the Self Issue
vice.

Appendix 7.2: Extracts from Marks and Spencer plc's interim report

The interim report for the half-year to 30 September 2000 is A5-size, surrounded by a colour photograph which forms the cover. However, if using this technique, make sure that your photograph adds value to your image and has a constructive impact. Marks and Spencer simply places a photograph of a woman's head and shoulders on its front cover, thus offering an example of commercial impact which should be avoided at all costs. Cover photographs should communicate information about your company. In this case, Marks and Spencer should have shown that the woman was modelling its products or directly contributing to the company's activities.

Although advertising specialists may argue that there is an ulterior motive here, subtle advertising through the use of so-called glamour photographs of models (whom the company suspects some of the shareholders or customers may wish to personally resemble) rarely works in this context. Likewise, the impression that this model 'may shop at our store so therefore you should' rarely works either. Just as with the main cover board for your annual report, you should select your interim report cover page or photographs with care.

Marks and Spencer starts its interim reports immediately with the trading 'highlights' and identifies three notable features concerning sales, profit and interim dividends. Do not select too many additional points or else you risk losing their impact and message.

A short statement by the company chairman is followed by a seven-page financial review covering important areas of the business. Key operational changes that highlight the supply chain, product appeal and availability and the environment of their stores are discussed. Extracts from the half-yearly financial statements form the remainder of the booklet. The inside of the back cover usefully contains information that shareholders might need, including dates when dividends will be paid, the company registrars and details about a share-dealing service that allows shareholders to buy or sell shares in the company.

Reference is also made to the company's Internet site for those shareholders who need further information about the company or their shareholdings.

The interim report extract on the following pages is reproduced by kind permission of Marks and Spencer plc.

Consolidated profit and loss account

	Notes	26 weeks ended 29 Sept 2001 £m	26 weeks ended 30 Sept 2000 As restated £m	Year ended 31 March 2001 As restated £m
Turnover				
Retained businesses		**3,222.0**	3,232.7	6,948.1
Operations to be discontinued		**516.2**	523.1	1,127.6
Total turnover	2	**3,738.2**	3,755.8	8,075.7
Operating profit				
Retained businesses before exceptional operating charges		**206.8**	184.3	465.7
Exceptional operating charges	6	**–**	–	(26.5)
		206.8	184.3	439.2
Operations to be discontinued				
Continental European operations		**(26.4)**	(19.4)	(34.0)
Less release of provision made last year		**26.4**	–	–
Other operations to be discontinued		**9.1**	8.4	35.3
Total operating profit	3	**215.9**	173.3	440.5
Loss on sale of property and other fixed assets	7a	**(7.0)**	(3.7)	(83.2)
Provision for loss on operations to be discontinued	7b	**–**	–	(224.0)
Loss on sale/termination of operations	7c	**(3.1)**	–	(1.7)
Less release of provision made last year		**3.1**	–	–
Net interest income		**4.4**	10.1	13.9
Profit on ordinary activities before taxation		**213.3**	179.7	145.5
Analysed between				
Profit before tax and exceptional charges		**220.3**	183.4	480.9
Exceptional charges		**(7.0)**	(3.7)	(335.4)
Taxation on ordinary activities	8	**(67.5)**	(59.3)	(149.5)
Profit on ordinary activities after taxation		**145.8**	120.4	(4.0)
Minority interests (all equity)		**(1.6)**	(0.4)	(1.5)
Profit attributable to shareholders		**144.2**	120.0	(5.5)
Dividends	10	**(105.2)**	(106.3)	(258.3)
Retained profit/(loss) for the period		**39.0**	13.7	(263.8)

All results in both the current and preceding periods are derived from continuing operations

Earnings per share	9	**5.0p**	4.2p	(0.2)p
Fully diluted earnings per share	9	**5.0p**	4.2p	(0.2)p
Adjusted earnings per share	9	**5.3p**	4.3p	11.2p
Fully diluted adjusted earnings per share	9	**5.3p**	4.3p	11.2p
Dividend per share	10	**3.7p**	3.7p	9.0p

Consolidated balance sheet

	As at 29 Sept 2001 £m	As at 30 Sept 2000 As restated £m	As at 31 March 2001 As restated £m
Fixed assets			
Goodwill	**–**	1.2	–
Tangible assets	**4,016.1**	4,281.5	4,118.9
Investments	**59.6**	66.9	58.3
	4,075.7	4,349.6	4,177.2
Current assets			
Stocks	**462.8**	493.9	472.5
Debtors	**2,642.1**	2,620.7	2,629.3
Cash and investments	**605.6**	419.1	414.4
	3,710.5	3,533.7	3,516.2
Current liabilities	**(1,930.7)**	(2,012.0)	(1,981.6)
Net current assets	**1,779.8**	1,521.7	1,534.6
Total assets less current liabilities	**5,855.5**	5,871.3	5,711.8
Creditors: amounts falling due after more than one year	**(932.4)**	(820.4)	(735.1)
Provisions for liabilities and charges	**(351.9)**	(178.5)	(395.3)
Net assets	**4,571.2**	4,872.4	4,581.4
Capital and reserves			
Called up share capital	**711.9**	719.3	716.9
Share premium account	**378.1**	374.3	375.6
Revaluation reserve	**453.3**	457.9	455.6
Capital redemption reserve	**8.0**	–	2.6
Profit and loss account	**3,003.2**	3,304.0	3,015.1
Shareholders' funds (all equity)	**4,554.5**	4,855.5	4,565.8
Minority interests (all equity)	**16.7**	16.9	15.6
Total capital employed	**4,571.2**	4,872.4	4,581.4

8 Corporate governance: explaining your procedures and controls

During the late 1980s considerable political pressure was placed on listed companies to explain their corporate governance procedures and controls. Some companies had faced vociferous public criticism because it was claimed that some directors were failing to explain in sufficient detail (if at all) how they corporately managed and controlled their companies. Some directors were accused of treating companies as a part of their own personal fiefdoms even though legal ownership of the company's assets belongs with the shareholders.

Troubled background

A decade ago, a comprehensive explanation of the corporate governance mechanisms of many companies was noticeable only by its absence. Then a number of high-profile company collapses began to cause considerable concern in political and accounting circles.

Some directors failed to give the concept of accountability (to shareholders) the degree of respect it was thought to deserve. Some companies had allowed their internal management controls to become so weak and incomplete that autocratic or charismatic chief executives or chairmen could unduly dominate or influence the board of directors by virtue of the strength of their personalities. There were also other serious difficulties. Some companies had limited checks and balances in their management and financial systems. Others had very few, if any, non-executive directors and little overall accountability. Other general management internal controls were often weak, non-existent or easily subverted.

There were other common criticisms concerning the level of directors' remuneration. In effect, the directors have their hands on the company chequebook and have full control of the company's key decision-making machinery. Some directors were accused of abusing their position and awarding themselves excessively generous levels of remuneration, implementing easily attainable senior management bonus schemes and ensuring that the company paid large sums into their personal pension funds. In addition, the determination of some companies' bonus schemes was often vague or even non-existent, with bonus payments apparently often being awarded when performance results were mediocre.

Other criticisms centred on the level of various forms of directors' share option schemes, many of which seemed unduly generous, with insufficient information explaining the underlying detail and the probable benefits that would eventually accrue to the directors.

In an attempt to 'clean up' some of the key desirable corporate governance practices, it was suggested that a number of committees be set up to improve the whole system of corporate governance and accountability.

Improving the reporting of governance issues

If your company is listed on the London Stock Exchange you should pay particularly close attention to the content of the codes and reports. Whilst these various codes do not have specific legal backing, they do nevertheless come with the full support of the stock exchange. So there is no point in making enemies of the stock exchange regulatory authorities by not complying with the codes' requirements. Do not pick a fight with the regulators. If you do not comply with all the codes' requirements, your auditors will be compelled to highlight this fact when they audit your annual report and accounts. Moreover, the political climate is now such that you should not court the adverse publicity that would almost certainly follow any non-compliance.

But these codes are not without their critics. Some companies argue that the detailed narrative explanations are unnecessarily time-consuming and occupy too much space in the annual report. The critics claim that the depth of the information merely confuses readers and, in many cases, fails to shed any new light.

Yet, however strongly you agree with this line of argument, you should not disclose your displeasure in the annual report. Take the requirements of the codes of practice as a challenge. Make the best you can of the situation. Do not underplay the significance of the corporate governance information from a political perspective. For example, do not relegate the narrative explanation to 'small print' at the end of the annual report. Give it the position of apparent authority that the stock exchange believes it deserves.

The content of your corporate governance information should be written to the same high standards as the rest of your report. Since the codes cover different areas, you may wish to devolve key sections of the various codes to three of four members of your team. You can almost regard the production of this governance information as a mini-project. You do not necessarily have to leave the writing of this section to the year-end. Large parts of the governance sections concerning committee structures, policies on the determination of directors' remuneration and information on internal controls can be written during the year, rather than in a last-minute rush.

The reports and codes of practice

The Cadbury Report

The principal attempt to introduce a better standard of corporate governance was contained in a report entitled the *Committee on the Financial Aspects of Corporate Governance* under the chairmanship of Sir Adrian Cadbury – the so-called Cadbury Report (1992). This report was a framework for sound corporate governance and was regarded as being of considerable significance by the stock exchange – in fact, so significant that listed companies were required to make an annual statement in their report confirming that they complied with the content of this report.

The implications of the Cadbury Report are important in terms of the explanations and discussions that have to be included in the annual report. In addition, the company's auditors will need to form an opinion on whether the company has complied with the Code of Best Practice. The Code requires companies to ensure the following:

- The board of directors have exercised control in respect of major decisions regarding such issues as investment programmes, borrowings and major acquisitions. There should be a clear division of the directors' responsibilities and the company's controls should ensure that no single individual has unfettered powers of decision. The Code also favours separating the roles of chairman and chief executive to maintain a strong element at board level. All directors should have access to the advice and services of the company secretary to assist in ensuring that board procedures are followed and to establish the company's compliance with all applicable rules and regulations.

- The board of directors includes non-executive directors of sufficient calibre and number for their views to carry significant weight in the board's decisions. The non-executive directors should bring independent judgement to issues such as strategy, performance, resources, key appointments and standards of corporate behaviour. The non-executives should be independent and free from any business or other relationship that could materially interfere with the exercise of their independent judgement.

- Executive directors' service contracts should not normally exceed three years without the shareholders' approval.

- There is full and clear disclosure of directors' total emoluments and those of the chairman and the highest-paid director, including pension contributions and stock options. Separate figures should be provided for salary and performance-related elements, and the basis on which performance is measured should be explained. Executive director remuneration should be subject to the recommendations of the remuneration committee.

- The company has established sound reporting and control measures. In particular, the Code requires companies to report on the effectiveness of the company's systems of internal controls.

The Code also requires companies to establish an audit committee compromising at least three non-executive directors. This committee concentrates, in particular, on the relationship between the company and its statutory auditors.

The directors should also explain that they are responsible for preparing the accounting statements. This statement should be placed next to a statement explaining the specific responsibilities of the auditors.

The practical effect is that directors are required to make their responsibilities clear and explicit. So you will need to insert a section in the annual report entitled 'Statement of Directors' Responsibilities' (see Chapter 6, 'Auditors' reports').

The Greenbury Report

In 1995 the Greenbury Report further added to companies' disclosure requirements. This report was an attempt to respond to considerable public criticism about the high level of directors' remuneration packages. Essentially, it tried to ensure that companies described how the level of directors' remuneration was set and how bonus schemes were determined.

Most of the requirements of the Greenbury Report were incorporated into the Listing Rules of the London Stock Exchange.

The Greenbury Report recommended, *inter alia*, the following:

- Companies should establish a remuneration policy and remuneration committee of non-executive directors to assist in determining an all-embracing policy on all forms of directors' remuneration packages.
- The remuneration committee should provide a yearly report to shareholders on this policy and full details of their directors' remuneration packages, including bonus schemes and pension rights, and any payments on early termination of directors' contracts.
- There should be more disclosure of remuneration issues to shareholders.

The Hampel Committee: the 'Combined Code'

An update to the initial Cadbury Report was implemented in 1998 under the auspices of the Hampel Committee. This committee, in conjunction with the stock exchange, published *The Combined Code – Principles of Good Corporate Governance and Code of Best Practice* (the 'Combined Code'). The report:

- reinforced the need to separate the chairman and chief executive roles
- recommended that directors should have contracts of no more than one year
- recommended that remuneration committees should consist of independent non-executive directors
- suggested that directors should be trained on formal courses.

In effect, this code was a combination of the Cadbury and Greenbury Codes but it also introduced some additional requirements specifically identified by the Hampel Committee (see also Appendix 8.3 at the end of this chapter). The end result was that the stock exchange incorporated the Combined Code into its Listing Rules.

The introduction to the Combined Code explicitly states that it has no fixed or prescriptive layout and content. Companies are given a free hand in explaining their corporate governance policies and in discussing any special circumstances that might apply to them.

The practical implications for the preparation of the annual report means that companies are required to include a number of corporate governance explanations. These include:

- a statement explaining how the company has applied the Principles of Good Governance as established in the Combined Code. A listed company should produce a narrative statement that allows its shareholders to assess how the Code's principles have been implemented thereby enabling them to evaluate the application of these principles.

- a statement that the company complies with the Code of Best Practice as stated in the Combined Code. A company that has *not* complied with all of the Code's requirements must give a full explanation for its non-compliance.

The remuneration committee

The provision of more details of directors' remuneration was a major recommendation of the Greenbury Report. Significantly, the Report stated that companies should establish remuneration committees to determine the company's policy on remuneration packages for executive remuneration. An increasing number of companies are now devoting separate sections to the discussion of directors' remuneration, including details of bonus and incentive schemes. Typically, many companies entitle these statements 'Compensation Reports', produced by the company's compensation committee. In the light of current political and accounting trends, it may be a good idea to follow this fashion.

Allow around two or three pages to discuss your company's policy and practice concerning compensation schemes. It is beneficial to place this discussion within the framework of the compensation committee's remit. Discuss the nature of this committee, its composition and its aims and also allocate a paragraph or two on such topics as:

- general remuneration policy for executive directors

- basic salary levels

- bonus payments and the benchmark measures and targets established

- share option schemes
- longer-term incentives for executive directors and senior employees
- payments, if any, on early termination of contract
- directors' pension scheme
- remuneration of non-executive directors.

In each section be clear and to the point. Resist any vague and spurious justification of remuneration schemes; instead, be open and honest and explain carefully how bonus payments and incentive schemes operate. Never state that bonuses are merely related to 'performance'. Explain what constitutes 'performance'. Provide the actual targets that directors have to achieve and discuss them fully. Evasive and incomplete details will be picked up quickly by the media. Figures relating to directors' emoluments of listed companies are *always* scrutinized by journalists, and distortion, selective details and misinformation (whether intentional or not) will provoke, at best, contemptuous or disparaging comments by analysts. You do not need this type of trouble – it would be a public relations disaster. You can avoid difficulties by being open, honest and fully informative in the first place.

It is also important to note that the Combined Code stresses that:

- these remuneration committees should be comprised of non-executive directors
- a statement should be made that the directors have conducted a review of the effectiveness of the company's internal controls
- minimum disclosures should be made about financial, operational and risk management controls
- the directors should issue a statement that the company is a going concern (supported with assumptions or qualifications if necessary). This statement is required to ensure that directors make an explicit statement that, in their opinion, the company will continue trading in the foreseeable future. If there is any doubt about the company's ability to continue as a going concern, the directors should identify all those factors which cast doubt on the company's ability to continue trading.

In the past, some directors would often attempt to place sole or undue responsibility for a company's collapse on their auditors. This statement is an attempt to make the responsibilities of directors more explicit. Confirmation of the going concern concept is now not just the responsibility of the company's auditors; directors must also play their part.

The Turnbull Report

In 1999 the Turnbull Working Party updated many of the internal control requirements in *Internal Control: Guidance for Directors on the Combined Code* – the Turnbull Report. Essentially, this Working Party recommended that companies discuss important features relating to their internal controls. These include:

- an acknowledgement by the directors that they are responsible for the company's internal controls
- an explanation that the system of internal controls can only provide a reasonable (not total) assurance against material misstatement
- a description of the key procedures that the directors have implemented to provide effective internal controls
- confirmation that the directors or a board committee have reviewed the effectiveness of these internal controls.

As part of the implementation of the Combined Code and the discussion of the internal management structures and internal controls, in your annual report you should particularly highlight the principal committee structures in your organization. From a contemporary political standpoint it is important to stress the existence and importance of these committees. Do not underplay or conceal the importance of their functions. Provide a full and detailed discussion on your committee structures. These committees are typically based on a number of key functions and include the following:

- **Audit committee.** This committee assists the board in reviewing the reporting of financial and non-financial information, discussing the system of internal controls and risk management, including key issues concerned with the audit processes.
- **Remuneration committee.** The task of this committee is to ensure that

directors and key managers receive an appropriate level of compensation for their skills, ability and effort.

- **Nomination committee.** This committee identifies and recommends to the board candidates for key executive and non-executive appointments; it is often concerned with senior management development and succession planning as well.

- **Ethics committee.** More and more companies are now establishing an ethics committee which considers ethical issues that may arise under a company's ethical trading code. The topic of ethics is another area that is becoming politically and socially more important. Large companies, in particular, are advised to provide a discussion about their ethics committee if they have formed such a body. (If your company has no such committee, you should give full consideration to establishing a corporate policy and committee to deal with these issues.)

- **Charitable donations committee.** This committee determines and monitors a company's policy towards charitable donations and community projects.

- **Environmental and social responsibility committee.** This committee considers all issues concerned with the impact of the company's activities on the environment and the company's commitment and responsibility to employees and to society generally. In the current political climate, the areas covered by this committee are politically and socially significant, so a full discussion of its work should be provided.

Auditors' confirmation

Where compliance can be verified objectively, the company's auditors must review the company's statement of compliance with the Code of Best Practice. The auditors are also required to review both the statement on internal controls and the 'going concern' statement.

In their report, the auditors will confirm this corporate governance information in the annual report, including whether the corporate governance statements are 'consistent with the audited accounts'. Until 1998, the Auditing Practices Board (which issues professional guidance and regulations for auditors) recommended that this confirmation should be included in the actual annual report. However, since the end of 1998, the APB has encouraged its inclusion in a statement of auditors' responsibilities – either as a separate statement or within the confines of an expanded auditors' report.

Future developments

The UK government is currently considering the introduction of new statute-based regulations on directors' remuneration that will apply to all listed companies. This means that companies may be required to produce a more comprehensive directors' remuneration report to replace the more limited report that they currently produce under the stock exchange Listing Rules. Directors may be also required to provide more detailed information on their total remuneration packages – particularly on share option schemes and long-term incentive plans.

'Conform to the fashion'

Given the increasing significance of corporate governance, especially in listed companies, you would be well advised to carefully study the nature and implications of the governance in your company and pay special attention to the Combined Code. Your company secretarial department should be contacted early in the financial year and you should forewarn the relevant staff that you will need a full report on this topic for inclusion in the annual report at the year-end. If you can lay out key areas that you wish to include in the year's annual report, the nominated staff can produce a more detailed and informative section.

Do not lightly dismiss the importance of your corporate governance information. In the current climate, the stock exchange and regulatory regimes are all concerned about providing more and better information. Do not go against the trend – even if you disagree. You will not be able to fight current political fashion. If you provide only the bare minimum information, it will rebound against you. It is best to conform fully.

It is important to incorporate both the letter and spirit of these various codes within your report. In conjunction with your company secretarial department, you should fully examine your corporate structures and conduct a full appraisal on their nature and structures. Clearly, you will also need to obtain copies of these codes and pronouncements and study them carefully.

Presentation

For many people, corporate governance is not the most interesting of subjects. However, although you must conform to the codes' requirements, you can improve on the rather dry, tedious style of writing and presentation of many companies. Do not regard the production of this section as a chore and do not show your lack of interest in the subject (as some companies do) by producing several pages of commentary in a small typeface, with cramped paragraphs and an overall unappetizing appearance.

As with the rest of your annual report, pay particular attention to your style of writing and presentation. The biggest mistake some companies make is to assume that readers already understand the nature and problems of establishing effective corporate governance systems and structures. You should explain, in non-technical language to begin with, your governing structures. Do not be pompous, overtechnical or patronizing. Create a balance between information overload and insufficient detail. Neither blind your readers with excessive detail nor leave them requiring more information. Explain why the structures and controls are important and how they operate in your company. Do not be afraid to use diagrams or charts and explain organizational, communication and reporting channels.

Colour diagrams and perhaps photographs of some of the personnel involved – such as the various committee chairpersons – would be helpful. Explanatory introductions and discussion by these chairpersons would be especially welcome.

Above all, make it a personal challenge to improve the abysmal standard of the content and presentation of the governance statements produced by many companies. Be innovative, be informative and try to make it interesting.

A necessary burden

Finally, a word of caution for some companies which believe that the seemingly ever-growing list of corporate governance requirements is an unnecessary burden. The management consultants McKinseys have reported that more than 80 per cent of investors would be prepared to pay a premium to invest in companies with good corporate governance structures. In some cases, the premium could be as high as 16 per cent.

Clearly, ignoring the importance of explaining your corporate governance principles is a high-risk strategy.

Appendix 8.1: Update on audit committees

The accounting scandals in America in 2001 and 2002 concerning global companies such as Enron and WorldCom have reverberated around the world. In the UK, the government was concerned that the financial and accounting scandals would expose weaknesses in the British system of accounting regulatory controls.

As a result, the Financial Reporting Council established an independent committee to enhance the role and responsibilities of audit committees. This committee was chaired by Sir Robert Smith, a member of the Financial Reporting Council, and reported in January 2003. In due course it is expected that this so-called 'Smith Report' will form part of the Combined Code.

Since this topic is becoming increasingly important in a political as well as in a business context, both your company and your annual report should certainly reflect these developments as and when they are implemented.

The Smith Report proposed that:

Composition of the audit committee

- The audit committee should include at least three members who are all independent non-executive directors

- At least one member should have significant, recent and relevant financial experience. Also suitable training should be provided to all members.

Role of the audit committee

Audit committees should:

- Improve the integrity of the financial statements and discuss significant financial reporting judgements

- Review the company's system of internal financial controls (and the company's risk management systems)

- Make recommendations about the appointment of the external auditor

- Monitor the external auditor's independence

- Develop and implement a policy on the engagement of the external auditor to supply non-audit services.

In addition, audit committees should be provided with sufficient resources to undertake their activities.

Source: *Audit Committee Combined Code Guidance: A Report and Proposed Guidance by an FRC-appointed Group Chaired by Sir Robert Smith*, January 2003, FRC, London.

Appendix 8.2: Update on non-executive directors

Additionally, in an attempt to increase the effectiveness of non-executive directors, the Department of Trade and Industry has recently issued proposals under the chairmanship of Derek Higgs.

The Report recommended, *inter alia*, that:

- The number of board of directors meetings and its main committees should be stated in the annual report.
- At least half of the board members (excluding the chairman) should be independent non-executives.
- The roles of the chairman and chief executive should be separated and the division of duties between the chairman and chief executive should be set out in writing and agreed by the board.
- A chief executive should not become chairman of the same company.
- The non-executive directors should meet as a group at least once a year – without the chairman or executive directive directors being present. The annual report should include a statement about whether these meetings have taken place.
- Prior to appointment, non-executive directors should satisfy themselves that they have the knowledge, skills and experience '. . . to make a positive contribution to the board.'
- A senior independent director should be available to shareholders – if they have concerns that have not been resolved through the normal channels of contact with the chairman or chief executive.
- There should be a nomination committee of the board to conduct the process for board appointments.
- Chairmen and chief executives should consider implementing executive development programmes to train and develop suitable individuals in their companies for future director roles.
- The performance of the board, its committees and its individual

members should be evaluated at least once a year. The annual report should state whether such performance reviews are taking place and how they are conducted.

- A full-time executive director should not take on more than one non-executive directorship.

- Non-executives should not hold options over shares in their company.

Source: *Review of the Role and Effectiveness of Non-Executive Directors*, ('the Higgs Report'), Higgs D, January 2003, DTI, London.

Appendix 8.3: Corporate governance discussions contained in the Combined Code

The extracts on the following pages are reproduced by kind permission of Tate & Lyle PLC.

Corporate Governance 2001: Tate & Lyle PLC

Combined Code

The Committee on Corporate Governance issued the Combined Code ('the Code') in June 1998. The Listing Rules of the Financial Services Authority require:

- a narrative statement of how the Company applies the principles of the Code, and
- a statement as to whether the Company has complied with the provisions of the Code throughout the accounting period, giving reasons for any non-compliance.

The paragraphs below describe how the Company applies the principles and complies with the provisions of the Code.

The Board

The Board comprises a non-executive chairman, four executive directors and six non-executive directors. The non-executive directors have a wide range of outside business interests. The posts of Chairman and Chief Executive are separated.

The Board considers the Chairman and all the non-executive directors to be independent, with the exception of Mrs Piwnica. Following completion of the purchase of the minority stake in Amylum, Mrs Piwnica stepped down as Chairman of Amylum Group but remained as a non-executive director of Tate & Lyle. She was also appointed to the Remuneration and Audit Committees. The Board meets at least nine times each year. At least one meeting takes place at an operating subsidiary or joint venture company. All substantive agenda items have comprehensive briefing papers, which are circulated five days before the meeting. The Board reviews regularly the strategy of the Group and at most Board meetings it reviews the strategy of one of the major units.

The directors have access to the advice and services of the Company Secretary and there is a procedure in place whereby, in the furtherance of their duties, directors can obtain independent professional advice at the Company's expense.

The Company's Articles require the re-election of one-third of the Board at each Annual General Meeting. Where this would result in a director serving for more than three years without re-election, the directors have agreed to submit themselves for re-election.

The Directors' Remuneration Report on pages 28 to 33 includes details of the Company's executive remuneration policy and practice.

The Board Committees

The Board has a formal schedule of matters reserved to it for decision, but also delegates specific responsibilities to Board Committees, all of which have written terms of reference. The current Board Committee structure is described below:

- The Chairman's Committee comprises the Chairman, the other non-executive directors and the Chief Executive, under the chairmanship of the Chairman. It meets before each Board meeting as required, and provides an opportunity for the Chairman and Chief Executive to brief and obtain the views of the non-executive directors.

- The Audit Committee comprises the non-executive directors under the chairmanship of Dr Hopkins and normally meets three times a year. It provides a facility for discussing with the Group's external auditors their report on the annual accounts, reviewing the scope and results of the internal audit work programme and considering any other matters which might have a financial impact on the Company. This includes reviewing the Group's system of internal control and the process for evaluating and monitoring risk.

  The Committee also reviews the objectivity of the external auditors, including the level of non-audit services supplied, and ensures that there is an appropriate audit relationship.

- The Remuneration Committee comprises the non-executive directors under the chairmanship of Lord Walker. It meets as required, usually before each Board meeting. The Committee makes recommendations to the Board on executive directors' remuneration policy and specifically approves the remuneration and other detailed terms of service, including the terms upon which such service is terminated, of the executive directors and the Company Secretary. The Committee also approves the salary and benefits of members of the Executive Committee and employees who report directly to the Chief Executive.

- The Nominations Committee comprises the non-executive directors and the Chief Executive under the chairmanship of the Chairman. It meets as required to consider candidates for appointment as directors and as Company Secretary and makes recommendations to the Board. It also makes recommendations to the Board on the processes for the appointment of the Chairman of the Board, the Board's composition and balance, the membership of the Board Committees and material changes in the responsibilities of Board Members.

Shareholder Communications

The Chief Executive and Group Finance Director, supported by the Chairman, maintain a regular programme of visits and presentations to major institutional shareholders. Some 250 shareholders normally attend the Annual General Meeting and are invited to ask questions and meet informally with the directors after the formal proceedings have ended. The Company aims to present a balanced and understandable assessment in all its reports to the public and to regulators. Key announcements and other information may be found on the Company's website at www.tateandlyle.com

Internal Control

The Board of Directors is responsible for the Group's system of internal control and for reviewing its effectiveness. Such a system is designed to manage rather than eliminate risk, and can only provide reasonable and not absolute assurance against material misstatement or loss. The Board of Directors reviews the effectiveness of the system of internal control annually. This review covers financial, operational and compliance controls and risk management procedures. The processes described below, which accord with the guidance 'Internal Control: Guidance for Directors on the Combined Code' issued by the Institute of Chartered Accountants in England and Wales, have been in place throughout the year and up to the date of approval of this Annual Report. These processes are reviewed on an ongoing basis by the Board and the Audit Committee.

The Group operates a management system that recognises the appropriate balance of risk and reward as a key part of the enterprise.

The system emphasises risk management as a responsibility of line executives, not only of staff specialists. The process is flexible and ongoing and is supported by a formal procedure for identifying and evaluating major business risks facing the Group. Senior executive management confirms to the Chief Executive and Group Finance Director, at least twice a year, that these risks are being managed appropriately within their operations. The Chief Executive requires his senior managers to maintain a regular dialogue by email. As a minimum, key points are emailed every Friday. He receives more comprehensive reports monthly from each major business group. The Group Finance Director undertakes quarterly reviews of the major operating units, which the Chief Executive attends at his discretion.

The Group has an internal audit department that supports the Board and the Audit Committee in maintaining procedures through a programme of regular reviews that focus on key aspects of the business. The Audit Committee receives regular reports on the progress and work of the internal audit department. It also receives reports from the Company's auditors on the effectiveness of the system of internal control and risk management.

An Executive Management Committee comprises the executive directors, the Company Secretary and other senior Group managers. It is chaired by the Chief Executive and meets in advance of each Board meeting and as required. Its members are appointed by the Chief Executive to assist him in overseeing the activities of the Group.

The Chief Executive and the Group Finance Director submit written reports to each Board meeting which include consideration of changing threats and opportunities within the business. The standard Board review of investments and disposals includes identification of major risks that could affect the outcome of each project, with a sensitivity analysis.

The Board also receives annual reports on certain areas of special risk. These include insurance, treasury management, commodity trading, pensions management, safety and environmental issues.

There is a comprehensive annual planning and financial reporting system comparing results with plan and the previous year on a monthly basis. Revised forecasts for the year are produced at least quarterly. Reports include a monthly cash flow statement projected for 15 months. The Company has defined procedures for the authorisation of capital expenditure and investment, granting of guarantees, trading and hedging of currencies and commodities and use of treasury products. The Group's businesses operate under mandatory written procedures to provide an appropriate control environment. The Group Operating Policies set out the Group's commitment to competence, integrity and ethical values. Each year, the Group's businesses are required formally to confirm that they are in compliance with these policies and the results of this review are reported to the Audit Committee.

Compliance with the Provisions of the Code

The Company has complied throughout the period with the provisions of the Code, with the following exceptions:

- Mr Pillard's annual bonus is pensionable, in accordance with usual North American practice.

- The Board does not consider it necessary to identify a single senior non-executive director, in addition to the Chairman, to whom concerns may be conveyed. The Chairmen of the Remuneration and Audit Committees may be consulted on any matters where investors feel an approach to the Chairman or Chief Executive would be inappropriate.

- Following the appointment of Mrs Piwnica to the Remuneration Committee on 14 August 2000, it did not exclusively comprise independent non-executive directors.

Directors' Remuneration Report 2001: Tate & Lyle PLC

The remuneration of the executive directors is set by the Remuneration Committee in accordance with a remuneration policy determined by the Board upon recommendation from the Committee. The policy is reviewed annually. The Committee, which is chaired by Lord Walker, consists solely of non-executive directors of the Company (whose biographical details are given on page 23). The Committee determines the detailed terms of service of the executive directors, including basic salary, incentives and benefits, and the terms upon which their service may be terminated. It takes advice from leading firms of compensation and benefit consultants.

Remuneration Policy for Executive Directors and Senior Executives

The Group's policy is to provide remuneration packages which:

- are competitive and commensurate with other international businesses of similar size, particularly those in the food processing industry;
- are designed to attract, retain and motivate high-calibre executives;
- reward above-average performance; and
- are based on local country practice.

The remuneration package consists of short-term rewards (base salary and annual bonus), long-term rewards (share options) and retirement and other benefits.

Base salaries take account of the median relative to similar companies and reflect job responsibilities, market rate and the sustained level of individual performance. The annual bonus is a short-term reward which reflects the performance of the Group, or appropriate division or subsidiary, against financial and other objectives. Annual bonuses are capped at 90% of base salary or lower, dependent on the executive's responsibilities.

Share option schemes provide long-term rewards that align with shareholder interests.

Retirement and other benefits reflect local market practice at median levels. Retirement benefits, in the form of pension and/or lump sums, are provided through tax-approved schemes, covering executives in the country and business sector in which they perform their principal duties. In certain circumstances where individuals are transferred from their home country to other Group locations but are likely to retire in the home country, pension benefits may continue to be provided on a home country basis. Where the promised level of benefits cannot be provided through tax-approved schemes, appropriate provisions are made in the Group accounts.

Remuneration of Executive Directors

Executive directors' salaries are reviewed on 1 December each year. Bonuses for the 53-week period ending 31 March 2001 are at the discretion of the Remuneration Committee. Such bonuses, which are capped, are determined by the Committee after considering the Group's performance relative to its competitors, the performance in relation to the previous financial period and particularly to profit before tax and improvement in economic value added (EVA), strategic achievements and cash management. No bonuses were earned by executive directors in the 53-week period to 31 March 2001.

The Company operates a discretionary Executive Share Option Scheme under which options over the Company's ordinary shares may be granted each year to executive directors and other senior executives. Option grants are based on individual performance and are phased over a number of years. A new Executive Share Option Scheme ('the 2000 Scheme') was approved by shareholders at the Annual General Meeting on 27 July 2000. The performance condition attached to the exercise of options under the 2000 Scheme is scaled such that, if over the first three consecutive years, the growth in the Company's normalised earnings per share has exceeded the growth in the UK Retail Price Index (excluding mortgage interest payments) by an average of at least 3% per year, then 50% of the options granted may be exercised. If it is exceeded by an average of at least 4% per year, then 100% of the options granted may be exercised. Options not meeting the performance condition in the third year may be exercised in subsequent years (up to ten years after the options were granted, at which time they will lapse) but only if the appropriate compound performance condition is met.

Prior to the approval of the 2000 Scheme, options were granted under UK and International Executive Share Option Schemes which were approved by shareholders in 1992 ('the 1992 Schemes'). The exercise of executive share options granted since November 1995 under the 1992 Schemes is subject to the Group achieving an increase in fully-diluted earnings per share of 6% more than the increase in the UK Retail Price Index during any period of three consecutive financial years over the life of the option. Following the approval of the 2000 Scheme, no further grants have been made under the 1992 Schemes.

The Company has a Savings Related Share Option Scheme ('Sharesave Scheme') that is open to all employees in the UK including executive directors. As permitted by the Finance Act 1989, exercise prices are normally set at a discount of 20% to the market price at the time of grant. The current Sharesave Scheme will expire in January 2002 and a new Sharesave Scheme will be submitted for shareholders' approval at the 2001 Annual General Meeting.

Retirement and Other Benefits of Executive Directors

Chief Executive

Mr Pillard is a member of the Tate & Lyle North America retirement plans. On retirement at age 60 he will be entitled to a payment from the plans that, when added to pensions due to him from the State and from a former employer, will total 52.4% (the 'retirement percentage') of his earnings at retirement. These are computed as the average of the highest 36 consecutive months' total compensation received in the preceding 120 months. Total compensation includes bonuses but excludes benefits. There is no provision for this pension to be increased during retirement. There is also a widow's pension payable on the later of Mr Pillard's death or his 55th birthday, and a lump sum death-in-service benefit. The Company makes matching contributions to Mr Pillard's 401 (K) plan (a tax-approved retirement savings plan in the US) up to 3% of the maximum compensation permitted for this purpose under the Internal Revenue Service Code.

As an expatriate, Mr Pillard receives a housing allowance and a travel allowance for his family. He also receives a car allowance, health insurance and other minor benefits.

Other Executive Directors
Executive directors other than the Chief Executive are members of the Tate & Lyle Group Pension Scheme and are eligible at age 60 for a pension equal to two-thirds of their basic pay in the highest of their last five completed tax years. Bonuses are not pensionable. The benefit also includes a widow's pension payable on a director's death and a lump sum on death in service. Once in payment to a director or his widow, the pension is increased each year in line with the Retail Price Index up to a maximum of 5%, with a minimum of 3%.

Executive directors are provided with a company car (or receive a car allowance in lieu) and health insurance.

Terms of Appointment of Chairman and Non-Executive Directors

Sir David Lees was appointed non-executive Chairman on 1 October 1998 for an initial period of three years. This appointment has been extended by the Board upon the recommendation of the Nominations Committee until 30 September 2002, and will continue thereafter, terminable by the Company or Sir David on not less than one year's notice. His fees are determined by the Board on the recommendation of the Remuneration Committee. Sir David has the use of a car, the running and associated costs of which are borne partially by the Company.

The fees received by the remaining non-executive directors are determined by the Board. The basic fee for each director is £27,500 per annum. The Chairmen of the Audit and Remuneration Committees receive an additional £2,750 per annum to reflect the extra responsibilities attached to these positions.

Mrs Piwnica received remuneration as Chairman of the Amylum Group up until completion of the purchase of the minority stake in Amylum on 14 August 2000. This remuneration was determined by the Amylum Group Board on the recommendation of the Remuneration Committee of Tate & Lyle and the representatives of Amylum's other shareholder, CIP. On 14 August 2000, Mrs Piwnica entered into a consultancy agreement with the Company for which she is paid €270,000 (£165,563) per annum. The agreement is for an initial three-year period and thereafter until terminated by either party giving not less than 12 months' written notice, such notice to expire no earlier than the end of the initial three-year period. In recognition of her consultancy services, Mrs Piwnica was appointed to the position of 'Non-Executive

Vice Chairman, Government Affairs' for Tate & Lyle. Mrs Piwnica also receives £2, 750 per annum in addition to her basic fee as a director.

The non-executive directors do not participate in the Group's incentive or pension schemes, nor do they receive other benefits except as described above. They do not have service contracts, but under the terms of their appointment they are usually expected to serve as directors for between four and eight years. The appointment of Lord Walker, who joined the Board in 1990, has been extended until the Annual General Meeting of 2001, when he will retire.

Service Contracts of Executive Directors

All executive directors have service contracts terminable by the Company on not more than two years' notice and by the individual directors on up to six months' notice. These notice periods take account of the international nature of Tate & Lyle's business and the need to remain competitive. Contracts for any new executive directors will specify a maximum of 12 months' notice except in special circumstances. Executive directors' contracts, together with summaries of their pension arrangements, are available for inspection at the registered office of the Company during normal business hours and at the Annual General Meeting.

External Appointments

The Board believes that the Company can benefit from its executive directors holding a non-executive directorship. Such appointments are subject to the approval of the Board and are normally restricted to one for each executive director. Fees may be retained by the executive director concerned.

9 Annual reports of other organizations: charities and housing associations

Although this book is predominantly concerned with the annual reports of limited companies, there are other organizations that still need to produce annual reports and accounts.

A considerable number of the topics that are discussed in this book are just as applicable to organizations that are not limited companies. Clearly, certain aspects concerning some of the legal, accounting and the Financial Services Authority provisions do not apply to organizations such as charities and housing associations, which often have to report under different or additional legislative or accounting requirements. Also, their target audience is not always as clearly identifiable as that of limited companies.

Even so, even in these other organizations you must not neglect the basic purpose of annual reports. As with all types of organization, you must still plan, prepare and consider the need to deliver key messages.

Charities: annual reports

Charities' annual reports usually have additional and specialized needs over and above the more conventional requirements of those of limited companies. In some ways, it is difficult to be very specific about the requirements of charities as there are many different forms of charity created for a vast array of different purposes, some of which have specific reporting requirements. In the UK, for example, there are over 180 000 registered charities. Nevertheless, many have common attributes.

The whole accountability process can be different in charitable institutions, and those differences can affect how you draft your report. A charity rarely has a body of shareholders in the traditional sense of a limited company. Often, a board of trustees will occupy the role reserved for the board of directors in a limited company. In addition, the trustees' responsibilities often extend further than those of directors of limited companies.

In a limited company, the directors represent the owners of the business – the shareholders. Clearly, in a charity, this extensive body of owners does not exist in the same sense, leaving the charity trustees with significant responsibilities. Accordingly, these trustees are all-important and, usually, a large degree of accountability rests with them. The auditors will report to the trustees at the conclusion of the year's audit, for the simple reason that there are normally no shareholders. Of course, other parties, such as the public and donors, may be interested in charities' reports, but there is no direct accountability channel – in practical terms it is just not possible.

In theory, the trustees occupy an all-embracing role, ensuring that the organization is run in such a way as to meet its charitable objectives. They also ensure that all the charities' assets and all its income – especially donations – are properly accounted for. As part of their remit, trustees are expected to ensure that payments and assistance to beneficiaries and claimants are in accordance with the charity's aims and trust deed criteria.

Charities are also required to consider the role of the Charity Commissioners who exercise a supervisory role over most charities in the UK. There are also the requirements of the Charities Act 1993 to consider. More specifically some charities have further restrictions or objectives imposed by their own articles of association or conditions attached to bequests by donors.

These differences and emphasis will have a varying degree of impact on the annual report. The chairman's statement and trustees' report will largely concentrate on the organization's charitable aims. You will need to highlight and express appreciation for fundraisers, voluntary assistance and new initiatives to generate funds and so on. Substantial attention should be paid to how your funds are spent and who are the beneficiaries.

In addition, you will certainly want to give prominence to the sources of funding and the effort put into generating funds, and provide specific examples.

As always, the principles of sound layout, design and image are important. Clearly, the image and messages that you wish to portray may be radically different from those of a commercial organization. Themes of commitment, devotion, caring and a benevolent philosophy should be paramount.

Fundraising and management costs

There is an important difference between most limited companies and most charities. The major objective of most companies is to achieve a healthy and increasing growth in year-on-year profits. Companies are normally judged by the level of, and the growth in, their 'bottom-line' profits. By contrast, most charities usually operate on different principles and have different performance measures.

The key determining factor that indicates a charity's performance is usually the management-expense ratio which compares the charity's total management expenses with the amount of income received. Although there are a number of valid exceptions, it is normally judged that charities are more efficient if this ratio is kept down to the lowest possible level.

Therefore, in attempting to deliver your message, you may wish to highlight the high level of efficiency in your charity and how, as a consequence of your low management costs, beneficiaries will share in the additional available funds. Emphasis on your low income/costs ratio will also encourage more money from donors who will see that their donations are not being 'wasted' on administration. Of course, a large proportion of administrative expenses and management costs are necessary and unavoidable, but you must remember that the public do not always appreciate their necessity. To many, administrative costs equate to wasteful 'bureaucratic' activity.

Conversely, if your charity's administrative or fundraising expenses are on the high side, you should perhaps consider offering a suitable explanation. Some charities have a few years of particularly high administrative expenses because they are establishing new initiatives to develop longer-term fundraising programmes. Other reasons for higher expenses include establishing new donation ventures and a particularly high level of advertising costs which will reap donation returns in future years. Whatever your reasons, explain the points and how these high levels of expenses will help fulfil the charity's objectives in future years. Never pretend that your expenses are typical of the sector's norm if they are not.

Another area where you need to tread carefully is if your charity appears to be retaining a relatively high proportion of its income, since the public might perceive that you do not 'really need' the funds that they donate. In fact, if the proportion of undistributed income, becomes excessively high there could be legal implications, and the Charity Commissioners may become concerned. In the majority of cases there are genuine reasons for large balances of retained income but, to allay public suspicion, you should provide an explanation – especially if you expect the situation to continue for more than a few years.

Warning: appearance of affluence

It is sometimes said that charities' annual reports should not give the impression of affluence or wealth. A glossy, high-quality report may suggest, to some, that the charity has funds that could be better directed towards potential beneficiaries or, alternatively, that it has inappropriate or unnecessarily large reserves of funds and is 'wasting its income'. As a result, potential donors might hesitate about making contributions. By contrast, a 'poorer-looking' report, with lower-quality paper and less attention paid to design, might attract more donations. It is difficult to strike the right balance. But, all things considered, avoid producing an annual report that looks very downtrodden and lacklustre. A scruffy, cheap-looking and poor-quality report may well reflect adversely on your organization in that these negative features may be attributed to the charity itself and the way in which you run it. Although there is no meaningful evidence to prove that either way is best, the better option is probably a 'reasonable'-quality report. You might not always use the best-quality paper and photographic images, but you should certainly not use the worst.

The layout of a charity's annual report and accounts has a number of similarities to that of a limited company and, consequently, much of the content of this book applies in the same way. There are more similarities than differences between the two types of organization.

Statement of Recommended Practice

However, in addition to conforming to charity legislation, many charities will need to comply with additional accounting requirements. Special accounting guidance has been issued in the form of a Statement of Recommended Practice (SORP), *Accounting and Reporting by Charities* (2000) which gives specific accounting guidance and recommendations that, although not legally binding, accountants should bear in mind when they are preparing a charity's accounts. Non-compliance may lead to some difficult questions being asked.

This SORP requires charities to produce a trustees' report explaining the charity's objectives and helping readers to understand how the accounts relate to its organizational structure and activities. The report should also explain the charity's key activities and significant developments and achievements during the financial period. The principal risks facing the charity should be identified and its investment policy discussed. A further requirement is a statement on the charity's policy on reserves and the level of reserves held – with justification for this level. In short, the trustees' report is seen as a vital communications medium.

If you are involved in the preparation of the annual report of charities you should certainly obtain a copy of this SORP from the Accounting Standards Board.

Types of annual report

Some larger charities follow the practice of limited companies and split their annual report and accounts into two sections – the annual review and the full report.

Annual review

The annual review section could contain an introductory statement from the charity's chairman followed by a description and explanation of the charity's activities and future plans. Pay particular attention to expressing appreciation to donors and praising the efforts of supporters throughout the year. It may well be appropriate to devote several pages to the charity's 'grassroots' volunteers who strive to initiate collections and generate income on a day-to-day basis. Fulsome praise is welcomed and usually deserved.

You will also need to comment fully on the beneficiaries of your investment and other spending. Provide plenty of examples and perhaps take a 'case-study' approach to finished ventures or projects in progress.

Since this part of the annual report will be the only document that some people receive, make it as interesting, readable and appealing as you can. Obviously, subject to our earlier discussion about not appearing 'too wealthy', you should make moderate use of colour, graphs and photographs to highlight your fundraising activities and beneficiaries.

Since many readers will not receive any other documentation about your charity you might wish to include your summarized accounts in this section. Other possibilities include: a brief extract of your income statement, often termed the statement of financial affairs (the term profit and loss account is perhaps inappropriate for a charity); a brief balance sheet; a cash flow statement; and perhaps a statement of your key investments and major capital expenditure projects.

Full report

The second section could comprise the full annual report of the trustees and a detailed report from the charity's chief officers, such as the treasurer and chief executive.

In these reports, a more detailed discussion on income, legacies, donations and other fundraising activities is normally expected. You would certainly be expected to comment on the ratio of management costs (or other fundraising and publicity costs) to income from fundraising projects and initiatives.

Another way in which charities differ from limited companies concerns reserves. A charity may have received funds to be used for different or restricted purposes. For example, in many charities you will often find some or all of the following:

- **Endowment reserves.** These are funds that are donated to the charity but under the legal restriction that they are invested in specified areas, and that the subsequent income from the underlying investments can only be used in accordance with the donor's instructions.

- **Restricted reserves.** These are general funds that can only be spent in accordance with the donor's instructions.

- **Designated reserves.** These are funds that are set aside at the discretion of the charity's trustees.

- **Free Reserves.** Many charities will disclose free reserves which are often funds set aside to meet expected future commitments. For example, the Royal National Lifeboat Institution, in its 2001 annual report, identifies its free reserves as being needed 'to provide assurance to those at sea ... [that it] will be able to sustain its commitment to provide a lifeboat service ... the trustees believe that this reserve should be set in the range of two to five years' cover of annual charitable expenditure.'

These funds are important for charities and you should certainly clearly explain their meaning and amounts to readers – this is an important message to convey.

Medium- and larger-sized charities will also usually supply full supporting accounting notes and an auditors' report. Auditors will be appointed, if required, and report under sections 43 and 44 of the Charities Act 1993. They normally report to the charity's trustees and give an opinion of whether the charity's accounts are 'true and fair' and comply with the Charities Act 1993. However, audit requirements can differ between charities – largely depending on the size of the charity, its legal status, its articles of association and its own governance rules. Your accountants will be able to advise you of the legal and professional requirements.

Splitting the report

Although a number of large charities split their annual reports and accounts into two sections (like limited companies), the choice must remain with your charity. There are no hard and fast rules. If you work for a large charity it may, on balance, be preferable to split the report as you may have a substantial number of potential readers who just 'want to see what the charity's been doing' and will therefore not be interested in the detailed accounts and trustees' report.

If yours is a smaller charity with a far more limited potential readership, it may be more expedient, and in fact probably cheaper in terms of a print run, to produce a complete annual report as a single document. It is very difficult to generalize, and you must examine the publication costs and the size of the potential readership.

See Appendix 9.1 at the end of this chapter, for an extract from a charity's report.

The future

The government is currently revising and modernizing the legislation relating to UK charities. Although it seems that the Charity Commission will be renamed the Charity Regulations Authority it does not appear, as yet, that there will be significant changes to the content of charities' annual reports.

Housing associations: annual reports

In the last decade there has been a substantial growth in the number of UK housing associations, largely caused by central government making a political decision to place most social housing development in the hands of housing associations rather than local government authorities. The majority of housing associations develop and rent accommodation to the public and to disadvantaged and minority groups in society. A smaller amount of accommodation can be purchased, often on specialized terms. Many housing associations receive financial support from the Housing Corporation.

Legal requirements

Housing associations are regulated by a number of legal requirements. Most associations report under the Companies Act 1985, Schedule 1 of the Housing Act 1996 and the Accounting Requirements for Registered Social Landlord General Determination 2000. Some associations may also need to report under the Industrial and Provident Societies Acts 1965–1978, and most associations will also adhere to the Housing Corporation's circular R2-18/96, 'Internal Financial Control and Financial Reporting'. (A Statement of

Recommended Practice on accounting by registered housing associations has also been issued by the National Federation of Housing Associations. This SORP should be consulted together with the legal requirements.)

Essentially, the annual reports of housing associations will be very similar to those of limited companies. However, like charities, there is a problem identifying the lines of accountability in terms of the users to whom you are targeting your annual report. The principal external users will be the Housing Corporation, other finance-providers and other local and political groupings. These groupings may include board members of the association, local politicians, local authorities (in the case of joint partnerships), the media and, sometimes, the housing beneficiaries.

Objectives

In some aspects, the points discussed earlier about charities are equally applicable to housing associations. The overriding objective of most associations is to use its funds to provide good-quality housing to as many people as possible. Accordingly, while you do not want to give an impression of undue extravagance in the quality of your annual report, on the other hand, you do not want to miss the opportunity of delivering your message. As with charities, it is probably preferable to aim for a reasonable, rather than the highest, standard of printing quality, paper thickness, binding, cover boards and so on. Above all, concentrate on your social housing objectives, housing targets and outcomes. A solid report of the 'good' works undertaken by your association, together with supporting photographs of, say, a new housing development, can convey far more positive messages than unadorned narrative.

It may be a good idea, subject to the tenants' permission, to consider including case-study reports, taking a selection of individuals or families and explaining how you have helped them solve their housing needs. If your tenants are unwilling to be named (or you choose otherwise), you could still relate the housing circumstances of 'typical' tenants, perhaps with 'given' names (but do point out the use of pseudonyms in the accompanying notes). Supporting and appreciative quotes from tenants would also be useful.

Your primary aim must be to convey the message and image of a caring organization that is trying to allay the housing worries of many socially disadvantaged and neglected groups of people. You could also point out the quality of the new housing developments and refurbishment and the benefits in terms of improving the quality of life for the tenants. However, take care not to sound patronizing. Always stress your caring, but professional, approach.

Some housing associations' annual reports are well explained, and their activities are competently discussed in a caring and benevolent tone. By contrast, however, the tone of some associations' reports can seem (not usually intentionally) as rather formal, remote and detached.

The fact that housing associations, unlike large listed companies, do not normally have substantial numbers of equity shareholders, does not justify neglecting your image or presentation.

The 'ideal' housing association annual report should be user-friendly, well explained, supported with photographs and predominantly centred on your key client group whom you are trying to assist with their housing needs. You could also refer to the 'value for money' benefits that the housing association has achieved with, if appropriate, the aid of public funds.

See Appendix 9.2 for an extract from a housing association's annual report.

Appendix 9.1: Charity annual report

The extract from a charity's annual report, on the following pages, is reproduced by kind permission of RNLI.

© RNLI/DK

Message from the Chairman

This has been an exciting and eventful year for the RNLI. Our highly successful 175th anniversary year in 1999 saw us looking back over a proud history of saving lives at sea. In 2000 we have been looking to the future and the way the lifeboat service will develop in the new century.

The RNLI Plan for 2000 and Beyond, published at the start of 2000, set out the purpose, vision and values that will guide our actions in the years to come. Looking at all aspects of the organisation, it lays out principles, goals and plans for us to work towards in everything we do. Clearly defined actions set out how we will achieve our vision of being recognised universally as the most effective, innovative and dependable lifeboat service.

New initiatives

Included in these actions are a number of key initiatives to develop our lifeboat service. These developments fall into two main categories: firstly, those aimed directly at saving more lives, and secondly, those which will greatly improve the service we give from our Poole headquarters to lifeboat stations, our volunteers and supporters.

The initiatives aimed at saving more lives concentrate on areas where lives have been lost or are at apparent risk and where lifeboats have not been in a position to help. These include beaches, inland waters, mudflats and the River Thames. Pilot schemes have started for beach rescue and inland waters, while trials of hovercraft in Poole Harbour are well under way. The plan to establish three lifeboat stations on the River Thames is the most developed, and we will see the first operational lifeboats on the river by early 2002.

At our Poole headquarters, the planned RNLI College will be a centre of excellence providing training tailored to meet the needs of all our crews, other volunteers and staff. We will establish a purpose-built store, to handle every item requiring distribution from Poole to our lifeboat stations and fundraising branches, and enhance the boat maintenance facilities with, among other things, covered workshops to ensure lifeboats operating from our Poole headquarters are kept in prime working condition. We are also planning a visitor and heritage centre to give members of the public a chance to gain a proper insight into the lifeboat service as a whole.

Thanks to the success of our fundraising over recent years, we are in the fortunate position of being able to undertake these new tasks, some of which we would like to have been able to do in earlier years but could not afford. Free reserves at the end of 2000 stood at £202m, leaving the RNLI in the secure position of having 2.8 years' cover of our charitable expenditure. Moreover, these new initiatives will in no way reduce the time and money we are currently spending on maintaining and improving our core business – that of running a lifeboat service second to none.

New technology

In 2000 our crews were once again extremely busy, answering 6,249 calls and rescuing 6,326 people. In support of them, we continue to lead the field in boat development. Our policy is to pursue continued improvement in the efficiency and safety of our boats and equipment. Trials of the experimental FSB2 fast slipway lifeboat have been highly successful and we hope to move on to a prototype vessel shortly. We are also developing a fast (25 knot) carriage boat to replace the Mersey class, a fast inshore boat to replace the Atlantic 75 and an inshore boat to replace the D class.

There is a lot of challenging and difficult work ahead but we have already made significant steps along the road mapped out in *The RNLI Plan for 2000 and Beyond.* It will not be long before our actions start to take effect. This promises to be an exciting time for the RNLI.

Peter Nicholson
Chairman
Royal National Lifeboat Institution

Annual report of the Trustees of the Royal National Lifeboat Institution for the year ended 31 December 2000

The Trustees submit their annual report and accounts for the year ended 31 December 2000. The Trustees have adopted the provisions of the new Statement of Recommended Practice 'Accounting and Reporting by Charities' issued in October 2000 in preparing this report and accounts.

1 Legal structure

The Royal National Lifeboat Institution (RNLI) is a registered charity, number 209603. Founded in 1824, the RNLI was incorporated under Royal Charter in 1860, with Supplemental Charters granted in 1932 and 1986. The address of the registered office is West Quay Road, Poole, Dorset BH15 1HZ.

2 Objects

The RNLI exists to save lives at sea. In furtherance of this, the RNLI has various powers including setting up and maintaining a modern lifeboat or marine rescue service, providing consultancy services in the marine rescue field and promoting the cause of the International Lifeboat Federation. The RNLI has defined its vision as 'to be recognised universally as the most effective, innovative and dependable lifeboat service'.

3 Review of activities

The RNLI maintains a network of 224 lifeboat stations around the coasts of the United Kingdom and the Republic of Ireland, which is served largely by volunteers (branch officials, coxswains and crew). In 2000, lifeboats launched 6,249 times and rescued 6,326 people.

The RNLI is funded entirely from voluntary contributions, with the active support of many thousands of volunteers. An important proportion of the RNLI's income arises from legacies. Funds are also received from activities and events arranged by 1,700 fundraising branches and guilds, and from many governors, members and other generous donors. The RNLI's profitable business in Christmas cards and souvenirs, through mail order and through RNLI branches, is operated by its wholly-owned subsidiary, RNLI (Sales) Limited.

The consolidated accounts for the RNLI and its subsidiaries for the year ended 31 December 2000 are reviewed in the Treasurer's Statement.

4 Future developments

The RNLI has embarked on a number of new initiatives in the course of the year. The introduction of competence-based training for lifeboat crew members will be supported by the modernisation and concentration of formal training in a new training college to be built in Poole. This investment will not only increase the quality of training but also be more cost-effective than the present arrangements. Plans are also being developed to improve and modernise the central stores and boat storage at Poole and provide proper visitor facilities there. In response to calls for better co-ordination and provision of rescue services on inland waters and beaches, the RNLI will be initiating pilot schemes in the course of 2001. Building on the Sea Safety campaign, further investment will be made in promoting sea safety for professional fishermen who have been identified as being particularly at risk.

5 Reserves policy

The RNLI's funds fall into the following categories:

Endowment reserves are capital sums which are donated under the restrictions that they are invested and that only the income arising is available for expenditure in accordance with the donors' directions.

Restricted reserves are only available for expenditure in accordance with the donors' directions.

Designated reserves are set aside at the discretion of the Trustees and comprise:

Fixed Assets in Use, which finances the fixed assets which are used in the RNLI's work.

Planned Capital Expenditure, which sets aside funds to assure suppliers that the RNLI can meet its planned capital expenditure. This is expenditure to which the RNLI is committed over the next three years in order to maintain the operation of the lifeboat service into the future and is principally on new lifeboats, lifeboat stations and shoreworks. The total amount set aside excludes projects funded by restricted reserves.

Free reserves are retained to enable the Trustees to provide assurance to those at sea and the Governments of the UK and the Republic of Ireland, that the RNLI will be able to sustain its commitment to provide the lifeboat service. The reserve is set at a level to withstand any short-term setback, whether operational, in the investment markets or in key sources of income, such as legacies. The Trustees believe that this reserve should be set in the range of two to five years' cover of annual charitable expenditure. When the free reserve falls outside this range, the Trustees will adjust the RNLI's fundraising strategy accordingly.

6 Governance and risk management

The RNLI is controlled by a Committee of Management and an Executive Committee who are its Trustees as set out on page 16. They are a body of volunteers who have had distinguished careers in a wide variety of activities; they come from all parts of the United Kingdom and the Republic of Ireland and many have first-hand experience of the working of lifeboat stations and fundraising branches. Trustees may be proposed by the Chairman or a Governor to the Membership Review Committee. This Committee, which comprises the Chairman and the Deputy Chairmen, reviews the names proposed and submits its recommendations to the Annual General Meeting for election by the Governors. Trustees serve a three-year term but may be re-elected for succeeding terms.

In addition, there are also several advisory committees, enabling specialists to contribute to every aspect of the RNLI's affairs, including operations, boat design, medical, public relations, fundraising, personnel and finance.

The Chief Executive is responsible for the day-to-day running of the RNLI and carrying out the policies decided by the Executive Committee.

... continued

... ***continued***

Company and charity law requires the Trustees to prepare financial statements for each financial year which give a true and fair view of the state of affairs of the charity and of the surplus or deficit of the charity for that period. In preparing these financial statements, the Trustees have:

- selected suitable accounting policies and then applied them consistently;
- made judgements and estimates that are reasonable and prudent;
- stated whether applicable accounting standards have been followed, subject to any material departures disclosed and explained in the financial statements; and
- prepared the financial statements on the going concern basis.

The Trustees have overall responsibility for ensuring that the charity has appropriate systems of controls, financial and otherwise. They are also responsible for ensuring that proper accounting records are kept which disclose with reasonable accuracy at any time the financial position of the charity and enable them to ensure that the financial statements comply with the Charities Act 1993, the Charities (Accounts and Reports) Regulations 2000 and the RNLI's Charter. The Trustees are also responsible for safeguarding the assets of the charity and hence for taking reasonable steps for the prevention and detection of fraud and other irregularities and to provide reasonable assurance that:

- the charity is operating efficiently and effectively;
- its assets are safeguarded against unauthorised use or disposition;
- proper records are maintained and financial information used within the charity or for publication is reliable; and
- the charity complies with relevant laws and regulations.

The systems of internal control are designed to provide reasonable, but not absolute, assurance against material misstatement or loss. They include:

- a strategic plan and an annual budget approved by the Trustees;
- regular consideration by the Trustees of financial results, variance from budgets and non-financial performance indicators;
- delegation of authority and segregation of duties; and
- identification and management of risks.

The Trustees have carefully considered the standards for corporate governance and the guidance of the Turnbull report and, as a consequence, have established an Audit Committee of Trustees in 1999 and in 2000 have appointed an internal auditor and codified the RNLI's internal controls, by publishing Standing Financial Instructions.

By its very purpose, the RNLI exposes its crews, support staff and operational assets to substantial risk. The Trustees have taken all appropriate steps to mitigate and manage these operational risks, principally through crew training, stringent design and maintenance of the lifeboats and equipment and insurance of third party risks. The further development of competence based training for lifeboat crew members and the new designs of lifeboat are major elements of this continuing process.

The Audit Committee commissioned a Risk Assessment during the year to codify the major strategic risks to which the RNLI is exposed. Action is being taken to ensure that controls exist and are operating effectively to mitigate these other risks.

7 Investment policy

The RNLI's investments are held as a reserve against any future shortfall in income against expenditure. The RNLI's objective is to maintain and, if possible, enhance the real value of the reserve represented by its investments. It seeks to do so by following an investment policy which is intended to maintain an appropriate balance between maximising long-term returns and avoiding undue volatility in capital values.

These objectives are pursued through a strategic investment policy which involves a broadly diversified spread of assets, covering UK and overseas equities, UK and overseas government and non-government bonds, and pooled property funds. Under this policy, approximately three-quarters of the investments are in equities, with the remaining one-quarter being in bonds and property.

Over recent years, the RNLI has sought diversification of investment management style and philosophy by dividing its investments between two portfolios, each of which covers the full range of assets. These portfolios are currently managed by Henderson Global Investors (who replaced Schroder Investment Management with effect from April 2000) and Phillips and Drew Fund Management.

Both of these managers operate by reference to a benchmark of the RNLI's strategic investment policy, but they have discretion to vary their asset allocation from that policy, within certain specified ranges. They also have full discretion over the individual securities to be purchased, subject to safeguards designed to avoid undue concentration of investment. The activities and performance of the RNLI's investment managers are monitored closely by the RNLI's Investment Sub-Committee, which reports to the Finance Committee.

The assets within the managers' portfolios are held by professional custodians who are entirely independent of the RNLI.

The performance of the RNLI's investments is measured by CAPS, which is one of the leading independent performance measurement services in the UK. The analysis of performance is carried out by reference to total returns, taking account of investment income and of movements in capital values, whether realised or unrealised, and allowing for the impact of cashflow to and from the investment managers.

Over the year as a whole, equity markets fell: although the strength of the US dollar and some recovery in the euro improved the results in sterling, returns tended to be negative. As a result, index returns from equity markets ranged from +1.5% in Europe to -2.5% in emerging markets; UK equities, which form the largest single asset class within the RNLI's portfolios, produced an index return of -5.9% over the year.

Against this background, the RNLI's investments produced a good return of 2.4% over the year to 31 December 2000, which was well above the benchmark return of -2.2%. The main source of this relative out-performance was the defensive stance pursued by one of the RNLI's investment managers, who had been particularly sceptical of the values reached by 'new economy' stocks early in the year.

Over the five years ending on 31 December 2000, the RNLI's investments returned 11.3% a year which was just ahead of the benchmark return of 11.2% a year. This has been well in excess of price inflation, which averaged 2.7% a year over the five years to the end of 2000, thus meeting the RNLI's basic investment objective.

Peter Nicholson

Peter C Nicholson
Chairman
4 April 2001

Annual report of the Trustees

The Treasurer's statement

The total cost of the lifeboat service increased to over £93m in 2000. The most significant increases were a £7m growth in crew and station costs and a £5m increase in lifeboat maintenance and running costs. Crew and station costs growth reflected the increase in full-time staff, the continuing roll-out of the new call-out and communications system and computer systems, and the completion of the programme to issue new protective clothing to crew. The increased costs of operating lifeboats arose principally from the increased complexity of equipment and consequently greater refit costs. These increases reflect the RNLI's sustained commitment to providing lifeboat crews with the best available equipment. Increases in other costs were incurred mainly by the depreciation of the recent heavy investment in new computer systems.

Income declined in the year by some £8m. The key factors were the reduction in legacy income, the anticipated step down from the high of 1999 celebrating the 175th Anniversary and reduced investment income. Legacy income fell by £5m, almost certainly as a consequence of the fall in stockmarket values: the weaker stockmarkets and a changed pattern of investment also reduced investment income by nearly £3m. The reduction in income from legacies had the effect of increasing the ratio of fundraising and publicity costs to fundraising income from 16.1% to 17.1%.

Investment valuations fell by £4m during the year, taking away some of the inflated gains at the end of 1999 which had added over £40m in that year.

These factors combined increased total funds by just £2m, but the increased investment in fixed assets and the higher level of investment planned in new lifeboats and other equipment over the next three years have the effect of reducing free reserves from £257m in 1999 to £202m at the end of 2000. This level leaves the RNLI in the position of having 2.8 years' cover of its charitable expenditure.

Iain R Bryce TD DL FCA
Treasurer
4 April 2001

Auditors' report to the Trustees of the Royal National Lifeboat Institution

We have audited the accounts on pages 4-15 which have been prepared under the historical cost convention and the accounting policies set out on pages seven and eight.

Respective responsibilities of the Trustees and the auditors
The Trustees are responsible for preparing the Annual Report. As described on page two, this includes a responsibility for preparing the accounts in accordance with applicable United Kingdom accounting standards. Our responsibilities, as independent auditors, are established in the United Kingdom by statute, the Auditing Practices Board and our profession's ethical guidance. We have been appointed as auditors under section 43 of the United Kingdom Charities Act 1993 and report in accordance with regulations made under section 44 of that Act.

We report to you our opinion as to whether the accounts give a true and fair view and are properly prepared in accordance with the United Kingdom's Charities Act 1993. We also report to you if, in our opinion, the Annual Report is not consistent with the accounts, if the charity has not kept proper accounting records or if we have not received all the information and explanations we require for our audit.

We read the other information contained in the Annual Report and consider the implications for our report if we become aware of any apparent misstatements or material inconsistencies with the accounts.

Basis of opinion
We conducted our audit in accordance with Auditing Standards issued by the Auditing Practices Board. An audit includes examination, on a test basis, of evidence relevant to the amounts and disclosures in the accounts. It also includes an assessment of the significant estimates and judgements made by the Trustees in the preparation of the accounts and of whether the accounting policies are appropriate to the RNLI's circumstances, consistently applied and adequately disclosed.

We planned and performed our audit so as to obtain all the information necessary in order to provide us with sufficient evidence to give reasonable assurance that the accounts are free from material misstatement, whether caused by fraud or other irregularity or error. In forming our opinion we also evaluated the overall adequacy of the presentation of information in the accounts.

Opinion
In our opinion, the accounts give a true and fair view of the state of affairs of the RNLI and its subsidiaries at 31 December 2000 and of its net incoming resources and cashflows for the year then ended and have been properly prepared in accordance with the Charities Act 1993.

PricewaterhouseCoopers
Chartered Accountants
and Registered Auditors
Southampton
4 April 2001

Consolidated statement of financial activities

for the year ended 31 December 2000

	Note	Free Reserves £m	Designated Reserves £m	Restricted Reserves £m	Endowment Reserves £m	Total 2000 £m	Total 1999 £m
Incoming resources							
Income from fundraising		**23.4**	-	**4.8**	-	**28.2**	27.6
Legacies		**33.4**	-	**18.6**	-	**52.0**	56.7
Merchandising and lotteries	2	**8.5**	-	-	-	**8.5**	9.2
Investment income	9	**9.1**	-	**1.6**	**0.3**	**11.0**	13.8
Total incoming resources		**74.4**	-	**25.0**	**0.3**	**99.7**	107.3
Resources expended							
Fundraising and publicity		**(13.7)**	-	-	-	**(13.7)**	(13.6)
Merchandising and lotteries	2	**(6.1)**	-	-	-	**(6.1)**	(6.3)
Investment management	3	**(0.9)**	-	**(0.1)**	-	**(1.0)**	(0.7)
Cost of generating funds		**(20.7)**	-	**(0.1)**	-	**(20.8)**	(20.6)
Lifeboat maintenance		**(37.2)**	-	**(3.7)**	-	**(40.9)**	(36.1)
Crew and station costs		**(18.8)**	-	**(4.9)**	-	**(23.7)**	(16.3)
Crew training		**(1.3)**	-	**(0.9)**	-	**(2.2)**	(1.6)
Sea safety		**(1.3)**	-	-	-	**(1.3)**	(1.3)
Dependants' pensions		**(1.5)**	-	-	-	**(1.5)**	(0.1)
Management and administration		**(3.1)**	-	-	-	**(3.1)**	(2.4)
Charitable expenditure		**(63.2)**	-	**(9.5)**	-	**(72.7)**	(57.8)
Total resources expended	6	**(83.9)**	-	**(9.6)**	-	**(93.5)**	(78.4)
Net incoming resources/ (resources expended) before transfers		**(9.5)**	-	**15.4**	**0.3**	**6.2**	28.9
Transfers between reserves	7	**(41.9)**	**46.1**	**(4.0)**	**(0.2)**	-	-
Net incoming resources/ (resources expended)		**(51.4)**	**46.1**	**11.4**	**0.1**	**6.2**	28.9
(Losses)/gains on investments	9	**(3.2)**	-	**(0.5)**	**(0.6)**	**(4.3)**	40.5
Net movements in reserves		**(54.6)**	**46.1**	**10.9**	**(0.5)**	**1.9**	69.4
Reserves brought forward		**256.6**	**201.1**	**46.0**	**10.0**	**513.7**	444.3
Reserves at 31 December		**202.0**	**247.2**	**56.9**	**9.5**	**515.6**	513.7

No activities were acquired or discontinued during the above financial years.

RNLI and consolidated balance sheet (note 2)

as at 31 December 2000

	Note	2000 £m	1999 £m
Assets employed			
Fixed assets	8	**155.0**	140.5
Investments	9	**350.2**	362.6
Current assets			
Stocks	10	**10.4**	9.1
Debtors	11	**10.3**	12.3
Short-term deposits		**4.0**	3.2
Cash at bank		**1.9**	2.4
		26.6	27.0
Creditors:			
Amounts falling due within one year	12	**(10.8)**	(12.2)
Net current assets		**15.8**	14.8
Creditors:			
Amounts falling due after more than one year	12	**(5.4)**	(4.2)
Net assets		**515.6**	513.7
Financed by			
Capital reserves			
Endowment reserves		**9.5**	10.0
Income reserves			
Restricted reserves		**56.9**	46.0
Designated reserves			
Fixed assets in use		**155.0**	140.5
Planned capital expenditure		**92.2**	60.6
Free reserves		**202.0**	256.6
		515.6	513.7

The accounts were approved by the Trustees on 4 April 2001 and signed on their behalf.

Peter C Nicholson
Chairman
4 April 2001

Andrew W Freemantle
Chief Executive and Secretary
4 April 2001

Appendix 9.2: Housing association annual report

The extract from a housing association's annual report, as shown on the following pages, is reproduced by kind permission of Manchester and District Housing Association Ltd.

MANCHESTER & DISTRICT HOUSING ASSOCIATION LIMITED
REPORT OF THE BOARD

The Board present their report and the audited financial statements for the year ended 31 March 2001.

PRINCIPAL ACTIVITIES

Manchester & District Housing Association Limited's principal activities are the development, management, maintenance and improvement of social housing.

LEGAL STATUS

The Association is registered under the Industrial and Provident Societies Act 1965, is a registered social landlord and on the 29 March 1999 became a subsidiary of Harvest Housing Group Limited. Full details of the parent and subsidiaries are detailed in note 27 to these financial statements. The Association, its parent and other subsidiaries are the Harvest Housing Group. Industrial & Provident Society registration number 16434R. Housing Corporation registration number LI423.

On 8 April 1999 the Association registered a change to Charitable Rules.

REVIEW OF THE YEAR

During the year 565 homes were rehabilitated or made available for reletting to new residents. The programme included shared ownership, rehabilitation for rent and special needs schemes. The Association spent £6 million on improvements, major repairs and adaptations on existing stock.

PERFORMANCE OF THE YEAR

The Association has achieved a surplus for the year on ordinary activities before transfers, of £0.6 million (2000 – £0.7 million). As a result a net amount of £1.7 million (2000 – £1.7 million) was transferred from designated reserves to fund maintenance and major repair programmes. The revenue reserve has increased to £11.6 million (2000 – £9.9 million).

FUTURE DEVELOPMENTS

The Association will continue to look at new areas of work and new sources of financing in response to both reductions in Government funding and to new opportunities for growth. We will continue to seek ways of improving services to tenants through developing our area network and reviewing existing services.

We are committed to providing housing to the frail and elderly, those with special needs as well as those in low-paid employment or unemployed. We are confident that we can meet these challenges and produce new initiatives that will ensure the Association continues to provide more housing for those in greatest need.

HOUSING PROPERTIES

The Association spent £11.3 million on the acquisition and development of housing. This was financed through Social Housing Grant of £3.4 million, total loans of £1.8 million and the balance through Association reserves. The Association has further loan facilities of £41.4 million with £12 million of security in place against these facilities for drawdown of additional funds. The balance is currently met from the Association's reserves although some will eventually be loan funded.

EMPLOYEES

The strength of the Association lies in the quality and commitment of its employees. Our ability to meet our objectives and commitments to tenants in an efficient and effective manner depends on the contribution of all employees.

The Association continues to provide information on its objectives, progress and activities through regular office and departmental meetings. The Association provides training programmes focussed on quality and customer service, seeks employees' views on how to improve services and on matters of common concern. As part of this process the Association was recognised under the Investors in People initiative in January 1996 and was reaccredited in January 1999.

The Association is committed to equal opportunities for all its employees in every aspect of employment. Targets are set and careful monitoring against these targets takes place.

GOING CONCERN

After making enquiries the Board has a reasonable expectation that the Association has adequate resources to continue in operational existence for the foreseeable future. For this reason, it continues to adopt the going concern basis in the financial statements.

STATEMENT OF THE RESPONSIBILITIES OF THE BOARD FOR THE FINANCIAL STATEMENTS

The Industrial and Provident Societies Acts and Registered Social Housing legislation require the Board to prepare financial statements for each financial year which give a true and fair view of the state of affairs of the Association and of the surplus of the Association for that period. In preparing those financial statements the Board has:

- selected suitable policies and then applied them consistently;
- made judgements and estimates that are reasonable and prudent;
- followed applicable accounting standards; and
- prepared the financial statements on the going concern basis.

The Board is responsible for keeping proper accounting records which disclose with reasonable accuracy at any time the financial position of the Association and enable it to ensure that the financial statements comply with the Industrial and Provident Societies Acts 1965 to 1978, paragraph 17 of Schedule I to the Housing Act 1996 and the Accounting Requirements for Registered Social Landlords General Determination 2000. It is also responsible for maintaining an adequate system of internal control and safeguarding the assets of the Association and hence for taking reasonable steps for the prevention and detection of fraud and other irregularities.

The report of the Board was approved on 3 September 2001 and signed on its behalf by:

Janet Harrison
Chairman

10 Environmental and social reports

Companies do not produce annual reports in isolation from their political, social and environmental surroundings. Over the last decade there has been a marked shift in the political climate concerning companies' commitment to environmental and social issues. A company can no longer just concern itself with financial and economic topics; it must also address issues concerning the company's wider role and responsibilities in society.

Background

Many of these social and environmental issues are often partially or fully outside the requirements of legal, accounting and regulatory control. Generally, the regulatory framework of annual reports has tended to ignore issues affecting political, environmental and social concerns but, nevertheless, these topics are often considered to be of vital significance by a large cross-section of society.

The potential environmental consequences arising from a company's trading activities are becoming a major social, economic and political concern for both a company's immediate neighbours and for the wider community. In many countries, and in many sections of the community, public perception and opinion has noticeably shifted towards increased recognition of the importance of green issues. As far as individual firms are concerned, ignoring this green trend has not provided a sound justification or rational basis for long-term corporate growth, or even perhaps ultimate business survival. Yet there are considerable advantages in being perceived by the public as a green company, one being that the public perception of being 'corporately green' can lead to substantial direct and indirect earnings benefits. There are also considerable political and public relations advantages.

Moreover, since the passing of the UK Environmental Protection Act in 1990, there are substantial legal penalties for companies that fail to comply with environmental legislation. This affects not only companies, who can be legally prosecuted for environmental damage in a corporate sense, but also individual directors who, if they are deemed negligent in their duties towards environmental protection, may face considerable personal penalties.

The incorporation of environmental issues into the framework of more conventional corporate reporting systems has been receiving increasing attention. In general terms, the emphasis that companies are attributing to environmental issues tends to differ widely in both breadth and depth. Developments have ranged from informal and rather superficial approaches to highly defined and structured environmental reporting systems.

For a long time environmental issues have often seemed to be a concern of a relatively small minority of more progressively-minded companies. Many of the companies that report upon environmental issues frequently do so on a rather superficial, largely unstructured and highly informal basis. You should try to avoid these errors and misguided approaches.

As regards industry and commerce, concern for environmental issues is frequently viewed as crucially significant because it:

- contributes both directly and indirectly to the quality of business and community life

- contributes both directly and indirectly to business and national economic development

- provides considerable business opportunities in areas such as leisure, tourism and pollution advisory services, and so on

- contributes directly to a more comprehensively-based measure of economic development.

For further information on these direct and indirect benefits, you are advised to read the so-called 'Pearce Report' (1989).

From a public relations perspective alone, it is a foolish company that neglects these issues, which can carry rapid and direct trading implications.

Corporate interest in, and recognition of, environmental issues and concerns have grown especially rapidly during the last five years, owing to changes in society and increasingly explicit pressure from vociferous pressure groups. This developing trend, and the growing emphasis on green issues, can be viewed as more than just mere altruism.

For many of the more progressive companies it is becoming fashionable to produce an environmental and, sometimes, a social report. The UK government is particularly enthusiastic in recommending companies to produce environmental reports. Currently, the publication of such reports is voluntary, but the European Union and the UK government have both indicated that legislation may be introduced if companies fail to publish sufficiently comprehensive environmental reports.

Forms of environmental report

In the absence of substantive legal or professionally supported rules there is no definitive form or content of environmental reports. The nature of their publication is heavily dependent on the judgement of individual companies. Some companies now publish an environmental report separate from their annual report. Other companies include a commentary on their environmental commitment as a subsection of their main annual report. Perhaps the most appropriate course of action is for companies that have a strong commitment to environmental issues to produce a separate report but also to discuss environmental issues more briefly in their main annual reports.

British Airways, for example, refers to the importance of environmental issues in the annual report and then produces another two separate environmental reports. One comprises a comprehensive discussion of complex and intricate environmental issues, and the other is a shortened discussion. These separate reports are freely available, on request, to shareholders or the public.

As a minimum, it is now usually regarded as politically sensitive and astute for companies to discuss their concern for the environment and how environmental protection and enhancement will be achieved. Again, as a minimum, companies should refer to environmental issues in their annual report. Many companies often include a short discussion of such issues in the directors' report. However, if your company does have a commitment to environmental issues, you should include more than a few sentences. Any worthwhile discussion of the topic should be allocated at least a page or two. Anything less may give the impression that your company's interest and commitment is only superficial.

For larger companies, it has now become politically more advisable to consider producing a separate and more detailed environmental report. However, it is not advisable for your company to attempt to produce these detailed reports itself. The numerous technical environmental issues to be addressed call for the advice of environmental consultants. These consultants who can become involved in establishing a comprehensive environmental management scheme in your company and assist in producing a year-end report. Clearly, a commitment to environmental reporting is more than just producing a report of 'good intentions'. Your company may wish to consider formulating environmental issues within its overall corporate objectives. A sound environmental strategy should also be developed and communicated to all levels within the organization.

You are also advised to provide specific quantitative and qualitative information such as: energy sources and usage; material usage; packaging material; waste management and recycling; transportation costs; noise and industrial pollution; environmental contingency and emergency plans, and so on.

Financial and political benefits

Direct benefits

Your commitment to green issues can be viewed on two levels. First, the direct benefits can be significant – for example, many sectors of industry, such as food supermarkets, have identified significantly increased earnings from customers who are given the choice of buying green products. Customers also indicate consumer preference in purchasing environmentally-friendly goods and services. Other financial benefits and cost savings may accrue to organizations that follow energy conservation measures, minimize packaging materials and implement green purchasing policies.

Indirect benefits

On an indirect level, companies can follow green policies for the simple, but fundamental, reason of altruism. Such policies lead to greater earnings benefits arising from an enhanced public perception of the company, conferring on it greater business status, community respect and political standing.

There is also emerging evidence that large institutional investors are taking a more active interest in the nature of the green policies of companies in which they place their investors' funds.

The scale of damage that can result when companies are not permitted to implement green polices can be seen in many countries, but particularly in the US where companies are experiencing massive legal claims for environmental damage. The monumental scale of the potential costs of neglecting environmental protection has been illustrated over the last 20 years by a number of large-scale damages awards against companies for environmental damage. For example the *Exxon Valdez* oil tanker spillage on the Alaskan coast is estimated to have eventually cost the owners over £2 billion. In addition, the Seveso dioxin gas release, which caused both environmental and personal injury, is estimated to have cost several hundreds of millions of pounds in compensation. It is against this background that many companies are now seeking to obtain environmental liability insurance cover. This trend has now become so pronounced that many insurance companies insist, as a condition of insurance, that the company conduct a full environmental audit prior to the granting of cover.

Environmental audits

The European Union is currently supervising an environmental audit throughout member states through the introduction of an Eco-audit Regulation. The adoption of the Regulation has meant that all member states can conduct an environmental audit within the context of a formally recognized scheme. Each participating company in each member state should have its environmental management system subject to independent verification by accredited environmental auditors.

The EU accepts that, at present, greater progress can be made if the Eco-audit is implemented on a voluntary basis. It believes that the option to participate voluntarily will give companies a greater impetus to examine their own environmental performance, encourage them to behave more responsibly and facilitate the flow of more information to the public.

To add authority to your environmental report, consider bringing in outside environmental auditors to examine your environmental management system. Attaching their report to your environmental statement can help you convey a more serious and higher-profile environmental message.

Audit framework

Independent auditors will examine the credibility of the information supplied in the voluntary scheme. To this end, each EU member state will ensure that steps are taken by 'a competent body' to introduce a system for the accreditation of auditors. The Regulation states that professional auditors accredited in one member state will automatically be recognized as being accredited throughout the whole community.

The EU proposals aim to facilitate management control of environmental practices, and assess compliance with companies' policies which would include, *inter alia*, the following features:

- plan of audit activities
- review of companies' environmental protection policies
- assessment of organizational controls, management and equipment
- collection of data and evaluation of overall performance
- identification of areas of improvement
- international reporting procedures to senior management.

The EU Eco-audit Regulation has, however, been subject to criticism. Currently, formal environmental accreditation can only be granted to companies operating in the 'industrial' sector – although the European Commission has noted that this category may be extended at a later date. But a significant criticism of the Regulation is the inclusion of the word 'voluntary'. The EU's initial plans contained no mandatory requirement for firms to conduct an eco-audit. However, the European Commissioner for the Environment has announced that, if the eco-audit is not taken up by a significant number of firms, then mandatory measures might be introduced.

Eco-audits in practice

During an environmental audit, the following areas (although they are not exhaustive) can be examined and reported upon in your company:

- relevant data on material and energy usage
- compliance with EU and national environmental standards
- significant incidents and events that have occurred and the nature and quantity of complaints received
- review of policy and management systems relating to:
  - control, monitoring and reduction of pollution discharge
  - other environmental nuisances

- energy choice and reduction in energy levels achieved
- raw material choice and type of transportation methods used
- waste transportation, elimination and recycling
- product planning, examining design, packaging and transportation
- staff training and prevention of accidents
- external information.

Environmental policy

Your company should formulate, and also publish, a comprehensive environmental policy. There are many different approaches that may be adopted but, in the pursuit of environmental reporting excellence, you should undertake some or all of the following actions:

- Develop and publish an environmental plan.
- Prepare an action plan.
- Organize and staff the programme.
- Allocate adequate resources.
- Invest in environmental science and technology.
- Educate and train, assess, monitor, audit and report.
- Monitor the evolution of the green agenda.
- Contribute to environmental programmes.
- Build bridges between various interest groups.

Suggested topics for inclusion

It may be feasible, at the minimum, to incorporate your company's environmental reporting commitment into the annual report under the following headings:

- An environmental policy: a statement and explanation.

- Problems and threats: any major problems and threats to the organization and to society that might give rise to a concern for environmental problems.

- Pollution control: any measures introduced to prevent, restrict or eliminate present and potential pollution damage.

- Environment report: the preparation and publication of an environmental report that is subject to independent audit.

Firms wishing to establish an environmental policy can refer to and draw heavily on the so-called Valdez Principles. In the aftermath of the *Exxon Valdez* oil tanker spillage, a large group of American investors established a set of environmental principles that covered, *inter alia*: the protection of the biosphere; the sustainable use of natural resources; conservation measures concerning energy and waste; the manufacture of safe products and services; compensation for environmental damage; the establishment of environmental managers and directors; and the provision of details in an annual environmental audited report.

Extent and quality of information

Some organizations tend to be highly selective, emphasizing only positive and favourable aspects, whereas other firms will provide detailed quantitative information on activities that have both positive and negative implications. Nevertheless, in the UK at present, the degree to which companies have introduced methods of environmental accounting is still rather variable, both in the extent of the provision and in its quality.

A few companies produce a separate report as a supplement to their main financial statements, but the majority simply produce a few pages – or even a couple of paragraphs – as part of their annual report. Over the last few years many larger companies have begun to publish an increasing amount of environmental information, although the published results are generally still of a low quality and are frequently incomplete. These are commonly characterized by a certain degree of superficiality and lack of structure rather than any detailed quantitative and meaningful information (see Appendix 10.1 at the end of this chapter).

Social and ethical reporting

During the last few years a number of the larger 'blue-chip' listed companies in particular have been including more detailed sections in their annual reports concerning social and ethical reporting issues. Like environmental reporting, this area is becoming increasingly important. Listed companies, in particular, should certainly consider including at least some reference to social and ethical matters in their annual report.

Social and ethical reporting will frequently include reporting on the impact of a company's operations on society generally. Social reporting moves away from the conventional annual report style, which is overwhelmingly based on reporting economic and financial activity, in that it discusses the importance of people generally and the impact of trading activity on society. This social concept can be extended to incorporate a wider discussion of ethical reporting.

Most companies that make reference to social and ethical reporting do so in the form of a section in their main annual reports, perhaps entitled 'Corporate Social Responsibility'. In this section you might wish to discuss such issues as: the ethical basis of your company's trading practices; sourcing of raw materials; investment in personnel; anti-discrimination policies; recruitment policies; health and safety topics; community involvement; product safety; and policies towards disadvantaged staff and customers.

A small minority of companies produce separate corporate social responsibility reports. However, currently, there is no legal or professional requirement to provide a social, ethical or environmental report (see Appendix 10.2).

Conclusion: the future

Many UK companies completely dismiss the concept of environmental reporting and environmental auditing as a passing political fashion. But this is unwise – at least in the case of listed and other large companies. It is best to go with the political flow and avoid antagonizing political or public opinion. At least for the time being, environmental reporting is a relevant issue.

If you have not ventured into the area of environmental reporting, then perhaps now is the time. You do not necessarily have to begin with a detailed and separate environmental report but at least you can consider devoting, at least initially, a few paragraphs or even a few pages to the topic. If you are contemplating introducing a more widespread system of environmental reporting you would be well advised to bring in a specialist firm of environmental consultants. Environmental reporting can benefit substantially from high-quality expertise – it is not a job for amateurs.

Appendix 10.1: Example of an environmental report

The extract from the 2001 environmental report on the following pages is reproduced by kind permission of British Airways plc.

Foreword

We have reported publicly on British Airways environmental performance for over 10 years and the consistently high standard of our reporting was recognised last year by the Association of Chartered Certified Accountants.

In previous years we have supported the concept of sustainable development and our views are developed in this report. In the last year we have made further public commitment through our adoption of the Global Sullivan Principles for corporate social responsibility. We have supported the new noise stringency standard proposed by ICAO and have led the industry in voluntary initiatives to reduce aircraft noise. We have actively promoted innovative solutions to environmental problems such as sponsoring work by the UK's Institute of Public Policy Research on emissions trading. Most recently we have signed as supporters of the Marine Stewardship Council.

We have now reported on environmental performance for over 10 years. The consistently high standard of our reporting was recognised last year by the Association of Chartered Certified Accountants. However, if we are going to continue to be a leader in the travel industry, we recognise that we must build on our record of improvement in our economic, social and environmental performance.

This means listening to our staff, our customers and other stakeholder groups. Our code of business conduct and supporting policies do not belong on the shelf. They must be incorporated into the business approach of the company. Last year we had three external groups look at the way we manage our social and environmental impacts. As a result we are now developing an integrated system for managing such issues, at the heart of which will be a revamped Environment and Social Council reporting through our executive Leadership Team to the Board on a regular basis. The Council will be charged with identifying targets and performance indicators for cross-functional issues, selected on the basis of agreed priority. In this way we hope to develop further our actions on sustainability issues.

Over the 10 years of reporting we have seen significant advances in major indicators of environmental performance. The overall noise generated by our fleet at landings and take-offs has decreased substantially despite a substantial increase in passengers carried. This has resulted from continuous and massive investment, more than $1 billion in the last year, in new aircraft which has reduced the average age of our fleet by 2 years. Our fuel efficiency in terms of accepted parameters has also improved over this period. Admittedly our overall emissions of engine exhaust gases have increased but at a lower rate than growth in overall passenger or tonne kilometres. The greater efficiency of our new aircraft and our strategy of concentrating on our core business have led to a decrease in overall carbon dioxide emissions for the last two years. Our community and social programmes have also shown significant advances. In that time we have improved our relations with our trade union partners. In the last 7 years our passengers have donated, through our on-board and related collections, over £12.5 million which is directed to UNICEF for projects helping children around the world. In 10 years our Assisting Conservation programme has provided travel assistance to more than 2,000 individuals working on conservation and environmental management projects around the world. In the last 18 months more than 10,000 students have passed through our Community Learning Centre.

These are examples of the ways in which we are moving forward. Our reports show that we do not move forward every year in every area. However, the overall trend is one of improvement and one that we are determined to sustain.

As CEO I must address short-term financial issues. Equally, however, we are in business for the long-term. Perhaps our most critical long-term issue is airport capacity, particularly in the south east of the UK. We are confident that the Government will give the green light for Terminal 5 at Heathrow later this year. Beyond that, the Government faces vital decisions on further airport capacity. We will work with the relevant parties to implement such decisions in a responsible way.

Next year will see the important Rio+10 World Summit on Sustainable Development in Johannesburg. Some may feel that not much has happened in 10 years. However, in aviation there has been growing recognition of the delicate balance between the benefits that aviation generates by bringing people together for social, cultural, economic and political interchange and any adverse environmental and social impacts. Our business faces a formidable challenge to make the most of limited capacity. We will address concerns such as climate change by building on our drive for efficiency and through innovative approaches such as trading in emissions of carbon dioxide, the principal greenhouse gas. We will continue to identify ways to avoid damage to the environment and make a full contribution to the development of an environmentally sustainable society.

Rod Eddington

Rod Eddington
Chief Executive

British Airways today

British Airways is the world's biggest international airline, carrying more passengers from one country to another than any of its competitors.

Our worldwide route network covers some 268 destinations in 97 countries, with two main operating bases at London's two principal airports, Heathrow (the world's biggest international airport) and Gatwick. British Airways is a co-founder of the **one**world alliance, which took off in February 1999. Fellow members now are Ireland's Aer Lingus, American Airlines, Cathay Pacific (of Hong Kong), Finnair, LanChile, Spain's Iberia and Australia's Qantas.

British Airways owns:

- 100% of Brymon.
- 100% of City Flyer.
- 100% of Deutsche BA.
- 25% of Qantas.
- 9% of Iberia.
- 18.3% of Comair *(its franchise partner in South Africa).*
- Additionally, 100% of British Regional Airlines (BRAL) has recently been acquired.

British Airways franchise family includes British Regional Airlines, British Mediterranean, GBAirways, Loganair, Maersk Air UK, based in the UK, Sun Air of Denmark, National Jet Italia and Comair of South Africa.

British Airways also code-shares with a number of other airlines – including Air Mauritius, America West, Crossair of Switzerland, Middle East-based Emirates, Malev of Hungary, and Poland's LOT.

Through **one**world and its other alliances, British Airways can offer passengers flights to some 566 scheduled destinations in more than 135 countries worldwide.

Key Group Statistics

Measure	1999–00	2000–01	Change
Turnover (£m)	8,940	9,278	up 3.7%
Employees	65,157	62,175	down 4.6%
Number of shareholders (as 17 May 2000)	264,191	265,107	up 0.3%
Passengers (000)	46,578	44,462	down 4.5%
Cargo (000 tonnes)*	897	914	up 1.8%
Overall load factor (%)*	66.6	67.4	up 1.2 points
Available Tonne Kilometres (ATKs) (m)	25,840	25,196	down 2.4%
Revenue Tonne Kilometres (RTKs) (m)	17,215	16,987	down 1.3%
Revenue Passenger Kilometres (RPKs) (m)	127,425	123,197	down 3.3%

Notes: Group statistics do not include those of associated undertakings (Qantas Airways, Comair and Iberia) and franchises (British Mediterranean Airways, British Regional Airlines, GB Airways, Maersk Air, Loganair and Sun Air (Scandinavia)).
* Mainline scheduled services include those operated by British Airways Plc, British Airways (European Operations at Gatwick) Ltd and Brymon Airways Ltd.

Sustainable development and corporate responsibility

"A better quality of life, now and for generations to come".

British Airways subscribes to the UK Government's definition of sustainable development "a better quality of life, now and for generations to come". We believe that this means taking into account the environmental and social impact of our activities as well as looking at their economic costs and benefits. Underpinning all interpretations of sustainability is the view that we should be aiming to leave our natural and social environment in a better condition and that we should avoid actions which could destabilise the physical and social systems on which we all depend.

We can only properly assess the sustainability of aviation by looking at its environmental impacts in relation to the net economic and social benefits it brings. We support the view that sustainability will involve ownership at all levels, government and individuals as well as in organisations. Business is important but no one organisation, business, government or other, can be sustainable on its own. This is particularly relevant for aviation. By bringing people together for social, cultural, political and business reasons, aviation is central to the global communication network. Thus, aviation has an important part to play in a sustainable society.

It is difficult to predict how society will transform and exactly what part aviation will play. Technological innovation will be one critical area for aviation, in order to overcome the challenge of climate change impact which our industry must face. We have outlined some possible ideas towards a solution in the section on climate change in this report. Of course we can't act alone to solve these issues but our company can offer some leadership for others within and outside our business sector to begin to work towards a more sustainable society. It is no coincidence that many issues covered in this report, in particular climate change, featured prominently in the recent UK Government consultation paper on the 'Future of Aviation'.

What we report here is not grounds for complacency but does give us confidence, particularly when we look back over 10 years of reporting on environmental performance. We are now moving into a wider area of transparency covering environmental, economic and social performance. There are clear hallmarks of a business which is properly contributing to a sustainable society:

- Robust environmental and social policies, reducing/minimising adverse impacts and promoting positive outcomes.
- Actions consistent with these policies.
- Active dialogue with stakeholders, such as Non Governmental Organisations and public authorities, which informs these policies.
- Promoting a positive social impact in the countries or localities in which it operates.
- Reporting in a clear and transparent way on progress.
- Vigilance to identify new significant issues.
- Demonstrating the economic and social benefits which flow from its activities, against which stakeholders can evaluate its contribution to a sustainable society.

An increasing proportion of corporate value is locked in reputation and worth to all stakeholders, including employees, customers, the communities in which we operate, as well as shareholders.

British Airways is no exception and we must address and anticipate these components of the sustainability agenda. Our Code of Conduct and supporting policies are integrated into our business strategy. Alongside the implementation of this strategy, we recognise that external stakeholders can exert great influence over the bottom line.

Aviation will only prosper if it pays attention to the relevant needs of stakeholders. Some of these groups have competing interests which require an appropriate balance and new issues are constantly appearing as a trap for the unwary. What aviation can provide, in part, and facilitate as an essential component of the global communication network, is creation of wealth necessary for education, health and welfare, which, in turn, prime a virtuous cycle leading to an overall more sustainable society.

1.0

To communicate and implement our relevant policies with key stakeholders and to demonstrate continuous improvement in our performance.

From areas where we can improve – to the progress that we have made.

Corporate management

Last year's report included comments from SustainAbility and our report verifiers CSR network. The following areas were amongst those identified for improvement:

- Further top level commitment to social and environmental issues.
- Over reliance on the Sustainable Business Unit.
- Management of cross functional issues.
- No overall documented commitment.
- Improve reputational enhancement.

In August 2000 a corporate review of compliance with legal requirements in safety, security and environment was completed. This review was carried out by an external legal expert.

The principal recommendations relating to the environment noted that a more formal Environmental Management System was being developed and that changes are being made to the Environment and Social Council.

It stated that "success will depend ultimately on clear, documented commitment from the Leadership Team".

In line with these reviews, a programme was accepted by the Leadership Team and Board which includes:

- Regular reporting to the Leadership Team on environmental and social issues – one such review has been made.
- Revision of the role of the Environmental and Social Council to identify priorities and thus focus on a limited number of cross functional issues – this role has been accepted by the Council.
- The Code of Conduct has been widely communicated, and with supporting policies, adopted as part of the overall business strategy.
- Ongoing discussions with key departments to identify issues and appropriate responsibilities.

Social and environmental management system

Consultants WSP have been engaged to assist in the design and implementation of this system. British Airways has committed to participate in the Sigma initiative, a multi stakeholder approach to managing sustainability issues in a corporate context.

Our developing system is based on the departmental organisation of British Airways. This is more consistent with the airline's overall management than a site based system. The system will be compatible with current formal environmental and social standards ISO 14001, AA 1000 and SA 8000. Business units and partners are encouraged to adopt such systems. For example, during the year our business centre at Waterside and management of Harmondsworth Moor parkland were certified to ISO 14001.

Last years actions

Last year we identified 6 key action points:

- Review of departmental objectives – a wide range of discussions relating to specific objectives have been held and many objectives implemented.
- Feedback from internal and external stakeholders – we have a wide range of formal and informal networks and contacts.
- Workshops with different teams – these have been held on various aspects of sustainability with departments such as Sales, Procurement and Strategy, as well as across departments.
- Review of progress at the Environment and Social Council – the Council met twice during the year.
- Targets – many environmental and social targets are set in the course of normal business. Some of these are reflected in the indicators in this report.
- A representative of the British Airways Trade Union Council, Bob Kirk, has been appointed to the Environment and Social Council and has attended one review at a meeting of the Leadership Team.

Departments

The two largest departments in British Airways, Customer Services and Operations (CS&Ops), and Engineering have both made significant changes. CS&Ops has established a new unit with responsibility for social and environmental issues and will have two supporting staff. Engineering is working to install a management system compatible with the corporate system. There are also active groups within departments such as Procurement, Property and British Airways Holidays.

Through our People department, our revised Code of Conduct and our policy on environmental and social issues are now included in all induction training programmes.

The Sustainable Business Unit

The aim of the Sustainable Business Unit is the integration of environmental and social considerations into the everyday business of British Airways.

The unit is responsible for policy on environmental and community relations matters and acts as a focus for the programmes within these areas. It is also charged with monitoring and reporting on performance across the company on environmental and social issues.

There are 16 British Airways positions within the unit, supported by contract staff, external consultants and internal British Airways staff on assignment from other departments. The overall expenditure in 2000–2001 was £1.8 million including corporate charitable donations, the Community Learning Centre and outreach programmes such as Assisting Conservation and Tourism for Tomorrow.

Students practising language skills at the Community Learning Centre.

Improving performance

We recognise that there are three main ways of improving our social and environmental performance:

- Regulation – compliance is our baseline.
- Market options – we are actively examining options such as emissions trading.
- Voluntary initiatives.

We believe that any measures taken must satisfy 3 basic criteria:

- Technically feasible.
- Environmentally beneficial.
- Economically reasonable.

Future needs of aviation

During the last year the provision of airport capacity has surfaced as a critical issue for aviation, in particular in the UK. There is a clear need to find a sustainable balance between increased capacity and environmental concerns. This has featured in our response to consultation documents including the British Airways input to government consultation on 'The Future of Aviation'. We believe that the Gatwick Airport Development Strategy provides a good indicator of the way ahead. The commitment of those involved from the industry, local government and consultative bodies has achieved an effective and timely agreement that could provide a model for future planning at airports in the UK.

External benchmarking

British Airways continues to be listed in the Dow Jones Sustainability Index.

The airline was ranked 13th of FTSE companies, and top of transport companies, in the 2000 Business in the Community survey – Index of Corporate Environmental Engagement.

British Airways was one of two UK companies recognised in the 2000 WorldAware Business awards, with special recognition of our Assisting Conservation Programme. We also received a Community and Conservation Award from the British Trust for Ornithology for work, with staff and residents, to monitor birds and conservation action in Harmondsworth Moor parkland at Waterside.

Compliance

There were no known legal proceedings against British Airways for environmental offences.

Reporting

With a network covering more than 200 destinations, we are not yet in a position to cover all of our activities at all relevant locations. This improves year by year; we are confident, however, that the report provides an accurate review of our overall performance.

3.2

Employees who feel respected, well managed, understood and able to do their best.

From health and safety performance and employee satisfaction levels – to safety training and employee relations.

Employee satisfaction

It is generally accepted that there is a clear link between customer satisfaction and employee motivation. It is important to our business therefore that employee motivation is measured on a regular basis. British Airways has run an employee opinion survey for all staff in 1999 and 2000. The questions are based on issues that matter to our staff.

The Employee Opinion Survey is designed with and implemented by an independent, external consultant. Results are provided at a high (company-wide) and low (e.g. departmental) level. Managers throughout the company set action plans and targets for the issues specific to their area.

Results

In 2000, employees were asked to rate items on both importance and satisfaction. The results showed a downturn in satisfaction across most topic areas of the survey. These results were taken extremely seriously, the Board and Trade Unions were briefed as the results were made available. The results were published in British Airways News and face to face briefings happened across the business.

The tough year in 1999-2000, that was experienced in the business, is reflected in the survey results. There were some areas that showed improvements but on the whole satisfaction declined. This was, of course, a major concern and significant effort has been spent in listening to employees. Over 500 workshops were held to explore further what was affecting motivation.

Employee Opinion Survey results summary for the whole of British Airways

	1999 Average satisfaction score	2000 Average satisfaction score
1. Current job in British Airways	4.2	4.0
2. Your work team	4.3	4.2
3. The way you are managed by your immediate manager	3.8	3.7
4. The way senior managers manage your department	3.2	3.1
5. The way Directors manage British Airways	3.1	2.7
6. Your training, development, pay and benefits	3.5	3.4
7. Customer satisfaction	3.5	3.4

Source: British Airways Employee Opinion Survey, 2000
Note: Satisfaction scored from 1 (extremely dissatisfied) to 6 (extremely satisfied)

Actions and commitments

The targets set from the survey were not achieved in 2000:

- Local action plans have since been developed with involvement of staff across the business. Each department regularly reviews and communicates its progress and the Directors and the Trades Unions meet to discuss actions.
- The Directors have set and communicated their commitment to:
  - Focus on key customer service issues that staff have highlighted as being critical.
  - Communicate more frequently and in greater depth.
- The Directors bonus scheme for 2000-2001 will be based on employee and customer satisfaction and operational performance, as well as financial performance.

Employee relations

In a company of over 60,000 people, relationships are crucial, and inevitably complex. British Airways is committed to creating an effective industrial relations environment at all levels of the business. We have been working with managers and Trade Union representatives to devise a strategy for 21st century industrial relations.

There is continued commitment to learning, and a range of education programmes are run jointly with the Trade Unions. For example, a one day introduction to industrial relations for all new managers, business awareness for Trade Unions representatives, and joint workshops to determine appropriate behaviours.

Approximately 70% of the British Airways workforce in the United Kingdom are Trade Union members. The Unions recognised at British Airways in the UK are:

- AEEU & MSF – Amalgamated Electrical and Engineering Union (including CC89 – Cabin Crew 89) & Manufacturing Science Finance Union.
- BALPA – British Airlines Pilots Association.
- GMB – General Municipal Boilermakers Union.
- T&G – Transport and General Workers Union (including BASSA – British Airlines Stewards & Stewardesses Association 2000).

The relationships we have with our Trade Union colleagues are developed

Employee at work.

3.2

via a network of negotiating and consultative opportunities including the European Works Council. This network ensures information and problem solving is quick, efficient and provides for active involvement at all levels.

Putting People First
Open to all British Airways staff across the network, this was a one day programme which gave everyone in the company the opportunity to learn about and discuss key business issues. The delegates also had the opportunity to ask questions of the CEO or one of the Leadership team. 15,000 delegates took part in the programme.

British Airways Trade Union Council (BATUC)
This monthly consultative committee at which key senior Trade Union representatives, from across the airline, meet with the CEO and other directors. BATUC provides an opportunity for linkage and consistency across the 6 National Sectional Panels. It also considers specific business issues and their resolution.

Employment Policy Consultative Committee
The Employment Policy Consultative Committee is responsible for ensuring all British Airways policies comply with UK legislation.

British Airways prides itself on caring for its employees and to this end continues to formulate policies which offer enhanced benefits and are highly valued by employees.

Parental leave
Although the new parental leave provisions give fathers scope to take unpaid leave at the birth of their child, many companies already offer some provision for paid or unpaid leave within their 'paternity' policies.

British Airways offers employees with one year's service at the time of the birth of their child five days paid paternity leave. We also offer up to five days paid time off for staff with dependants in the event of an emergency such as a dependant being taken ill. Both of these provisions go beyond what legislation currently dictates.

Change to Gatwick operations
British Airways worked closely with the Trade Unions in preparing the announcement of change to our Gatwick Operations including the consolidation of City Flyer Express into the mainline business. Although the difficult message included job losses, the collective work combined with excellent communication ensured that the news was understood and accepted.

Trade Union recognition was granted during the year to two wholly-owned subsidiary companies, Brymon and City Flyer Express.

Drug and alcohol testing
In October last year, British Airways announced plans to introduce a drug and alcohol testing programme, the first to be introduced by a major European airline. A working group has been set up to develop the details of the programme, in consultation with the trade unions.

The airline has very clear policies on drug and alcohol use which it believes the vast majority of its staff adhere to rigidly. For flying staff the rules are very specific. However, it has been looking for some time at the successful implementation of testing programmes in other industries, in particular the railway and chemical sectors and believes this approach is the right way forward.

Diversity

It is our policy to promote equality of opportunity regardless of gender, marital status, sexual orientation, race, colour, nationality, ethnic or national origins, disability, religious or political affiliation. Dignity at work and mutual respect are already incorporated in our working practices and the way we behave towards each other at work.

We have appointed a team of 26 Equal Opportunities and Diversity Champions. Their role is to act as the focal point for issues within their department and to provide departmental action plans. They meet regularly to share information and initiatives, and to create, review and amend policies.

We have recently introduced family-friendly policies, including parental leave, time-off-for-dependants, and paternity leave.

Since 1998 nearly 1,500 employees have attended the Equal Opportunities and Diversity workshops. More than 5,000 staff will complete the programme over the next 18 months. These workshops are now mandatory for all people managers. We have also started a regular communication programme to all employees regarding equal opportunities issues.

In 2001, the Chief Executive committed the airline to the Commission for Racial Equality's Leadership Challenge. British Airways has publicly committed to put racial equality issues high on the

British Airways currently employs 119 female pilots and 3,060 male pilots

agenda and to steer the development of programmes of practical action that will help prevent discrimination and unequal participation.

This year British Airways has successfully secured the 2-tick 'positive-about-disability' symbol. This means we have agreed to meet commitments regarding the employment, retention, training and care of disabled employees. The airline has also recently set up a Disability Working Group which meets regularly to take responsibility for the improvement and understanding of disability issues within British Airways and to ensure corrective action is taken.

The fact remains that women are still under-represented in higher levels of management and we are failing to attract sufficient applicants from ethnic minorities into our Graduate Management Training Programme. To meet these challenges the Equal Opportunities team has been strengthened and allocated additional resources for the coming year.

Health and safety performance

Lost Time Injuries

A Lost Time Injury (LTI) is classified as one which results in the employee having one or more days off work through injury. This rate is used as an indicator of performance by many industries and enables us to benchmark against other companies worldwide.

The past 5 years has seen an increase in the level of reporting and we see this rise as a positive feature. Since the last report our incident reporting system has been updated and, as a result, a number of new LTIs have come to light. This is reflected in the fact that our reported LTIs for 1998-99 and 1999-00 have increased over those reported last year. The last two years have seen a steep decline in LTI rates and we are still on target to reach our goal of 0.23 LTIs per 100,000 man-hours worked by the end of 2002.

Over the last 12 months we have ensured that the issues contained in two Health and Safety Executive Improvement Notices served on British Airways Engineering have been comprehensively addressed and lessons learnt are being spread to all areas of the business. We have completed the development of an Intranet package to facilitate the management and implementation of general workplace and manual handling risk assessments. This package is now being rolled out across all business groups within the company.

Risk Levels

All incidents reported are assessed for their potential severity and allocated a risk level. We operate a system of 5 risk levels from Severe to Minimal. A 'Severe' incident would be one in which we believed there was the potential for a fatality or serious injury combined with a high likelihood of the event occurring again, whilst a 'Minimal' incident would have little or no potential to cause injury and be unlikely to re-occur. Between these two extremes we have a further three categories based on judgements around these two factors.

Incident reporting – risk levels

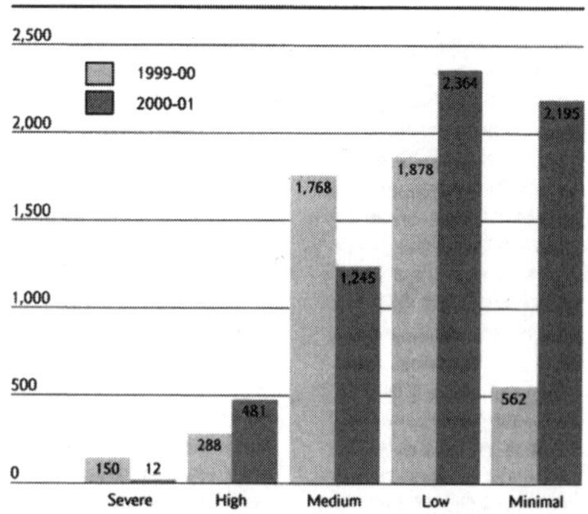

Our chart shows the number of incidents reported in each category over the last twelve months. The vast majority of incidents fall into the lower risk categories. Within the 'high' category the major cause is manual handling where there is the risk of a major injury. Few of these incidents resulted in injury; however, we have used this topic as a focus for our internal training.

Safety Training

In 1999 we launched a new programme of safety training aimed at all managers and supervisors. This training is building on a series of 9 CDROMs covering health and safety, developed internally. Two courses have been developed – one covering the initial requirements for scene preservation and evidence gathering and the second covering questioning and interviewing skills.

4.2

To minimise fuel and energy consumption and the associated emissions of exhaust gases.

From options for emissions trading – to fuel jettisoning and ground emissions.

British Airways

Global emissions and fuel efficiency

Our overall emissions of CO_2 have decreased for the second successive year. This has resulted from the company business strategy of reducing its overall operations, allied to the continued investment in new aircraft with better environmental performance. Our overall fuel efficiency increased by 4% and we continue to be in line to achieve our target of 30% improvement by 2010.

Following the setting of our target, IATA member airlines, including British Airways, have adopted a goal of achieving 10% improvement over the period 2000-2010. The Association of European Airlines has estimated that the AEA fleet will be 22-24% more efficient in 2012 than in 1990. The AEA estimate does not, unlike our target, allow for improvements in air traffic systems.

Fuel jettisoning

It is occasionally necessary to jettison fuel in order to reduce weight of some longhaul aircraft in emergency situations to below the legal safe maximum weight for landing. Operational procedures require that, whenever possible, this is done at a height and location where there will be no impact at ground level, often in areas specifically prescribed for this purpose. Incidents of fuel jettisoning decreased from 40 to 28 with a 39% decrease in the recorded fuel discharged at 837 tonnes. As in past years, in no case was any fuel jettisoned close to an airport and there were no reports of any fuel reaching the ground.

Ground energy consumption – Climate Change Levy

While the vast bulk of the emissions come from aircraft, the airline consumes significant amounts of energy on the ground. British Airways is liable to the Climate Change Levy, which came into effect in April 2001, for relevant energy consumption in our ground facilities. Although our record in improving ground energy consumption is outstanding, our Property department will use this as an incentive to take further initiatives over the next year.

Ground emissions

British Airways is sponsoring development of a model for estimating aircraft contributions to local air quality. Work is concentrating on Heathrow where the programme is being developed in consultation with a multi stakeholder group including local authorities, BAA, CAA, DETR and academic experts. In advance of completion of this work our best, conservative, estimate of the contribution from aircraft is substantially less than that suggested by published inventories, such as that of BAA Heathrow. Generally, such inventories have been based on emissions up to 3,000 feet; however, there is increasing evidence that a large part of such emissions has no impact on local air quality.

APUs

As with noise, APUs are a source of emissions on the ground. We have reduced emissions beyond the 10,000 tonnes reduction of carbon dioxide estimated last year. These reductions have been achieved through reducing the running time of APUs and have been established through a series of 6 audits. However, more accurate estimation depends on installation of the tracking system mentioned in the noise section.

Aviation and Climate change

International

Under the Kyoto Protocol (an international agreement on reducing greenhouse gas emissions), ICAO was charged with developing mechanisms for reducing or limiting emissions from aviation. Under Kyoto, domestic emissions from aircraft, accounting for close to 50% of the total, were allocated to relevant national inventories. Many individual countries, including the UK, have agreed to set targets for reduction in CO_2 emissions within the inventories. Allocation of international aviation emissions has not yet been decided. The protocol directed the parties to work through ICAO to reduce or limit emissions from aviation.

Aircraft painting

Verification statement

Objectives

csr network was commissioned by British Airways to conduct an independent verification of the social and environmental information included in the 2001 Social and Environmental Report, which has also been published on its corporate internet site. The objectives were to verify claims and review the systems for the management of social and environmental issues and collection of data. We were also asked to comment on the completeness of the reporting and on the company's social and environmental programme.

Responsibilities of British Airways and the verifiers

British Airways has sole responsibility for preparation of the Social and Environmental Report. This statement represents our independent opinion. We were not involved in the preparation of any part of the report and have no other contract with British Airways.

Method and scope

The verification process was conducted through meetings at British Airways premises at Heathrow, London, with managers responsible for the areas of information and data on which the report was based. At these meetings, specific claims were discussed and substantiated, and data checked. The assessment of performance data was confined to air emissions, fuel efficiency, energy, waste, employee relations, and charitable donations. We also reviewed the system for collection of data presented in the report, under these headings. We did not have the opportunity to witness any stakeholder dialogue.

The process was linked to a broader review of the overall arrangements for social and environmental governance and related management systems, in particular: i) the response to last year's compliance review, (ii) development of a sustainability management system, and (iii) social and environmental issues of strategic importance.

Opinion

Accuracy and completeness

For the air emissions, fuel efficiency, energy, waste, employee relations, and charitable donations report sections, we have found the data collection systems to be robust and that the underlying trends are substantially correct. However, the report does not present a complete account of the social and environmental performance of British Airways. We welcome the commitment to a wider scope for future reports, including further reporting on non UK social issues, and other areas where reporting is currently limited such as suppliers and communities close to Heathrow and Gatwick.

In our environmental verification statement last year, our main concern in the area of completeness related to a lack of clarity regarding the provenance of data. This concern remains as the coverage of data for wholly owned subsidiaries is variable, for example in the areas of fuel consumption and efficiency. It is not currently clear how reporting priorities have been determined. Linked to this issue, is the absence of a clear set of objectives and targets to support progress towards an overall vision for sustainability.

Recommendations for future British Airways reporting

Reporting itself can be a catalyst for change, and British Airways should use this report to reflect on how reporting priorities should be identified. We recommend that further social performance indicators, associated targets and benchmarks be developed, including those derived from consultation. The results of this work should then be discussed with the parts of the organisation from which key data and information will be provided. This report is to be commended for consideration of some real issues (eg deep vein thrombosis and immigration). Future reports need to make clear how stakeholders and their concerns will be systematically covered over time.

Recommendations for British Airways Social and Environmental Programme

British Airways faces a significant challenge if it is to integrate corporate social, environmental and economic sustainability into its business processes, in partnership with its stakeholders. The Leadership Team has yet to issue a clear and documented commitment towards social and environmental issues, or to develop a mechanism by which it is encouraged to consider issues of long term strategic importance to the company.

Progress on development of a sustainability management system has been slow. The Sustainable Business Unit can only make progress if accountability and responsibility for integrated management of social and environmental issues is accepted by key business departments.

British Airways has acknowledged the importance of business principles through the development of its Code of Conduct. For the Code to succeed however, wide acceptance and ownership will need to be developed through further careful communication. We welcome the study of the implementation of the Code in Nigeria as a positive step towards greater understanding of the complex social issues surrounding the company's operations in an overseas context. Priorities for social and environmental issues are currently set by different teams and departments in the absence of an overall framework of stakeholder consultation. It is recommended that a 'stakeholder panel' be created comprising representatives from each of British Airways key stakeholder groups. This would provide an important mechanism for gathering information about stakeholder expectations, demands and values.

In last year's statement, we made recommendations concerning: the process for establishing goals, performance measures and objectives and targets; definition of a limited number of Key Performance Measures for regular performance reporting; and the processes for management of issues that arise through cross departmental activities. Whilst the role of the Environmental and Social Council has been revised, there is little other evidence that any action in response to these recommendations has been taken.

csr network ltd

Mark Line – Director

Jon Woodhead – Director

Deborah Seamark – Associate
Adrian Henriques – Associate

UK June 2001
www.csrnetwork.com

Appendix 10.2: Example of a 'corporate social responsibility' section of an annual report

The extract on corporate social responsibility issues shown on the following pages is from AstraZeneca's 2001 annual report and is reproduced by kind permission of AstraZeneca plc.

Corporate Social Responsibility

With a global business comes global responsibility and this means ensuring consistently high standards in the three areas of sustainable development: environmental, social and economic. Earning and maintaining the trust and confidence of shareholders and society in general is essential to our continued success.

We aim to set, promote and maintain high standards of corporate social responsibility (CSR) worldwide, which will, at a minimum, ensure that AstraZeneca meets national and international regulations. At the heart of our responsible approach is our CSR policy, which is being overseen by Board member Dame Bridget Ogilvie. The policy will be widely communicated within the Company during 2002 to ensure consistent and appropriate behaviour worldwide. In addition, key corporate policies, such as the AstraZeneca Code of Conduct and Safety, Health and Environment policy, support our commitment. We do not consider CSR to be an optional activity – it is an integral part of all that we do and we are determined that we will continue to be a company that is welcomed as a valued member of the global community.

As part of our integrated approach to CSR, AstraZeneca has invested $10 million in new laboratories in Bangalore, India, which will focus on the discovery and development of a new treatment for tuberculosis (TB). TB is the single largest cause of adult death from infectious disease in the world.

In 2001, AstraZeneca was included in the FTSE4Good Index and the Dow Jones Sustainability Index following independent assessment of our approach to CSR.

At the World Economic Forum in January 2002, AstraZeneca made a commitment to the Global Health Initiative which focuses on the role that businesses can play in reducing diseases which contribute to global poverty and hold back economic development.

Further information about our CSR commitment, policies and performance is published each year in a separate report and is available on our website: www.astrazeneca.com

Safety, Health and Environment (SHE)
At the core of our CSR agenda is our commitment to good safety, health and environmental performance. Backed by a clear policy and set of standards, we are beginning to see the benefits from the implementation of our new SHE related management systems. During 2001 much work was done to obtain regular reporting of relevant SHE statistics and to progress to full implementation of our SHE standards.

Following the annual review of SHE at the end of 2000, the Board set five new SHE objectives:

Objective 1 To improve the safety, health and wellbeing of all our employees by introducing behaviour-based programmes at all locations before 1 July 2002;

Objective 2 To have no accidents or incidents and to minimise our environmental impact. During 2001 we will identify the key areas where improvement is a priority and the most useful indicators to measure our performance. Progress against these key performance indicators will be published from 2002 onwards;

Objective 3 To publish information about our SHE performance using the internationally recognised guidelines produced by the Global Reporting Initiative;

Objective 4 To conduct auditing as an essential part of continuous improvement. We began a global SHE management audit programme in April 2001 and programmes for local SHE audits were in place at all locations by the end of 2001; and

Objective 5 To achieve a reduction in the growth of carbon dioxide emissions from our facilities by 2005 – this will be by an amount equivalent to 20% of 1998 emissions.

Our SHE management audit programme is now fully operational. The objective of this programme is both to ensure that all facilities are operating to a consistent standard and to seek opportunities to share best practice and learning across AstraZeneca.

The annual review of SHE at the end of 2001 involved all facilities reporting their current performance, any significant SHE issues and plans for future improvement. This review found that there are currently no significant liabilities or areas of non-compliance but identified a number of areas where improvements are necessary to ensure that performance is maintained and emerging issues are properly resourced.

The demands made upon our industry to deliver improved environmental performance together with greater openness are increasing. We are therefore developing a strategy for the future that we expect will allow us to meet these challenges effectively. The major areas under consideration are the change in culture necessary for full engagement of all our people, improvement in our systems of risk recognition and assessment, and enhancing the provision of relevant information to all our stakeholders.

Community involvement
We recognise the importance of good relations not just with shareholders, customers and employees, but with all those in society who have an interest in AstraZeneca's activities and progress.

We aim to be responsible members of our local communities through charitable donations, sponsorship and other initiatives that help to make a positive difference. In particular, we focus on bringing benefit in ways that are consistent with our business aim of improving human health and quality of life and on promoting the value of science within the community.

We also support a wide range of health education initiatives designed to increase awareness of major healthcare problems, such as breast and prostate cancer, heart and respiratory diseases and gastro-intestinal disorders.

In 2001, AstraZeneca responded to the India earthquake appeal with a donation to the International Red Cross.

In the US, following the terrorist attacks in September 2001, AstraZeneca made significant donations to the American Red Cross and to the United Service Organization in Delaware as well as product donations to hospitals treating victims and rescue workers. Product donations were also made for the care of Afghan refugees.

To encourage young people's interest in science, we sponsor a range of science based school programmes. In the UK, the AstraZeneca Science Teaching Trust, an independent charity with a total trust fund of $32 million, supports a programme of projects designed to help build the knowledge, skills and understanding required to promote and teach science effectively in primary schools. In 2001, the Trust sponsored a 'Little Book of Experiments' which was distributed to UK primary schools as part of the National Year of Science programme.

Last year, AstraZeneca donated $19 million to charity.

People

AstraZeneca's success depends on the quality and performance of all our people worldwide and we value the individuality, diversity and creativity that every employee brings to our business.

Our commitment to promoting a culture of equal opportunity is embedded in our core values:

- respect for the individual and diversity
- openness, honesty, trust and support for each other
- integrity and high ethical standards
- leadership by example at all levels

Managing and rewarding high performance
We aim to build and maintain a performance-led culture in which everyone recognises the need to add value for customers and shareholders and understands the link between individual contribution and business priorities. Our business performance management systems support this objective. Our reward policy and practice link individual and team rewards with business performance at each level, aligning the interests of the Company, our shareholders and our employees.

Personal development
We encourage and support our people in developing their potential to the full. All AstraZeneca managers are responsible for working with each member of their team to agree a personal development plan for that person which is aligned with business needs and tailored to the individual's skills and aspirations. Employees contribute to the identification, delivery and evaluation of their subsequent learning and development. In addition, an online global centre for learning and development provides information, materials and ideas on personal development planning.

Developing global leaders
The AstraZeneca leadership capabilities defined by our Senior Executive Team continue to be applied throughout the Company. Global leadership programmes are designed to strengthen commitment to AstraZeneca's culture and values, enhance leadership capabilities and help leaders develop good working relationships across the organisation. Programmes include GOAL – a leadership programme for senior managers in global roles, 'Developing Leaders' – a programme for staff moving into key leadership or functional roles and 'Senior Induction Programme' – an accelerated induction opportunity for senior managers new to the Company. These are complemented by local leadership and development programmes.

Global succession planning ensures that a pool of leaders is available to support our long term success and that succession plans are in place for key positions. The importance of international experience is recognised as a key development requirement for our future leaders.

Building the talent base
One of our top priorities is to attract and retain the best talent to meet existing and future employee and business needs worldwide. To support this aim, in 2001 we introduced our employer of choice initiative which focuses on three global themes that set the agenda for local implementation:

- energising work environment
- excellent development opportunities
- competitive and flexible reward

Employee communications
We aim to maintain an open management style, keeping our 54,000 employees in 45 countries informed of all major business decisions and events.

We use our intranet to provide leaders with the information and tools they need to share relevant information with their teams. Other media, online and print, are also used to keep employees informed and enable them to enhance their contribution to business success. A regular global employee survey provides employees with a comprehensive feedback channel and enables us to respond to the views of employees and monitor the success and impact of ongoing global initiatives.

As part of the ongoing response to the 2000 employee survey, in 2001 members of our Senior Executive Team undertook a number of employee presentations worldwide to foster open dialogue and leadership visibility.

Within Europe, employee consultation arrangements are in place and elected representatives form an employee consultation forum, which is chaired by the Chief Executive.

Wellbeing
We believe that if we are to expect people's energy and commitment at work, we must provide the right environment and ensure the physical and psychological wellbeing of our employees. AstraZeneca's WellBeing programmes around the world are designed to ensure the wellbeing of employees and complement existing occupational health and safety programmes, including physical development, stress management and healthy nutrition. WellBeing programmes are underway in Brazil, Canada, France, Philippines, Sweden, the UK and the US. Best practice is being shared across AstraZeneca to encourage and help with similar activities in other locations.

Part 3
Planning, design and production

11 Planning the annual report

The one thing that can be said with certainty about planning the annual report is that no two organizations will prepare their annual reports in the same way. What can also be expressed with a considerable degree of confidence is that, however good you believe your company's planning process to be, there will never be enough time for preparation. An annual report must be produced and delivered to all the interested parties on time, every year. There can be no excuses.

Deliver without fail

A limited company that fails to deliver its report in a timely fashion can suffer serious consequences in terms of legal regulatory issues, but also in terms of adverse public relations. The consequences of being perceived as 'incompetent' or 'disorganized' by failing to deliver your report on time are immense.

Media analysts and large shareholders in particular will be highly suspicious about any excuses offered concerning delays to your company's report. They will immediately ask themselves: what do these delays and excuses hide? Is there more to these delays than initially meets the eye? Is the company hiding something much worse? Is the delay symptomatic of a serious underlying problem?

Since time is of the essence, detailed planning of the annual report is vital. You can never plan too soon. But make sure that your planning is more than a statement of 'good intentions' by producing a realistic and attainable timetable.

Responsibility

The first stage of the process must be initiated by the department that takes overall responsibility for the report. The level of responsibility can differ amongst organizations. In some companies, the responsibility for the report lies ultimately with the finance department; in others, it rests with the company secretarial department, or with the corporate affairs or corporate communications department, or even with the chairman's office. In some organizations, most of the pre-planning process may be contracted to an outside agency.

There are no hard and fast rules on where the centre of responsibility should lie. You must decide which department is to take overall responsibility and clearly identify which individual manager or team is responsible for the whole process. And make sure that you choose the lead manager with care. This job is not for the fainthearted. Do not allocate the job to a manager as a 'project' for him or her 'to do,' perhaps pending retirement or while waiting reallocation to another role. It should be treated as a senior role with demanding responsibilities.

The lead manager

The role demands a manager who can see 'the big picture'. Whilst no single manager can possess all the attributes necessary to produce a report, there are nevertheless certain qualities and experience that are essential. The manager should understand key aspects of accounting and legal issues, possess sound company secretarial skills, and display impressive interpersonal and management skills. He or she must be able to control a large-scale complex project competently and to a tight timetable, so the ability to persuade, motivate, coordinate and encourage other people is crucial. In addition to all this, the manager should have solid experience in a cross-section of the organization's functions and departments and be able to deliver a project successfully on time and on cost. Above all, you should select an individual lead manager who 'can get things done'.

A team approach

The manager should organize the formation of an appropriate team or committee to produce the report through to its final completion. Although you may be slightly hesitant about forming yet another committee in your organization there is usually no suitable alternative. Since there will be an input from many departments and sections in your organization, it is a good idea to bring in representatives from these areas at an early stage.

Your team should include some representation from functions that encompass finance, company secretarial, corporate communications, legal and design. If your design function is outsourced, rather than in-house, you should involve any outside parties at an early stage. You should also include a representative from the chairman's office and/or another member of staff from the chief executive's department and from the corporate/shareholder relations department.

The timetable

Initially, you should agree a strict timetable. If you start the initial meetings early in the financial year you can get away with only fortnightly or even monthly meetings for the early part of the planning process. However, if you only start to actively prepare your report a few months before your year-end, time will be of the essence. Monthly meetings may well give way to discussions on a weekly basis or even every few days.

Ensure that, in the early meetings, managerial responsibilities are clearly allocated with timetabled dates for completion. In fact, the more successful organizations tend to implement their planning procedures for the next annual report almost as soon as the last report has been produced. It is never too early to put the annual report's preparatory wheels in motion. Whatever you do, never leave the production of the report to the last minute. It never works and it always shows in the quality of the finished product.

Whoever is eventually allocated responsibility for the annual report must place time management and cost control at the top of their agenda. The report's timetable must be produced early in the financial year. Always build in appropriate contingencies for mishaps, overruns, other delays and last-minute changes.

The budget

At an early stage discuss the size of the budget that your company is going to allocate to the report. In your (hopefully) high-quality, image-conscious and message-driven report, costs will not be low. Although a cheap and cheerful report may satisfy all the legal and other regulatory requirements, as this book stresses, this is the incorrect approach. However, there are compromises and 'in-between areas.' For example, the use of lower-grade paper or perhaps the use of fewer colour photographs can substantially reduce costs. But as explained in Chapter 13, 'Design, printing and distribution', go for the best your company can afford.

Determining the size of the budget will not be easy. There will always be some members of the committee who regard the annual report as being an 'evil necessity' and have an attitude of 'Why bother? Nobody is really interested in it anyway'. Do not merely dismiss such views; instead, explain to the individual why this opinion is as old-fashioned as it is simply wrong. Your crucial goal is to explain why the annual corporate report is an important means of delivering both explicit and implicit messages, so show the dissenting committee member the error of his or her ways! Of course, people who hold such negative views are not really the most desirable team members, but you may have no choice – in many organizations the members are nominated by their own departments. You will need to use all your managerial abilities and powers of persuasion to convert these people.

Try to obtain an overall budget for the annual report as early as possible in the year. Always ask for the largest amount of funding possible but also provide reasons why you need a more expensive, high-quality product. Aim at least for the use of top-quality design and production techniques – neither of which come cheap.

Although you cannot do much about some of the costs (many of which are outside of your control), you can influence others. For example, the layout, content and theme of your report can carry relatively minimal costs. The costs you will need to consider can be allocated in many ways but, typically, they will be centred on five key areas:

- design and preparation
- photographic
- materials (essentially paper)
- printing
- postage and distribution.

The procedures for the approval of the budget for the annual report vary widely in companies. But whatever the practice in your company, it must be re-emphasized that it is vitally important to obtain approval of the budget limit at an early stage. Once the cost constraints have been established, the whole nature and quality of the project can be determined.

Establish leadership

You need to break down the work involved in preparing the report into major functional areas. Under the overall leadership of the report's manager, a leader should be appointed to take direct responsibility for the key areas of:

- supervising, facilitating and coordinating the report's main sections
- establishing the report's theme
- design and layout
- in-house or outsourcing issues
- content – this area will be obviously constrained by legal, accounting and stock exchange/Financial Services Authority Regulations
- photography – consider such issues as type, theme, image portrayal, relationship to text, in-house or outsourcing, and so on
- printing – consider such issues as in-house or outsourcing, quality, technical details, spacing, and so on
- distribution – consider method, means, costs, and so on.

In-house versus outsourcing

Costs relating to design, photography and printing can sometimes be reduced by using your company's own in-house facilities. But be warned. Unless your company is large, experienced and well-organized, some of these in-house functions can be variable in terms of quality and reliability. In fact, even in large and experienced companies, the in-house design, photographic and printing departments are not always as competent or as imaginative as they may sometimes like to think they are.

You will also need to investigate the costs of distributing the report. The timing and means of distribution should not be left until the end of the financial year. It may sometimes be cheaper to outsource all of the distribution process. Early negotiations with final delivery agents, such as the postal authorities, may yield worthwhile cost savings. In addition, it may be beneficial, at this early stage, to establish the costs of packaging and the cost of inserts into the packaging (such as information relating to AGMs). Having this information to hand will help you decide whether to leave the distribution in-house or to outsource the work.

You need also to assess, honestly, the quality of these in-house functions and whether they have the capacity and specialist skills for the work required. At the same time, you should examine the options if these areas of work are to be outsourced.

In many ways, a specialist design agency or printing company may produce a much better finished product. And the costs are not always necessarily much higher. It is always a good idea, when you are considering issuing tenders for outsourcing contracts, to ask for examples of work, or perhaps a presentation, from potential firms. The potential outside contractors can then explain just exactly what they can do for you.

A useful tip is to examine the annual reports of other companies. Examine the use, nature and quality of their photographs and graphic design, and decide which company's report is particularly appealing. Usually, in very small print at the bottom of the back cover will be the name of the design agency (if one has been used). If you are sufficiently impressed by their work, contact them to see just what they can do for your company and the cost of their services. Whatever you decide, in-house or outsourcing, once you have made a decision, try to build up a working relationship with your selected contractor over several years. No one gains if you persistently jump between internal and external service suppliers. Likewise, whichever you decide, discuss your ideas and presentation early in the process. Try to formulate your ideas and avoid continually changing direction as this is very costly. You and your report committee should decide on themes, presentation, design, printing and so on at an early stage. But always bear in mind that, in practice, arriving at these decisions can take much longer than you originally anticipate.

Quality over cost

Whatever you do, do not try to economize too aggressively on the quality of design, printing or photography. It is simply not worth it. The quality of the finished product is just too important for your organization to cut costs too harshly. Some companies believe that it is a waste of resources to produce a glossy high-quality report. Their argument is that most shareholders are not interested in the final product and that professional analysts only want the actual numbers and information, without the supporting presentation and image generation. This view is wrong. As discussed earlier in this book, the annual report is a crucial 'shop window' for the company. You need to concentrate not only on content, but also on the presentation of the report. A high-quality and professionally produced report sends out both explicit and implicit signals. It is a vital document and it is equally vital that your company gets it right. Production values are critically important.

It is not only leading blue-chip companies that need a high-quality report. Other smaller-sized companies, either with a stock exchange listing or perhaps on the smaller alternative investment market, should consider the future. You may be a small and seemingly relatively insignificant player today, but tomorrow may be so different. Your annual report can help reflect and project your hopes, aspirations and messages. So if you work for a smaller but ambitious company, you should take just as much care in preparing the annual report as a leading FTSE 100 company.

Remember: quality of printing matters
Be warned: never necessarily choose the cheapest quote for any work you require. Ask to see annual reports that the design and printing firms have produced and printed for other companies. There are important quality issues at stake. As we have already discussed, it is vital that the report conveys your corporate message and theme. A cheap and poor-quality print run will create unwanted and negative images of your company. Do not compromise high standards of design and printing for the sake of being able to boast to the finance department just how much money you have saved. It is so often a false economy. Never forget: image matters.

Avoiding 'indifferent' reports

Although the defining characteristics of a 'good' or 'bad' report are clear, there is another category that should be particularly noted – and avoided.

In some ways an annual report that can be classified as 'indifferent' can ultimately result in more long-term problems for companies and organizations than being considered as 'bad'. At least with a 'bad' or poorly designed annual report there is a fair chance that sustained criticism will eventually result in the company implementing substantial changes. But if users consider your annual report to be 'indifferent', there is a distinct possibility that any criticism will be vague and lacklustre and the company will continue to produce its reports in a similarly unattractive fashion. Users will just implicitly accept your indifferent report as the 'norm' for your company.

The 'good' sections of an 'indifferent' report may often be 'netted off' against the 'poorer' sections in users' minds. Since there may be nothing too adverse that attracts vociferous criticism, the company will continue to produce an 'indifferent' report in future years – with dire consequences. 'Indifferent' reports are sometimes produced because some companies do not believe that annual reports are particularly significant and therefore choose to conform merely to the minimum regulatory requirements. As a consequence, insufficient resources and effort are devoted to the production and design processes. But as this book emphasizes, annual reports *are* a significant corporate asset, and resources must be allocated to enable the production of a high-quality report.

Some companies operate on the basis that the indifferent quality of their annual report 'will do' or 'serve its purpose'. This view is utterly misguided. There is never an acceptable excuse for producing an indifferent annual report.

'Indifferent' reports can so easily lead to the stagnation of ideas and produce no real incentive to improve. It is an unattractive picture, which should have no place in any organization.

Learning from mistakes

Even in the best-managed organizations mistakes and mishaps will occur in producing the report. It is clearly important to learn from these mistakes. Once this annual report has been finalized, you should not only review the report itself but also the procedures leading to the report's production. Establish where you went wrong, show how you could do better, identify the causes of any delays, and analyse working relations between team members. Always take a critical, but constructive, approach to ascertain how matters can be improved next year. But, most importantly, it is not only sound management practice, but also plain courtesy, to send a note of appreciation to all the people involved in the report's production. Make sure that your team members' work is fully appreciated – you may need their help again next year.

The production framework

Although most organizations have their own procedures, a framework for the production of your report could take the 12-stage form discussed below.

Stage 1
First, review the successful features and problems arising from last year's report. Identify the strengths and weaknesses of the report and establish, in general terms initially, how it can be improved.

Stage 2
Construct a timetable for the preparation of this year's report. Set deadlines for the completion of various sections of the report and also ensure that you have (or will have) the necessary staff resources to prepare the report and, of course, an appropriate production budget.

Stage 3
Allocate responsibilities to staff. You should ensure that each member of the team is made fully aware of what is expected of them, the nature of their responsibilities and their own allocated deadlines. It is imperative that team members are made aware of the consequences of failing to adhere to their allocated targets and timetable.

Stage 4
Set the framework and theme for the report as early as possible. It will be so much easier to construct the rest of the report once this task has been done. Decide on the overall corporate message that you wish to convey to your audience this year and make sure that it is firmly fixed in the framework.

Stage 5
Highlight your presentational and design requirements.

At an early stage, make key outline decisions about the way in which you intend to present and design your report in terms of size, nature and use of photographs, graphs, charts, colour and, of course, content. Within the remit of your budget, you will also need to start, on a preliminary basis, discussing matters pertaining to paper type and quality, and so on.

Stage 6
Start seeking information from design agencies and printing firms about how they can assist in the production of your report. Enter into discussions with a selection of firms to establish what they can provide within the limits of your budget. Also, try to ascertain the underlying ideas and aspirations that these firms have for your report. It is a sound idea to solicit the ideas of several agencies and firms as both design consultancy fees and printing costs can vary substantially. It may be worth considering taking advice from a printing specialist about quality levels and costs and then seeking a printing company that will undertake a competitive print run. Alternatively, some design consultancy agencies have their own in-house technical printing experts or can recommend a competent and reliable printing firm. In consultation with your chosen design specialists, you

should also explore opportunities that might involve printing the report in another country with lower production costs.

At the same time, you should consult with your typesetters on issues such as presentation, typeface and deadlines for completion.

Stage 7

After receiving cost information and, perhaps a presentation from the prospective design and printing companies, estimate the size of your print run. Clearly, you will need to look at the number of copies printed last year and adjust accordingly for any likely increase or reduction for the current year. You can then begin to seek formal tenders from the design and printing companies.

You may also wish to discuss other associated issues with your printers. Some printing firms offer additional services dealing with enveloping, postage and distribution. However, it may sometimes be cheaper to use a separate packaging and distribution company. You should investigate the respective costs. Additionally, if your report is to carry paper inserts, such as details about AGM resolution voting forms or admission forms for entry to the AGM, you should ascertain these add-on costs. Most printers will undertake the complete package for you.

Stage 8

Liaise with the key contributors of the report, making sure that the individuals and departments who will be writing sections of the report are briefed and ready to start writing when required. By necessity, some parts of the report cannot be written until the latter stages of the process when all the final information becomes available. However, although the structure and some of the content can often be started at an earlier stage, many contributors may be tempted to leave the writing of all of their submissions until the last possible minute. Try to ensure that this does not happen, perhaps by asking for periodic progress reports from key departments. At first, diplomatically suggest that contributors might let you have sight of the outline of their input to date. A disappointing response will suggest that very little has happened so far, so it might be necessary for you to take a more assertive approach.

Stage 9

With the financial year-end on the horizon, it is now time to check that typesetting design and printing quotes have been received and accepted. The printers should know, by now, when you will expect to receive the final printed report back from them. Ensure that the printing contract clearly contains a deadline when the print run is to be finished. You may wish to consider including financial penalty clauses for non-completion by the due date. Your legal department can advise.

While you are checking your printing arrangements, it is crucial that, even at this stage, you check and recheck and proof and reproof the draft submissions. Never be complacent and never underestimate the possibility of errors creeping into your report.

In many organizations, the chairman's statement or a commentary by the chief executive are often left until last. If this is the practice in your organization it may be difficult to change the habit overnight, in which case you should send reminders to, for example, the chairman's office stressing the deadlines and explaining why you are introducing earlier deadlines.

Finally, once you have done everything humanly possible to eliminate errors, you can now pass the edited proofs to the typesetters.

Stage 10

By now you should have received the final typeset proofs from your typesetters. Check the details once more and carefully proofread, yet again. Look for errors and omissions that are so glaring and so obvious that everybody has missed them. It is a good idea to use the services of some individual who has had no connection with the report's preparation. Their sole purpose will be to look for 'obvious' errors such as:

- incorrect dates
- missing dates
- use of the 'wrong' year
- incorrectly titled photographs
- missing paragraphs or pages
- non-sequential page numbers.

The list is almost infinite (see also Chapter 14).

Technical accounting details received from your finance department should be given special emphasis. Although the company's accountants should have proofread the details carefully before you receive them, it is nevertheless a sensible idea to read the accounting information again – just to make certain. If you are in the slightest doubt about the structure or content, refer it back to your company's accountants.

Stage 11
It is important to establish the 'signing-off' date for the report. You need to ensure not only that the relevant directors have approved the financial statements but also ensure that the auditors have signed off the accounts. Again, just before issuing the final proofs to the printers, you should check once more with all the team members and the contributors, or their representatives, to ensure that there are no final problems, errors or alterations. Once the report has been printed, any mistakes found will not only be extremely embarrassing, but may also be astronomically expensive to correct.

Stage 12
In the absence of any last-minute difficulties you can now give the final instructions to the printers and authorize the printing of your report.

Afterwards, it is imperative that your appreciation and thanks are conveyed to everyone involved. If any particular individual or department has been especially helpful, then acknowledgement of their assistance should be notified to those personally concerned. You will need the help and cooperation of many of these people again next year, so do not be sparing in your appreciation.

As a final point, if any significant problem has arisen this year, make a note of it. You will need to take it into account when you prepare next year's report.

Common problems

Most projects in business will cause some problems and the preparation of the annual report is no exception.

Common complaints about the annual report are that it can become too introspective, too complacent, too self-satisfying, too pious and almost patronizing to the external reader.

Some public relations agencies will testify that many companies can create reports that are monuments to self-consciousness, defensiveness and opaqueness. Often, so many people contribute to the production of the report that the finished product becomes a poor compromise. The danger is that the finished report pleases no one and irritates everyone.

Sometimes the actions of the chief executive cause problems. In some organizations the chief executive does not become involved at an early stage. Sometimes, he or she will wish to study the report at the final draft stage and then attempt to implement last-minute changes; at other times, he or she, or a representative from his or her department, will be sent draft versions but leave any input or amendments until the deadline is imminent.

On other occasions, external design agencies and printing companies are unsure of their responsibilities and deadlines. Sometimes, the financial statements that will need to be incorporated into the report are late arriving from the accountants, or the auditors cause delays by discussing key issues with the finance department.

Your principal defences against these problems are planning, clear allocation of responsibilities and continual monitoring of the preparation of the report. Never be complacent for a moment; vigilance at all times is essential.

12 The new age: electronic reporting

The use of conventional methods of delivering accounting and other corporate information to shareholders and other users is undergoing vast upheaval. The electronic information age is already here. Legislation now permits companies to communicate electronically with shareholders, if they so wish. The vast majority of listed companies have already used electronic reporting in one form or another. Many other large and medium-sized non-listed companies have also adopted the new reporting technology. Throughout this chapter it will be assumed that your company already has a website and makes use of it to convey information on the organization – for example, sales, corporate profiling, share price information and general contact details.

Whatever the size of your company, you have no choice. If you have not done so already, you must adopt this technology and adopt it rapidly.

An opportunity for communicating

The potential scope of the Internet to deliver faster, clearer and specifically targeted corporate information is enormous. Soon, the means by which information has been traditionally delivered over the last half-century will change beyond recognition. Even the current methods and quality standards of Internet delivery will be surpassed by technological leaps in electronic reporting.

Even if delivering annual reports in electronic form becomes the norm, there will still be some users who will want to receive their report in written form. Anyway, even if the legislation is changed again in future years to abolish annual reports in written form, there will still be a need to continue to process and deliver messages. In fact, in the overwhelming majority of cases, many of the planning, procedures and publication issues associated with written reports will apply in just the same way with electronic reports. The nature and content of the report remains just as important; quite simply, the only significant difference is in the mode of delivery of your report's news. The new technology is merely another, but important, way of distributing your report.

As highlighted earlier, many organizations will already have a form of electronic reporting in the shape of a corporate website. Indeed, some companies already display their annual report as part of their websites, normally locating it under a section entitled 'Shareholder Information', 'Corporate Communications', 'Investor Relations' or similar title. If your company has not, as yet, put the annual report on the web, now is your opportunity to consider doing so.

Although larger organisations have already made many of the necessary changes to accommodate electronic reporting, adoption by some smaller and medium-sized companies is still embarrassingly slow.

Legislation

Government recognition of the changes brought about by new technology has been incorporated in the Companies Act 1985 (Electronic Communications Order 2000). Under this Act, which came into effect on 22 December 2000, companies are permitted to send documents (which the company previously sent out in hard copy) to shareholders in electronic form. Section 238 of the Act now allows companies to send electronically copies of the annual report and accounts to those entitled to receive them. Companies are also permitted to e-mail the report directly to shareholders or, alternatively, to send notification to shareholders that they can now access the information on the company's website. If the latter option is chosen, publication on the website must take place at least 21 days before the AGM. Section 239 goes further by allowing a demand from other stakeholders for a copy of the annual report and accounts to be satisfied by electronic means.

The Electronic Communications legislation does not just apply to shareholders. It also includes electronic communication with debenture-holders, registrars of companies and auditors. For specific advice on the more technical and legal points of communicating electronically with shareholders, you are strongly advised to make reference to recommendations produced by the Institute of Chartered Secretaries and Administrators (ICSA). This professional organization for company secretaries has published specific technical guidance (see ICSA, 2000).

The ICSA recommended best practice is as follows:

- Companies should amend their articles to facilitate the use of electronic communications.
- Invitations by the company to shareholders to use electronic communications should identify any computer equipment specifications that are needed.
- The initial invitation to use electronic communication should be sent by post to each shareholder and explain which documents will be available.
- Companies must state that shareholders can receive all material in the form of hard copy if they so wish.
- Companies should repeat the offer to use electronic communications at least once at year to those shareholders who have decided to receive hard copies.
- The initial invitation to register for electronic communications should include clear advice on how to register. New shareholders should have the opportunity to register for electronic communication within three months of registration.
- The company should clearly identify any statutory information on its website and whether it forms part of the audited accounts. It is also recommended that clearance is obtained from the company's auditors prior to displaying the statutory information and the auditors' report.
- A routine should be established for checking the statutory information on the website to ensure that the information has not been tampered with by computer hackers.

Even if you intend to continue to distribute your report predominantly in hard-copy form for the foreseeable future, you should still ensure that your company takes advantage of the flexibility and opportunity offered by electronic communication. As an initial step, put the annual report on your website and draw attention to its existence in the hard copy of your annual report and other documentation. Then, for the next year or two carefully monitor the number of 'hits' your website receives to assess its take-up rate and effectiveness. Only after a full appraisal should you move to adopt the provisions permitted by the Electronics Communications Order in full.

No obligation

It must be stressed, however, that neither companies nor shareholders are legally required to use electronic communication. Equally, it is important to realize that there must be agreement between the company and each individual shareholder. Many shareholders will almost certainly still prefer to receive their annual report in hard copy, at least in the foreseeable future.

In the medium term, there are no indications that the legislation will be changed to compel shareholders to accept their annual report in electronic form and remove their option to receive it in written form . Nevertheless, the UK government seems committed to increasing the use of electronic means to deliver annual reports. The government is also proposing to require certain categories of companies to make their annual report available within four months of their year-end. Electronic processing may assist companies in meeting this more onerous deadline.

The website

Assuming that, almost certainly, your organization already has a website, make sure that your annual report is placed on it. Even nowadays, a number of large listed companies have impressive websites but do not include their annual report. Do not waste your opportunity. If your organization already uses its website for, say, sales purposes, your current website designers may be able to help you create additional pages to display your annual report. If your organization does not have a permanent website designer, ask prospective designers what other websites they have recently designed and then test the sites out for yourself. What do you think of the site? What improvements could be made? Does the standard of site design suit your company? Once you have answered these questions to your satisfaction, act without delay.

Design

Putting your annual report on the website is not, in itself, too problematic. But you should have higher ambitions. Given that presentation and ease of use must be paramount in designing your website, discuss with your designers how to improve such features as the use of colour frames, hyperlinks, portals to other sites, ease of navigation and a quick search facility.

There are also other technical details which you should consider and discuss with your designer. Areas that should be kept under continual review include, for example, your monitor resolution, colour settings and data throughput. Indeed, data throughput – that is, the length of time that the web pages take to be downloaded and displayed on the user's computer – is often the most crucial factor. For most users, speed is of the essence. If they have to wait more than about ten seconds for a web page to be displayed, they often move on to a faster and more user-friendly site.

It will often take some time to download the full annual report on a website, even for the fastest data throughput. In some instances, there will be a trade-off between the complexity of your website design and the speed of its transmission. The situation is compounded if users have a 'slow' or outdated modem. You will also need to discuss with your website designers other technical hardware and software interrelated factors such as the type, age and bandwidth of your company's web server.

When discussing these issues with your designer, be clear about your aims. And do not attempt to do too much too quickly – it is best to start simply and robustly, then build complexity as your technological development and commitment increases. Beware of creating an overcomplicated site that can only navigated with extreme difficulty.

You may also wish to include your summary accounts. If your company does not produce summary accounts, you might consider asking your designer to install a quick and simple search facility so that users can easily access what they are seeking from the mass of the more complex information contained in the detailed and full annual report.

If your website is located on your own company's computer you should certainly consider security issues, although the nature of the information you will be placing on the web will not generally be regarded as particularly high-risk. If, on the other hand, your website is hosted externally, the security of the site should be ensured by the host company.

As you are (presumably) not selling your annual report to 'customers', you will not need to consider the high level of security needed, for example, for credit card payments. In fact, the information in the annual report will already be placed in the public domain (or soon will be), so the principal consideration is making the website secure against mischievous or malicious computer hackers intent on causing disruption to your site. A hacker may regard it as a personal challenge to crash a large company website or post 'unofficial' or unwanted material on to your site or report. This means that you will need to discuss with your computer advisers how to implement some suitable and secure firewalls (barriers) and other security measures. Do not, however, neglect general security issues – these are important whenever computer systems are used to distribute information.

Hyperlinks

Since there is a large amount of information in the annual report, make sure that there are a number of hyperlinks on your website. Hyperlinks will allow the user to 'click' on key words (often underlined) so that they can 'jump' to associated supporting sites and later sections of the report. Above all, make the site clear, uncluttered and easy to navigate.

As your website develops, you might also consider placing on it other information that might be found in your annual report (or which perhaps provides additional supplementary information). You could, for example, follow the lead of certain companies and include all, or extracts, of your environmental report or perhaps any ethical trading statements that you issue. However, remember that the more information that you place on your site, the more difficult it may be for some users to find the section they seek. As a necessity, you must include a powerful search facility in your site so that users can track down the chosen section of information by entering a key word or phrase.

Refresh frequently

Remember to keep your website up-to-date. Do not establish it and then neglect it. Keep the site fresh with new information. Obviously, the annual report will be on your site for a year, but other information can be included, if necessary, on a more frequent basis. This information could include interim reports, preliminary announcements and perhaps movements in your daily share price. There is a variety of general and business trading information you can provide – if you wish.

PDF files

Many companies place their annual reports in what is termed an Adobe Acrobat PDF file. This is a Portable Document Format (PDF) file and is often the simplest way to place a lengthy document on the web. Essentially, most Word and other document files can be formed into a self-contained PDF file that comprises your annual report and accounts.

All the layout, text, fonts and images are kept intact when they are moved into a PDF file. A major advantage of PDF files is that they confer a high degree of file integrity. They are also relatively robust in security terms and can resist most attacks by hackers.

A PDF file is particularly useful if you are e-mailing the annual report direct to shareholders. It is not easy for the recipient or anyone else to change the form and content of a PDF file, so its integrity is more or less guaranteed. You should certainly discuss the use of this type of file with your website designers.

Conclusion

Failure to place your annual report on your website will speak volumes about your company's inability to adapt to the new electronic age. You will rapidly acquire a prehistoric image – not something that your company will be keen to convey. Even if you still intend to send out hard copies of your report, you should still place your annual report on your website. This is not a case of pointless duplication – the website gives the user an additional source from which to access information during the year, and sometimes a user may well mislay his or her hard-copy report.

Just a final word of warning. Electronic technology is developing so rapidly that the whole nature and means of distributing information is almost certain to change within a few years, if not months. It is imperative that you keep up-to-date with these changes.

But, whatever you do, do not ignore the march of technology. The consequences for your company will be dire if you do.

13 Design, printing and distribution

In preparing your annual report on an in-house basis you should pay particular attention to the quality of design and printing. The preparation of the annual report must be conducted to a high standard, and sometimes the quality standards of some companies' design and printing leaves room for improvement. However, even if you are using outside specialist sources to undertake the work, you should at least be aware of some of the issues that will concern your appointed agencies. A well-designed and printed product will rarely turn a report of mediocre content into a well-received document, but a good design can put extra polish and 'sparkle' on a company's image and perceived business standing.

Design

Predetermined content

The content and, to some degree, the layout of substantial parts of the annual report, such as the financial statements and supporting information, are determined by your accountants. For example, your profit and loss account will be in the format specified by the Companies Act 1985 and will normally comply with Format 1 or Format 2 (see Chapter 4, 'Content of financial statements'). The content and layout of many other financial statements are also heavily dictated by legislation and accounting regulation. You will, for instance, have to provide (legally) the comparative financial figures for last year alongside this year's figures. Also, some companies prepare what is termed 'multicolumn' profit and loss accounts whereby items, such as exceptional items, are shown separately in additional columns. As a result, the layout of the profit and loss account may end up consisting of many columns across the width of the page – a rather complex presentation that does not lend itself to innovations in design and 'readability'. Many of these problems are unavoidable – they are intrinsic to the nature of corporate reporting.

Clarity of design

Fortunately, you will be able to play a role at the design and printing stage in selecting a clear, readable typeface and perhaps in choosing an alternative shade of background colour (on which to print last year's comparative figures) and so on.

The key word must be clarity. You should try your utmost, within the confines of legal and accounting constraints, to design the layout of the financial statements so that they appear clear, well structured and informative. But, generally, it is not always possible to be very imaginative with, for example, the design of a cash flow statement. (See Chapter 15, 'A winning report', for a discussion of some of the better (and worse) features of annual reports.)

Pictorial content

There are other specific areas, often neglected, in which you can apply your design and presentational skills. These areas particularly concern the use of photographs, graphs and diagrams.

Photographs

The general adage that 'a picture is worth a thousand words' is certainly applicable to annual reports. Nowadays, most companies use photographs in some context. Strategically placed and relevant, they can be used to break up pages and sections of often mind-numbing technical facts and accounts, as well as appropriately capturing corporate images, style and presence. Long after mundane accounting information has been forgotten, the themes and images in photographs will be remembered and be associated with the company's profile. But care must be taken. Too many companies waste the opportunity to convey their message. All too often directors monopolize photographic opportunities in order to portray themselves in some narcissistic and overbearing way.

Most companies cannot resist showing photographs of their chairman and directors. While there is nothing intrinsically wrong in this approach, there are limits that should not be crossed. Passport-type photographical presentation, portraying a passive, regimented and dull board of directors (and company), almost never works. Conversely, photographs of directors in action, at work, on the shopfloor, discussing matters with other employees, and so on, tend to work much better. Most design agencies will commission the photographs for you. Use their services. But if their finished photographs fail to satisfy your requirements, insist on a reshoot. Photographs are too important to leave to chance.

Do not stop at photographs of the chairman and directors. Far too many companies believe that these are the only people worthy of having their photographs displayed. Other employees are important to a company's success. The imaginative use of photographs of more junior staff can convey a more inclusive, more equitable and a more all-embracing message about the company. Most importantly, do not forget that these more junior employees have an identity too. Even companies that do show photographs of employees at work often leave them 'nameless', in stark contrast to the directors who are invariably credited with their names. Treat more junior staff with the same courtesy accorded to the directors. Disclose their names and job duties and try to ensure that their photographs, in terms of size, context, and even position, are not perceived as 'inferior' to those of senior employees.

Even photographs of company products, use of its services and its customers can contribute to the corporate image. Used constructively, photographs can convey useful impressions and help send valuable messages.

Graphs and diagrams

As well as photographs, some companies use graphs and diagrams to highlight information. If your company chooses to do likewise, key presentational points must be borne in mind. First, pay careful attention to the nature of the information and what message you are trying to convey in the graphs and diagrams. The information might range from sales growth or growth in earnings to a geographical and diagrammatical split of turnover. You may wish to indicate large increases in the value of turnover over the last five years or the annual percentage increase in dividends. But always think carefully what your diagrams and graphs are trying to achieve. Do not include them just for the sake of it.

Second, always choose your presentational modes with the aim of ensuring that readers easily understand your message. Decide whether you are going to use graphs, bar charts or pie charts and choose the appropriate scale. A common mistake is to select a totally inappropriate scale for graphs and charts. If they are too small, few readers will take the trouble to decipher your message. Additionally, do not make the graphs or diagrams too complex. Keep your message clear, simple and even blunt. Be selective and only portray the really key issues.

Also consider the significance of using colour. Many companies fail to put their message in the best light because they fail to make imaginative use of colour in their diagrams and graphs. Dull, but important, information can be livened up by using a few clear and bold (but not too intense) colours. However, take care not to overdo the colour – you are not necessarily aiming to win artistic awards!

As with photographs, it is essential to clearly caption the graphs and diagrams and also to refer to them in the accompanying narrative. Do not leave them 'floating' around the page; they need to be anchored firmly in the context of the explanatory text and your overall message.

Printing

Paper size and type

The first practical consideration in preparing your report is to determine the size of paper. Nowadays, the most commonly used paper size is A4. A small minority, largely comprising smaller companies, do use alternative and smaller sizes, but most of the leading UK listed companies have adopted A4 size as the 'industry norm'. On balance, the A4 size tends to be the most appropriate size for optimal presentation and the use of a mixture of text, diagrams and photographs.

Smaller-sized reports tend not to do justice to the image and message that your company should try to put forward. In more mundane practical terms, non-A4 size will often pose difficulties in terms of printing costs, packaging, enveloping and even filing on library and analysts' shelves. Some printing specialists have argued that a page width larger than A4 allows better presentation of the multicolumned financial statements. But, on balance, the benefits of using non-A4 size paper do not outweigh the extra costs, and the A4 size ends to reign in the end. As a rule, you should have a very good reason for choosing *not* to adopt the conventional A4 format.

Many companies fail to appreciate the importance of the nature, type and quality of the paper used for the report. It is often held that paper is a minor issue. Do not believe it. The type and quality of your paper will speak volumes about the image you are trying to project. In general, select the highest quality specifications you can accommodate within your budget. It is money well spent.

Paper weight

In conjunction with your printers, you should decide on your paper weight. In overall terms, the cost of the made-up weights of paper, expressed in grams per square metre of paper sheet (gm^2), is comprised of the cost of the wood pulp plus the cost of the paper coating. The cost of the paper and coating, together with ink costs, are especially important in terms of postage and distribution costs. You will need to calculate the total weight of the report print run and then pay careful attention to postage rates. There are distinct 'cut-off' postage pricing levels, based on weight, and, in some cases, the jump into the next postage band can be steep in terms of cost. Do not forget that inserts and other documentation may further add to the overall postage weight.

Sometimes a slight reduction in the weight of your report may push it back into a lower postage rate level. Doing this can yield very significant overall savings. However, there is an important trade-off to consider. By reducing the weight of your report you may be reducing quality and diminishing that all-important image. It can be a difficult decision but, on balance, you should do your utmost to avoid compromising on quality. You should even return, if necessary, to the ultimate budget-holder of the annual report and plead for additional funding, if the report's quality appears to be at stake.

Exceptionally, as discussed in Chapter 9, 'Annual reports of other organizations', some organizations, such as charities, might consider it inappropriate to select the highest grade and costliest paper. These types of organization have other issues to consider.

Other considerations

Another factor to consider is the opacity of the paper. Text, figures and photographs must not 'show through' to the reverse of the page. 'Show through' should only be noticeable when the page is held up to an especially bright light. The best way of eliminating, or at least minimizing, 'show through' is to select the appropriate thickness of paper. But clearly, the thicker the paper, then the greater the weight and the higher the postage charges. Of course, the solution is, again, a compromise between an acceptable paper thickness and weight, yielding acceptable postage costs.

Ask your printers to show you samples of paper thicknesses used by their other clients. Paper thickness can be decided on early in the year, so it is wise to avoid a last-minute panic and discuss the issue as soon as possible.

Your printers should also advise you on the surface coating of the paper. In general terms, it is possible to have a matt (dull), semi-gloss or full-gloss (shiny) coating. In many ways, a 'glossier' paper may be preferable. Matt finishes can sometimes look uninspiring and unimpressive, whereas a degree of 'shininess' can be more attractive and inviting to the reader. A higher-gloss finish also makes it easier for printers to ensure that colour photographs have more visual impact and 'stand out' better. But choosing an extremely glossy paper can cause difficulties. High gloss, resulting from a high level of coating and polishing, can cause a substantial degree of light reflection which, in some cases, can make reading the report more difficult and tiring.

Also consider the use of coloured or tinted pages. For example, you may decide that the financial statements should be printed in black but perhaps on a beige or light blue tinted background. Different tints for different sections of the report can help not only to create an aura of importance and identify key areas or figures, but also to 'split up' a long document for ease of reading. Some companies tint part of the page or only certain sections of figures in the financial statements. For example, it is possible to print this year's financial figures in a tinted background colour column so they stand out from last year's figures, which might be printed on a white background.

Tinted paper has the best effect when you are simply imposing a single colour print on to the tinted paper. But do check the colour of the print against the tinted background. Some companies are now experimenting with non-black printing on to a variety of different coloured backgrounds. Be careful – some colours should just not be used together. Even if you select a white background, think twice before using a non-black colour. For maximum impact and readability you normally will not go too far wrong if you always stick to black (or dark) print on a very light background. If you are thinking of choosing a different colour print on a tinted background, always ask to see samples of the effect. This point may appear obvious, but it is apparently not to some companies – as evidenced in the poor outcome of their reports.

Some companies are now using two print colours on a tinted background for the financial statements. For example, this year's figures are printed in a straightforward black print but last year's comparative figures are printed in a different colour, often grey. Always look at examples first. Sometimes, grey is too faint on a tinted background. Again, you should consult your printers on how the use of gloss or matt coating may affect the 'readability' of the text.

Binding

As well as the actual printing you should also discuss the frequently forgotten topic of binding. The last disaster you wish to have on your hands, after all the hard preparatory work, is faulty binding. If you choose a binding that is too cheap, you run the risk that the report's pages will separate and fall out if they are fully opened. Most reputable quality printers, nowadays, are aware of this risk and will point it out if you express a preference for cheaper binding methods.

However, this may not be the case if you are negotiating a printing and binding contract priced at the lower end of the market, where some printers may cut corners in terms of costs and quality in order to remain 'competitive'.

If in doubt, once again, look at other work the printer has undertaken. Even more simply, if you were satisfied with the type and quality of the binding used for last year's report, why change it this year?

Cover boards

The front and back covers of the report – the cover boards – are critical. You should think long and hard about the type, quality, covering, print and images that you will use. As in so much of business life, first impressions matter. Moreover, many people still judge a book by its cover and, obviously, this will be the first feature a reader will use to form a judgement about your company. So do not waste this opportunity. A badly drafted and poorly prepared report will be made infinitely worse by having a poor-quality front cover, but an inviting, impressive and thought-provoking cover can substantially improve a moderately well prepared report. Give the impression that you care, that your company cares and that you care about conveying your corporate message.

Many readers will not necessarily be interested in, and will ignore, large chunks of the technical accounting and legal details inside. But what they will not ignore is the front cover. Even if they merely open the envelope containing the report they will at least see the front cover. So make an impact; make a statement about your company. Be bold, create a presence and make a clear corporate statement.

The cover needs to be designed with great care over several months. Use imaginative application of colour, images and messages. In an explicit and, indeed, subliminal sense, what you place on the front cover will make powerful statements about your company, its mission and its whole ethos. In conjunction with your design agency and graphic designers, you should come up with perhaps five or six possible covers. Involve the whole team in deciding which cover best reflects your corporate message. If appropriate, also consider perhaps placing your corporate slogan or objective on the cover page. But, by necessity, these statements must be brief. A long rambling corporate slogan will have little beneficial impact.

You might even want to make imaginative use of design techniques, perhaps choosing to have part of the cover 'cut away'. For example, in 1999, the food giant Heinz had a large photograph of its leading-brand tomato ketchup being poured from its bottle. Part of the cover sheet was cut away and set against a ketchup-coloured background on the underlying and following page. The idea was clear, simple and different. Try to avoid being 'too gimmicky' as this will 'cheapen' your product and company in the eyes of your readers. But if it is well thought through and tastefully executed, an innovative cover design can make an impressive impact.

You might even want to consider using a different texture for the cover. A high-quality non-gloss, but textured, cover not only has an impressive tactile impact but also conveys the 'feeling' of a quality company.

Do not make the mistake of some companies in wasting the cover. British Telecommunications, for their 2001 annual report, simply used a bluish-green coloured sheet bearing only their corporate name and the title. Such an approach is a completely wasted opportunity; the cover lacks visual impact and conveys no message – apart from tedium and an utter lack of ideas. British Airways likewise uses a bland, blue cover. There are so many better ways to make use of such a high-profile document.

A good example of a cover board is that of the advertising conglomerate, WPP plc. Their cover is a graphic illustration of creativity and originality, displaying drawings and images representing ideas and imagination. It is eminently suitable for a business directly concerned with creating fresh advertising ideas for its clients.

Other companies, such as the clothing retailer Arcadia plc, have, in the past, used impressive photographs of models displaying their clothing range. Sales advertising, the corporate message and the annual report were rolled up into a high-impact cover board.

Whichever cover board you eventually select, it is usually a sound idea to choose a 'glossy' edge. Matt finishes can seem lacklustre and are best avoided. The most successful reports, in terms of initial impact, usually have a glossy and 'inviting' cover.

Most importantly, however, contact your printers early in the year. If you leave negotiations to the last minute you will have little or no time to investigate the various printing, binding and cover options. Once you hit upon what you consider to be a winning printing and binding version, it is usually a good idea to stick with your decision for a few years. However, there may be scope to improve a cover board with a 'winning theme' that you can build upon, improve and adapt as the years progress. But do not be complacent. Printing, binding and design techniques are changing fast. What may seem uneconomic one year may well become financially acceptable a few years later.

Useful information

There is one final point to consider with cover boards – or the inside of the cover boards to be precise. Many companies are increasingly placing 'useful' information for shareholders on the inside front or back covers. Some companies place the name and contact details of their company's registrar. You could also include key dates in the company's calendar such as the date of AGM, dates of dividend payments and dates when your interim results are released. It is also possible to provide contact details of brokers or other share-dealing facilities, to make it easier for shareholders to buy or sell their shares. In addition, some listed companies, in particular, often provide an analysis of the composition of their shareholders (for example, by retail or institutional holdings), as well as a range of shareholder accounts indicating the number and value of shares in each banding.

An increasing number of companies now use the inside front cover to highlight key financial information for both this and last year. You could include, for example:

- turnover
- operating profit
- earnings per share
- dividends per share
- interest cover.

The inside front cover could also carry a list of contents – an often forgotten, but valuable, aid for readers.

You could even use the outer back cover board to perhaps put the name and address of your design agency (if used), the name of your company's registered office and your company's registration number. But a word of caution. Do not swamp the reader with too much information or spoil the design and impact of your report – take a balanced approach.

Packaging

The packaging of the report is often the most overlooked area of the whole process.

Nowadays, most companies select sealed plastic envelopes as their preferred medium. These plastic envelopes are strong, durable and allow good colour printing and design on the outside. Very few listed companies continue to use white or manila paper envelopes.

Since the envelope will find its way to shareholders, debenture-holders and other interested parties, do not ignore its importance. Some groups and individuals, such as professional investors, analysts and large shareholders, will read the report whatever the type or colour of the envelope or packaging in which it arrives. But for many shareholders, the annual report is not always their most eagerly awaited mail. After all your hard work in preparing and designing the report, you certainly do not want the recipient to throw away the envelope containing the report without even opening it. The inherent danger is that, when the mailing reaches its intended destination, the envelope is simply disregarded as being 'junk mail' and thrown away unopened. To avoid this, include, on the envelope, rather dull but fundamental information such as your company registrar's name and address (for undelivered mail to be returned to) and an indication of the importance of the contents (such as 'Contains Important Material' printed on the outside).

Just as you will want to produce a top-quality report you should also select top-quality packaging to contain it. A scruffy and unappealing envelope is guaranteed to take the edge off even the best report. Some companies do not accord the envelope design the high degree of importance it deserves. Do not fall into this way of thinking. You may even want to specifically employ a professional designer. But whatever your final decision, at least ensure that the finished product matches the high quality of your report.

Distribution

The actual distribution procedure is an important event that must always succeed. Missing and late deliveries must be avoided at all costs. At the outset, you should have a clearly defined distribution day. Firmly announce this date – and stick to it!

The distribution process can be fraught with the internal politics that are inherent in all large corporate organizations. For example, you should avoid giving senior managers or directors their copy of the report after other employees who may be perceived as having positions of lower status.

'Special' or 'priority' list

To pre-empt some of these difficulties, it is important to have a clear timetable concerning the countdown to the report's distribution. About a month before the intended distribution date you should make arrangements to send out the report to people on your favoured 'special' or 'priority' list and for those who need special distribution arrangements.

The 'special list' should comprise those individuals and institutions that must have a copy immediately on release. These 'special' people will clearly include the chairman's office and the chief executive and all the directors, including all non-executive directors. Do not send only the bare minimum of copies for the chairman and directors themselves. Most chairmen and directors have, in turn, their own special lists of contacts to whom they have promised a copy as soon as it comes off the press. You should contact the secretaries of these directors to ask discreetly how many copies they need and then add a few more for good measure. There is always someone whom the chairman or directors have met on the golf course and has been promised a copy. It is not worth antagonizing your top management by neglecting to supply sufficient copies.

Two other important groups on the 'special' list are the large shareholding institutions and key media contacts. Large fund managers and institutional investors should also be given top priority. After all, if they control a large chunk of your company's shareholding, there is no point in upsetting them. Likewise, key media contacts, especially financial journalists and influential business writers, should be among the first to be sent a copy. In fact, it is usually a sound idea to arrange a courier to deliver personally a copy of your report to these named individuals.

If newspaper and other business reporters do not receive a copy, they will certainly go looking for the report, perhaps in a more investigative frame of mind. Again, there is no value in irritating this group.

Since the stock exchange regulators will also want a copy, you might as well send a priority copy to them as well. There is no advantage to be gained in making the stock exchange wait until the mass of reports are sent out.

Other groups that may need some form of special delivery will include any influential and important readers of the report located overseas. These groups may include key executives and directors of major subsidiaries and divisions, as well as influential large shareholders, institutions and foreign media correspondents. To ensure rapid delivery to these groups you should not rely on ordinary postal deliveries. Select a speedy courier service, even if their services do cost more than conventional post office rates. The extra costs are worth the additional goodwill and interest generated.

Crucial final checks

On the actual nominated day of distribution, the remainder of the reports will be issued. As a last-minute check, before the reports are put into the envelopes, make sure that the correct names and addresses have been supplied from your share registrar. Most established share registrars are normally efficient and competent, but it is foolish to take chances at this stage.

Also check and recheck that the correct inserts are going into the packaging envelopes. It is expensive in terms of both cost and time, as well as an adverse reflection on the company, if these details have to be sent out separately at a later date because of errors or omissions.

Constant vigilance

Things can go wrong at any point during the design, printing and distribution stage. It is during these final stages that complacency can set in and leave space for simple, practical errors that can have many serious repercussions. So be alert at all times – a moment's inattention can result in heavy extra costs and embarrassment.

14 Problems and challenges

Even in the best-run operations things can 'go wrong'. When you have checked, double-checked and then carried out one final check there will still be something, somewhere, that is missing, misspelt, in the incorrect location, uncaptioned, in appalling English and poor grammar – or, sometimes, just plain wrong. You can never eliminate all errors and mishaps – just try to reduce them to the absolute minimum that is humanly possible.

Even the normally best-organized company cannot take anything for granted. For many shareholders and other readers the annual report *is* the company. It is all that readers see about the company. To them, the annual report is not the 'tip of the iceberg' – what they see represents the company, no more and no less. If you make mistakes or if they find omissions in the report they will naturally assume that this carelessness is indicative of the rest of your company. The corporate message you wish to convey will be sadly diluted. Even relatively simple mistakes can be acutely embarrassing and some mishaps will make you the laughing stock of the business world. Nothing spreads as fast as news about your failings.

Company chairmen naturally take a grave view of their company being brought into ridicule, so you must do your utmost to ensure that the report is sent out, as far as is practical, in a perfect condition. But what can go wrong and just how can you prevent simple mishaps and downright blatant errors from occurring?

Avoiding the rush

The principal problem with annual reports is that they are frequently prepared in one almighty hurry. At the year-end, most of the company's accountants are rushing around trying to finalize the accounts and seeking the auditors' seal of approval. Further complicating matters can be delays by the company's senior management in writing their input. The chairman and chief executive can sometimes be slow in drafting their inputs to, for example, the chairman's statement and the operating and financial review. They frequently have other demanding roles and responsibilities and believe that they can 'do' their submission for the report when they have a few spare moments. And, of course, they often fail to find the time and continually postpone the delivery of their input – not always being aware of your looming deadline. It is at this often panic-driven stage that mistakes arise.

Politics and pressure

You must also be prepared for the internal politics and pressure created by the production of the annual report. Too often, the chief executive or managing director believes that he or she has an almost automatic right to make their opinions or views dominant in the report. Sometimes they will have no strong feelings about the report's message at the start of the process but, towards the conclusion of the project, they come up with all manner of suggestions, which might or might not have been useful at a much earlier stage. It is often difficult to explain to a senior figure in the company that his or her opinions have arrived too late. As a result, some reports attempt to incorporate the chief executive's last-minute suggestions – just to keep on the right side of senior management. The outcome is usually a report that resembles a rather poor and disjointed compromise.

You must try to resist these final changes. At this stage, there is no easy way of, or solution to, saying 'no' to your chief executive. The best way to avoid this situation is to stress strongly, at the outset, that all ideas and suggestions from everyone must be submitted early in the year. Emphasize that fundamental changes are utterly impossible during the closing stages of production. Politely, but firmly, stress this point to senior management early in the year, pointing out such last-minute changes can so easily destroy the theme of the report and seriously distort the company's message.

The report should be prepared in as much detail as is practically feasible before the final rush. All supporting photographs, diagrams, trend figures, directors' bibliographies and other material that can be considered well in advance should be checked a month or two before the deadline. Make a checklist of items and of work that is still outstanding. Clearly indicate the date by which you expect this work to be completed and indicate the name of the colleague responsible for chasing up the outstanding material.

If the chairman or chief executive has failed to complete his or her submission, there is no excuse for not politely reminding these individuals of their role and obligations. Repeated but discreet telephone calls to their secretaries will usually secure their cooperation eventually. If need be, the deadlines can always be exaggerated a little in order to get the work done. The chairman's secretary can even be informed that the deadline is a fortnight earlier than it actually is. You will then have a two-week margin of safety to play with.

Problems can also occur with members of the annual report's committee. Personality clashes, policy differences and a lack of shared goals can easily undermine the nature and form of the report. If there are significant problems in the committee they must be ironed out sooner rather than later. Individuality, creativity and a variety of opinions are welcome in the initial stages, but there comes a point at which a consensus has to be obtained. If dissident members cannot agree on key issues, then the lead manager must ultimately take charge. The dissident members must then either conform to the corporate view or consider instead whether their career could best be served by moving to another project or even to another part of the organization. Organizational in-fighting has no place in preparing the annual report.

Avoiding accounting delays

You should also monitor the progress of the work of your accountants. At the year-end, time is at an absolute premium. In many companies outright panic sets in. Since the accounting input is one of the key features of the report, it is self-evident that nothing can proceed without the financial information.

Even when the accountants have finished their work, it will need to be approved by the auditors, and therefore further delays may follow. In some companies, constant delays, last-minute alterations to the figures and also discussions over accounting policies can potentially delay publication by days or even weeks.

The financial systems of most large companies nowadays are normally designed to be kept up-to-date on a continuous basis. However, there is still important work to finalize at the year-end. Nevertheless, most large companies will expect to have their accounts completed and 'signed off' by the auditors within the space of a few months after the year-end. Time is now of the essence for accountants.

Since you should have already set your report deadline many months ago, you should convey this date to your accountants. Stress that the deadline must be hit, even if the accountants need to work a seven-day week. Once the accounts have been prepared, it is normal practice for the figures to be carefully checked and rechecked and then to be presented to the finance director for his or her approval. The finance director will usually also carefully check the key figures in an overall, or global, sense. But even in the best-operated companies, which are audited by leading auditors, mistakes can still creep into the financial picture. A notable case occurring a few years ago springs to mind, when positive cash balances ended up being classified as an overdraft – and agreed by the auditors.

Once you receive the typed proofs of the financial statements make sure that they have been annotated by a senior member of the accountants' team and countersigned by the finance director.

At least it will be easier to apportion blame later if there are delays or mistakes. But apportioning blame is not your primary aim. You need to ensure that all errors and omissions are eradicated first time.

It is useful to ask the accountants for a copy of the accounting checklist when they send you the accounting proofs. This checklist is used by the accountants themselves to ensure that they have included all the accounting statements, notes and details. You can then, if need be, carry out some spot checks of your own.

The manager charged with taking overall responsibility for the report should also inspect the financial statements, which by now should have been signed off. Place these with the rest of the report so that the whole document can be inspected in context.

If your company is additionally publishing summary financial statements, then make sure that they include the correct extracts.

Although it is helpful to have some accounting background or training to read the accounting content, it is still possible for non-accountants to identify glaring errors in the financial statements. You should also read the report in its entirety. Reading only segments can lead to areas being omitted.

Although it is not normally the lead manager's explicit responsibility to check the figures for accuracy of additions or layout, it is nevertheless wise to adopt some random checks on a selection of various figures across a number of pages. If errors are found at this stage, the organization has certainly got significant problems. The accountants must be recalled now from whatever they are doing – correcting any errors in the annual report must be the top priority.

Other final checks

Check the narrative content for your corporate theme and message in sections such as the chairman's statement, directors' reports and operating and financial review. Read all the sections together. Do they all fit together to make a coherent discussion and convey the message you originally intended to make?

It is now probably too late if parts of the message have 'gone astray' but if the full sense of the message seems to have been partially lost this year, you should ask yourselves 'Why?'. You can then incorporate remedies and changes next year.

Contents checklist

Check the very obvious – some areas are often overlooked in the checking process, just because no one ever dreams that there could be mistakes of that nature. This, of course, is the very reason why you should do it. In particular, you should:

- Read the whole document for good English and sound grammar.
- Ensure that the page numbering is correct.
- Check headings and subheadings.
- Check cross-referencing, especially any supporting notes to the financial statements.
- Check the dates, especially the dates of the profit and loss account, cash flow statement and balance sheet. Check that the correct date appears on accounts when they are approved by the directors.
- Ensure that all photographs are appropriately titled and all individuals in the photographs are correctly identified.
- Check that all diagrams, graphs and illustrations are to scale, clear, well explained and cross-referenced to the text, if applicable.
- If applicable, check that your summary financial statements have been properly prepared and correctly signed off.

External checks

There are other checks you should make on your report, externally to your organization. The next stage in producing the report is the printing and, even at this stage, it is still possible for mishaps to occur. Normally, if properly ordered and correlated pages are submitted to the printers, an acceptable finished product results. But what can understandably confuse printers are the last-minute changes or inserts of new text. Often your instructions in respect of these changes can easily be misinterpreted.

Although printers understand that their clients may sometimes wish to change some sections of the report just before final printing, this practice should be avoided. Most printers will do their utmost to incorporate your alterations, but you are treading on dangerous ground. The risks of errors appearing will multiply exponentially at this stage. Only request changes if absolutely necessary. Put it another way: will you or your company be made to look foolish if you do not make the amendments? If you are going to be open to ridicule then you may reluctantly have to consider these eve-of-publication changes.

You might also wish to inspect some early copies of the report once the printing process has begun. If convenient, visit the printers and watch a few copies come off the print run. Most printers will run off a small initial print run and you should meticulously inspect the form and content of the report. Sometimes the mistakes are not yours. However careful your company is, printers can and do make mistakes, or misunderstand your instructions. Clearly, if the mistakes lie with the printers then the remedial expenses are down to them, but these are of little concern if a mistake delays your report. So, a check at this stage helps prevent last-minute errors creeping in and keeps your report on schedule.

Paper and packaging checks

Do not forget to check the cover pages, binding and the quality of paper and coating. Admittedly, it is often extremely expensive to change any factor at this stage, so if you do discover that some feature is not to your preference you will have to consider whether the errors justify the remedial costs. In many cases they will not. But you should bear in mind the points for next year's report.

Remember to make a final check of the suitability of packaging material. Is there enough? Is it the right quality? Always remember to check the obvious – even down to making sure that your reports will actually fit in the envelopes. Check that you have the correct names and addresses of your shareholders for addressing the envelopes. The list of shareholders' names and addresses will normally come direct from your share registrars, most of whom keep exemplary records. But watch out for human error. Even check that the list of shareholders is your company's list (and not another company's). Spot-check a few names and establish that they are your current shareholders – you do not want to use an outdated list submitted in error.

Check with the company secretary that all appropriate inserts concerning AGMs, resolutions, voting forms and so on have been included. If you are also sending out summary statements for the shareholders who have not requested the full report, make sure that the company registrars have correctly identified this group of shareholders. You do not want to send out the summary accounts to those shareholders who requested a copy of the full report.

Finally, as discussed in Chapter 13, establish that the report is immediately distributed to those groups on your 'priority' or 'special' list such as the chairman, large institutional shareholders and key media outlets. It is so easy to forget one of these key groups. Tick them off on your prepared checklists. Do not rely on memory alone.

Learning from mistakes

If you do find that mistakes have been made, learn from them. Some of the mistakes may not necessarily be within your immediate control. Many may lie within external agencies such as design consultants, graphic designers and printers. Fortunately, with these groups, you do at least have some power in the longer term. You can always select another firm or agency. However, in some ways, internal mistakes and problems may not always be simple to overcome. Organizational structures, internal office politics and divisional arguments will often take time to resolve. But, if there are difficulties, do not let the issues fester and deepen. You must grasp the issues and, if necessary, take the matter to the highest levels. The annual report is just too important to be spoilt by unnecessary, and largely pointless, internal disagreements.

Place any problems you have encountered before the report committee who will be preparing next year's report. Like most things in life, preparing the report is a continuous learning process. Never accept that your report cannot be improved; never believe (because of your checks) that mistakes cannot happen in your report; and *always* accept that you can do better next year. There is always room for improvement.

Preparing for 'difficult' questions

There is another related matter of concern. On the day when the first copies of the annual report are issued, your public relations or corporate communications (or the equivalent) department in your company must be on standby for any enquiries. But not only should your PR department be primed; there must also be back-up advice available from other technical support operations. As some of the public and press enquiries can be very technical with regard to, for example, accounting or company secretarial issues, your finance department and company secretary should be ready to provide your PR department with technical answers to complex enquiries.

It is best to channel all enquiries through named representatives in the PR or corporate communications department. In this way, sound working relationships can be established with institutions and media groups. Individual departments should not normally respond directly to enquiries. Fragmented replies may lack the authority and comprehensive response of a more clearly defined and properly channelled corporate voice.

However, there are a few stock issues and questions that are often pursued when the report is actually issued. And the level of corporate earnings (profits) is not usually one of them, as the company's earnings figures will have been published some months earlier in the company's preliminary announcements. The issues that the media focus on are usually more specific and politically sensitive areas concerning the level of the directors' remuneration packages and chairman's thoughts on future business.

Directors' compensation packages never seem to fail to generate interest from media groups. Whether through envy, spite or just to discover what the directors have done for their remuneration, this topic attracts a high degree of media interest. The notes on directors' remuneration are regarded, rightly or wrongly, as key areas of public interest.

As discussed in the directors' report (see Chapter 5, 'Major reports, statements and reviews'), the legislation requires companies to give a reasonably detailed breakdown of both the chairman's and highest paid director's actual emoluments, and also the remuneration of the rest of the unnamed directors, in bands of £5000. Journalists will certainly be interested in this – especially if your company is listed, has reported poor results for the year and your directors have received a seemingly generous remuneration package.

The other area that often attracts enquiries is the commentary on future trading prospects contained in the chairman's statement. Most chairmen deliberately portray themselves as eternal optimists in their reports, and some of their predictions need to be treated with a high degree of caution. Nevertheless, there are still analysts who seize upon the future trading projections. Expect, therefore, to be asked to enlarge on some of these comments. You should be even more concerned, and prepared for more detailed questions, if your company has reported disappointing earnings and your chairman has still insisted on painting a healthy financial picture of the company. Such questions should be anticipated and replies prepared. Almost certainly they will be needed.

Finally, never give a 'no comment' response to any question or enquiry. Such a response will certainly lead to even greater media interest; journalists will want to know just what you are hiding.

Annual report preparation checklist

To re-emphasize some of the key topics discussed in earlier chapters, you should refer to the points listed below in formulating, or reviewing, the systems and procedures for producing your own high-quality annual report. These points will also help minimize the chances of problems and errors occurring.

In particular, you should:

- Initially, and crucially, ensure that the production processes of your annual report are coordinated and led by an effective and committed manager.

- Allocate clear responsibilities to the team of contributors involved in producing the annual report.

- Issue a timetable and ascertain budgetary limits.

- Establish the nature of the corporate message and themes that you wish to deliver this year.

- Ensure that all contributors to the annual report are also clearly aware of this year's corporate message.

- Decide how this message or theme will be delivered in terms of writing, style and the inclusion of supporting examples relating, for example, to your products, customers or employees.

- Identify any opportunities for outsourcing of work, if appropriate.

- Ensure that the lead manager keeps all targets and deadlines under close review.

- Monitor and continually check that vital input from major contributors, such as the finance department or company secretarial department, are not falling behind schedule.

- Do not neglect the importance of design. Just concentrating on content is insufficient in today's business environment. Nowadays, form is often just as important as substance.

- Ensure the draft annual report can be read in a smooth and seamless fashion and is made as interesting as possible.

- Be self-critical at all times.

- Check and recheck your draft report. Annual reports are notorious for errors arising from the pressure of producing the information at the last minute. Never be complacent.

- Carry out one last check just before the proofs are dispatched to the printers. You can even ask a person not involved in the report's production to read through the report looking for glaringly obvious errors – so obvious, in fact, that everyone else involved in the report has missed them.

- Carry out a self-reflective review of the annual report soon after it is published. How successfully do you believe that your message was conveyed to your audience?

- Establish how you can improve in the future. You always can!

- Pass your appreciation to all contributors involved in the annual report – you will need their help again next year.

- Be original, be different and be certain (as far as possible) that your message is being successfully delivered.

15 A winning report

Many companies often seem to adopt an indifferent or an 'it will do' policy towards their annual report. These companies appear to believe that it does not really matter how the design or layout of the report finally turns out at the year-end. As long as the legal, accounting and stock exchange requirements are met, some companies are content to let matters rest. But how wrong they are! The attitude that only the minimum legal and accounting contents of an annual report really matter belongs to a bygone era. At the beginning of the twenty-first century so much of an annual report – as in so much of business life generally – is highly dependent on image, presentation and appearance.

Clearly, if your company fails to meet legal, accounting or stock exchange requirements, the various regulators will pounce extremely quickly. Consequently, all companies must, by necessity, conform to the rules. But along with compliance with the rules, in many areas it is relatively easy to improve radically the overall message that your company conveys.

Evaluate other companies

Unfortunately, originality can come at a high price in terms of cost and time. Designing and projecting a novel approach to the form and content of your report can demand a tremendous input of resources and commitment. Once you have an approximate framework as to your themes, design and messages, you should examine other companies' reports to see whether there are any themes and styles that you could perhaps modify and use. In many instances, there is no mileage in constantly reinventing the wheel. Of course, you do not need to copy exactly your corporate neighbours' ideas and approaches, but you should continually look for new ideas and consider how these might be used or adapted and put into practice in your company.

Your first step should be assess the 'feel' of other companies' reports. The messages of these companies' reports should be clear and unambiguous. For example, examine the cover page. Is it inspiring? Does it make an unequivocal impact? Is it in keeping with the nature and image that the company wishes to project? Study the use of colour. Is the use of different coloured pages confusing or helpful? Are the chairman's statement, the operating and financial review, and the directors' report written well, giving clear direction? Is there the 'right' balance of text, photographs and diagrams?

What makes you impressed with that company's overall report? Are there any parts, presentation or design you believe would benefit your company? Examine the text, layout, spacing, typeface and paper quality. Are there any features that you could improve, or adopt or perhaps find totally unacceptable? Does the nature and quality of binding meet your high standards?

In short, take a long critical examination of a cross-section of a variety of companies' reports. And do not limit your selection to just companies in your own business sector. There may be many acceptable ideas in non-related businesses. Examine the reports of some of the more progressive companies in up-and-coming advanced technological areas. Many of these high-tech companies are using particularly imaginative and unusual styles of presentation. And do not just restrict your examination solely to 'good' examples. Identify companies that produce (what you consider to be) poor, undemanding and unimaginative reports. Ask yourself just why you consider these reports to be particularly lacking in some way? Be precise and detailed.

Keep an open mind

The second key point is to always be open-minded and receptive to new and different ideas. Never reject an idea on the grounds that 'we don't take that sort of approach in our company'. Have no preconceptions and bear in mind changing fashions, not only in the style and content of reports themselves but also in new printing techniques and layouts. Be prepared to recognize the views of experts in areas such as printing, design or the use of professional writers. Do not be afraid to be different for a change, even if only for one year. Experiment, be novel and be different. If it does not work out, or if there is too much adverse criticism, you can always revert back to your previous format next year.

Always discuss your findings and ideas with other members of your annual report team. Regard your appraisal of other companies' reports as an iterative process. Do not rush your learning experience.

Try to be objective and simply ask yourself just what makes you prefer company's X's report to company Y's. Some companies may produce a colourless, bland and dull report but, in contrast, they may also publish a more informative and interestingly presented annual review and summary financial statements. Some companies argue that, since only so-called professional investors and more financially sophisticated readers will study the full report, then there is no need to spend time and effort in producing a top-quality designed main report. Instead, these companies devote much of their efforts to designing an easily 'readable', informative and well-presented annual review and summary financial statements. Although only a limited number of the top 100 blue-chip companies produce summary accounts this is no excuse. All companies, even if they also produce summary financial statements, should ensure that their full report conforms to the highest standards in terms of design, content and production. There can be no exceptions. Remember that reports convey both explicit and implicit messages. A bland, dull and poorly produced report will elicit an equally bland, dull and negative reaction from most people who may only casually read it. The quality of your main report is just as important as the standard of any annual review and summarized financial statements that you produce.

Never be tempted to cut corners; always produce a prestige annual report.

It's *your* message

Do not spoil or undermine your message by issuing a report that is deficient in terms of layout or presentation or displays poor production standards. When you look through a selection of annual reports from different businesses, establish what type of messages each of them is trying to deliver. How effective and successful are their messages? How could you improve the messages and images that are projected? What would you avoid doing (or including) if you were producing that company's annual report? Evaluating the messages in other companies' annual reports will help you evaluate your own message.

Of course, all companies must conform to the various regulatory requirements, but your organization can, and should, go far beyond this obligation. Be honest with yourself. What characterizes your organization and how does it wish to portray itself. Often, your style, design and presentation will project stronger and more influential messages than the mere technical content of the annual report itself.

With commitment and enthusiasm, virtually all companies of all sizes in all business sectors can produce excellent, if not outstanding, reports. There are no excuses for producing anything less than a first-class annual report, every time.

Your annual report is a valuable document. It is an important shop-window for your company. It reflects your company's whole standing, reputation and image and, significantly, shapes the public's and industry's perception of the company as a corporate entity. All this means that it is of paramount importance to effectively deliver your company's corporate message in the annual report.

Do not waste the opportunity – it's your message, and your message matters.

References

Department of Trade and Industry (DTI) (2001), *Modern Company Law for a Competitive Economy*, London: DTI.

Department of Trade and Industry (DTI) (2002), *Modernising Company Law*, London: DTI.

Institute of Chartered Secretaries and Administrators (ICSA) (2000), *Electronic Communications with Shareholders – Recommended Best Practice*, London: ICSA.

Pearce, D. et al. (1989), *Blueprint for a Green Economy*, London: Earthscan.

Report of the Committee on the Financial Aspects of Corporate Governance (the Cadbury Report) (1992), London: Gee & Co.

Index